The World's Most Mysterious Places

Lionel and Patricia Fanthorpe

The World's Most Mysterious Places

HOUNSLOW PRESS
A MEMBER OF THE DUNDURN GROUP
TORONTO · OXFORD

Hounslow Press
A Member of the Dundurn Group

Publisher: Anthony Hawke
Editor: Kathy Lim
Design: Jennifer Scott
Printer: Transcontinental Printing Inc.

Canadian Cataloguing in Publication Data

Fanthorpe, R. Lionel
The world's most mysterious places

ISBN 0-88882-206-5
1. Curiosities and wonders. I. Fanthorpe, Patricia. II. Title

AG243.F36 1999   001.94   C99-930910-2

1   2   3   4   5   03   02   01   00   99

THE CANADA COUNCIL | LE CONSEIL DES ARTS
FOR THE ARTS | DU CANADA
SINCE 1957 | DEPUIS 1957

We acknowledge the support of the **Canada Council for the Arts** for our publishing program. We also acknowledge the support of the **Ontario Arts Council** and the **Book Publishing Industry Development Program** of the **Department of Canadian Heritage.**

Care has been taken to trace the ownership of copyright material used in this book. The author and the publisher welcome any information enabling them to rectify any references or credit in subsequent editions.

J. Kirk Howard, President

Printed and bound in Canada.

Printed on recycled paper.

Hounslow Press
8 Market Street
Suite 200
Toronto, Ontario, Canada
M5E 1M6

Hounslow Press
73 Lime Walk
Headington, Oxford,
England
OX3 7AD

Hounslow Press
2250 Military Road
Tonawanda, New York
U.S.A. 14150

CONTENTS

*This book is dedicated to
Lionel's sister, Jane Fanthorpe,
with much gratitude for all her help
in so many ways*

Foreword
by Canon Stanley Mogford, MA

The Reverend Lionel Fanthorpe and his wife, Patricia, have been friends of mine for many years. It is hard to say which astounds me the more, their range of intellectual interests, which seems never ending, or their capacity for meticulous research into those differing interests. This book is the third of a trilogy of like writings, all researched and written in under two years. The first introduced us to a series of bizarre events, some well known, others less so, and examined their possible causes and consequences. The second of their books concentrated on a series of strange, mysterious people, again some better known than others, and explored the effect they had on their generation. This latest book of theirs highlights sites, buildings, and places, in this country and elsewhere, each of which had influence, for good or for ill, on the lives of those around them.

At the heart of the book lies a question they pose and seek to answer. Have places an influence? If so, how far reaching is it? People, we know, have exercised power over others, and, maybe, always will. The coming of Christ, all of two thousand years ago now, must have seemed, at the time, of small consequence. His was a simple life and it was like that to the end. He never travelled more than a few miles in any one direction. He never wrote a book. His circle of friends was small. He died, apparently humiliated, on the cross. At the second millennium of his birth we now acknowledge the way that simple life transformed the world. It reshaped our calendar. Architecture, painting, literature, and music came to new life through his words and his influence. Others, too, have transformed the lives of millions of us and, sadly, not to our good. The rows of the silent war graves and the bitter remains of concentration camps brook no argument. Some people can, and always will, affect the world of their day. We dare to hope it will be to the benefit of others and not to their harm.

Events, too, have probably always had their influence. Nothing could ever be the same once the atomic bomb had been dropped on Hiroshima. The whole world now knows it stands in peril of extinction if such bombs fall into dangerous hands. That event, of long ago now, has left the world in fear. Events, of course, also have influence for good. Those of us who love reading, and cannot imagine life without books, do well to value the services of those who invented the way to print books for great companies of readers. Reading, once only for the few, became possible for all. Again, there is no argument. Events have affected all our lives.

But can places have similar influence? In general terms, of course, they can and do. Those who live on a tropical island, in constant sunshine, with food easy to gather, are never likely to know the stresses of competitive living. Tomorrow will be time enough for what they need to do. Those who live in a large block of flats in a deprived area with vandalism and graffiti as facts of life will be hard put to it not to surrender to the squalor of their surroundings. Can it be equally true that separate buildings, places, sites also have had power over the thinking and actions of those for whom they were built and for generations to follow? Our authors have introduced us to a variety of such places. They have travelled to them for us, and have described them in detail. They have researched their past, breathed in their atmosphere and speculated about their origins and their secrets.

All my travelling now, at eighty-five years of age, is done from an armchair. Through the pages of this book, I have been to every one of these places with Lionel and Patricia as my guides. Some have left me bewildered. How could generations, with only primitive tools to use, have constructed Stonehenge and the monuments of Easter Island? Some have been a consolation to me. Those of us who are house-bound, and sometimes feel the burden of a restricted life, will find it a relief to go with the authors to the hermit's cell in a lonely part of Cornwall to share the peace of one who chose such a restricted way of life as his way to serve God and his fellow beings. Places have influence; they can dominate people's

Foreword

lives. This book takes us to such places one by one. It is the result of much travel and close study. Very few of us can ever hope to go to Easter Island. None of us will be privileged to penetrate the deepest dungeons of the Tower of London. Not many of us will welcome a walk through the serried ranks of the dead in Highgate Cemetery, however distinguished the company of those buried there. Fewer still will risk the jaws of the Bermuda Triangle. These places, and many more, are all here for us in this book.

Canon Stanley Mogford, MA
Cardiff, Wales, UK

(Footnote: Once again, the authors are deeply indebted to their friend Canon Mogford — widely acknowledged as one of the leading church scholars in Wales — for his massive help, support, and encouragement. It is a great privilege to be able to include a Foreword from such an outstanding thinker.)

Introduction

From the farthest reaches of intergalactic space to the mistiest origins of geological time, the universe is inhabited by unsolved mysteries — none greater, though, than the mysteries of the human mind, and its eternal striving to make sense of its environment.

In this present volume, we have looked at just a few of the mysterious places on this one tiny planet – but even those few can provide more riddles than the human life span can hope to answer.

There are ancient rings of massive stones whose purposes are still a matter of conjecture. There are intriguing hints and pointers to lost lands, concealed by oceans, deserts, or impenetrable tropical rain forests. Who lived there millennia ago? And what destroyed them?

There are curious "magnetic" hills – where gravity seems to work backwards – or are they only optical illusions? Gigantic figures of men and horses are carved into ancient hillsides. Who went to all that trouble, and why? What was it that exploded over Tunguska in Siberia in 1908? Only a comet — or a nuclear-powered, extraterrestrial ship? Is there a sinister secret room in Glamis Castle — and what does it contain? So many fascinating places pose an equal number of fascinating questions.

Yet all of these strange and unusual places are *different*: each has its own characteristics. It is only their mystery that unites them.

The search for mysterious places can be like a pilgrimage: an echo, or a reflection, of the great pilgrimage of life itself. We all need something worthwhile to *do*, and we all need somewhere worthwhile to *go*. We need a quest, a journey, and a purpose.

As you turn the pages and travel with us to these enigmatic locations, we hope that you will share the same pleasure and excitement which we found in visiting, researching, and speculating on them.

Lionel and Patricia Fanthorpe
Cardiff, Wales

Chapter 1
Stonehenge

Thomas Stokes Salmon wrote a poem about Stonehenge in 1823. The following lines are significant:

With breathless gaze, and cheek with terror pale,
The lingering shepherd startles at the tale,
How, at deep midnight, by the moon's chill glance
Unearthly forms prolong the viewless dance …

In Salmon's time the farmers and shepherds of Salisbury Plain, and the villagers of neighbouring Upavon, Shrewton, and Durrington, were not enthusiastic about visiting the Stonehenge area after sunset.

Barely a dozen miles north of these awesome old sarsen stones lie the equally strange and ancient ruins of Silbury Hill, one of the famous White Horses, the Avebury Circle, Oldbury Castle, and a long barrow.

What is the real history of these places, whose origins are lost in the mists of time?

The archaeological and historic significance of Stonehenge would be hard to exaggerate. It is generally regarded by scholars as the most important prehistoric structure in the United Kingdom, and, as far as is known, there is nothing quite like it anywhere else on earth.

It must be emphasized, however, that even the best archaeological evidence and the most logical and scholarly interpretations of it can provide nothing more substantial than theories about the origins, construction techniques, uses, and purposes of Stonehenge. New evidence from improved research methods often leads to older theories being challenged: the most reasonable of today's explanations may well be overturned by tomorrow's discoveries.

Taking the contemporary academic, archaeological suggestions as a starting point, the first Stonehenge seems to have been a wide, roughly circular earthwork dating back to approximately 4000 BC. In all probability it served as a formal meeting place on ceremonial occasions. During the next few centuries, it looks as if wooden structures were added. Considering the location of Stonehenge on Salisbury Plain, the next stage is a very surprising one indeed: the so-called bluestones were apparently brought all the way from Preseli, a range of mountains in Wales — a trip of nearly 250 miles. Weighing up to four tonnes each, and standing over six feet high, the sixty or so bluestones were arranged in a double crescent formation well inside the original earthworks.

There is some evidence on site that the original bluestone structure was deliberately dismantled after a century or two to facilitate the construction of the famous sarsen ring of trilithons. However, there is a geological possibility that with the recent revision of the previously estimated extent of the ice sheets, these bluestones

Stonehenge. Photo © Mr. and Mrs. M. Wentworth.

may have been nearer the Stonehenge site than was previously thought, having been deposited there by a convenient glacier.

It is generally estimated that some three centuries elapsed between the bluestone construction and the start of the work on the prodigious sarsen feature. From the Marlborough Downs — some twenty miles to the north — each sarsen stone (weighing between twenty and thirty tonnes) was dragged to Stonehenge. Five huge trilithons (consisting of a lintel supported by two uprights) were set in the centre of a circle consisting of some thirty uprights topped with an unbroken ring of lintels. Each of these was not only shaped in accordance with the curve of the circle but was painstakingly mortised to give extra strength and stability to the structure. When this mammoth task had been completed, the earlier bluestones were set up again *inside* the sarsen circle.

Three great Portal Stones marked the main entrance, which was in the northeast. Only one of these, the Slaughter Stone (which has fallen) can be seen today. The Heel Stone and its partner were set outside the main entrance — apparently to mark the position of sunrise at midsummer.

An interesting question arises with this Heel Stone because unlike the central structure it was not dressed or trimmed into shape. Did it predate the circle? The four Station Stones that, it has been suggested, mark the positions of cycles of the moon together with sunset on the winter solstice are also natural rather than dressed. They, too, may belong to an earlier period than that of the carefully trimmed sarsen circle.

The processional avenue seems to belong to the same period as the sarsen ring and may well have been the original route along which these great stones passed. Parallel banks and ditches indicate the position of the avenue that connecting the entrance to the Heel Stone and the Portal Stones.

What makes Stonehenge so different from all similar prehistoric monuments?

The dressing and squaring of the great stones seems to have been carried out by a process of pounding them with heavy stone hammers. Thor Heyerdahl's experimental work on Easter Island (dealt with in detail in another chapter) certainly proved that it was possible to shape stone by this technique in a comparatively short time. The Easter Islanders were also able to overcome the logistical problems associated with moving vast masses of stone over long distances.

At Stonehenge, vertical tongue and groove joints were cut into the interfaces between the ends of the ring of lintels that ran all around the top of the great circle of sarsen stones. Mortise and tenon joints were used between the lintels and the uprights, and the making of such joints must have presented those early stonemasons with a formidable challenge. Perhaps the greatest feat of all achieved by these neolithic craftsmen was the curvature of the sides of the lintels to create the sarsen circle. Among other theories, experts have suggested that the structural ideas and techniques the early stonemasons used were based upon methods that had been employed previously at Woodhenge.

What may be thought of as the last phase of Stonehenge continued until approximately 1500 BC and lasted for some seven hundred to eight hundred years. During this time the great sarsen stones remained where they were — but the bluestones were modified and relocated on at least three or four further occasions. Had the original users moved them in imitation of the sarsen settings, laying them out as a circle and an oval? It seems that some time later a circle and horseshoe were preferred. These constant rearrangements and alterations of the bluestones are one of the strangest and deepest mysteries at Stonehenge.

Although very slow relative to the breakneck speed of contemporary technology, it must be remembered that there were, nevertheless, significant alterations and developments together with marked social changes in the lives of the people in the Stonehenge area during this period. Flint and stone were replaced by metal tools and weapons. Round barrows began to appear — usually in groups. Kings or other important leaders were placed inside them accompanied by what their followers believed they would need for their journey to the hereafter.

Unless the outcome of Stone Age hunting expeditions and agriculture were far more prolific than contemporary evidence suggests, Stonehenge and its environs would not have been able to cater to a very large population. Paradoxically, whoever lived there — irrespective of their numbers — were well organized and presumably effectively and firmly governed. How else could these massive communal building enterprises have been carried out? The work of constructing Stonehenge was not a matter of days, weeks, or even months. Under the most favourable conditions possible, it must still have taken several years.

The most widely accepted construction theory is that the great stones were eased along with ropes and pulleys and the lower end of each upright was dropped into a suitably positioned pit or sump. It was then pushed from beneath with wooden props while other workers heaved it upright from the far side of the sump using long ropes or strips of rawhide. Although this is by no means impossible, it would seem to be less efficient than some of the methods put forward in other theories suggested from time to time. One of the best of these theories depends upon climatic conditions during the period when the structure was put together and considers the use of ice and snow for both the transporting and elevating stages. Very gently sloping inclines of hard packed snow could have been arranged to lead to the foundation holes into which the uprights of the trilithons were to be dropped. The beauty of this technique would have been that the ramps and slides used by the construction workers would simply have melted away in the early spring thaw. A

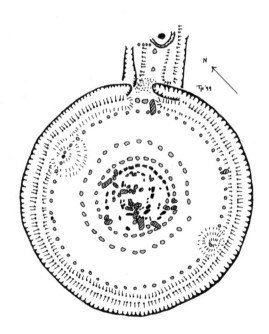

Stonehenge plan. Drawn by Theo Fanthorpe.

variant of this theory suggested that fine sand or gravel was used instead of snow and ice. The problem would then have been to dispose of the material after the work was completed. It would have seemed logical for the workers to scatter it over an area of the downs and the plain not too far distant from Stonehenge. Admittedly, after the passage of the centuries, such layering would be virtually undetectable, but a skilled petrologist using sophisticated modern equipment could almost certainly find evidence that such layering had taken place.

The most intriguing theories suggest that the structures could have been raised by extraterrestrials with tractor beam technology, by survivors of the advanced civilization that Graham Hancock postulated in connection with Antarctica in *Fingerprints of the Gods*, or by some form of "magical" levitation or telekinesis employed by Merlin, Morgana, or some other "enchanter" of their period, or of a much earlier period. Objective researchers are prepared to give a fair and open hearing even to the wildest and most imaginative theories: nothing should ever be laughed out of court until it has been properly examined.

As is to be expected, a monument as strange and as ancient as Stonehenge has attracted numerous myths and legends. The Heel Stone or Sun Stone may have well have derived its name from the Greek *helios* meaning "sun" or "sun-god" — but according to legend it was thrown at a monk or friar by the Devil or one of his minions. It struck the holy man, whose sanctity gave him divine protection, although it left a scar on his heel.

The word *sarsen* (applied to a type of sandstone found on Marlborough Downs) also has an interesting etymological background. From the eleventh to fourteenth centuries, when the Crusades and pilgrimages to the eastern Mediterranean were much in people's minds, the Saracens were regarded as strangers or unknown people. Allowing for the irregular orthography of the period, the term *Saracen* (possibly rendered *sarsen* in the case of Stonehenge) came to mean the "strange" or "unknown" stones.

It is thought by some researchers that the five great trilithons represented the five most powerful tribes ruled by the Wessex chieftains. Other theories suggest that they are connected with the five planets visible to the naked eye: Saturn, Jupiter, Mars, Venus, and Mercury. Another possibility is that Stonehenge was a vast sepulchre and the trilithons had originally formed part of a gigantic five-chamber burial place.

John Aubrey was commissioned by Charles II to carry out a survey of both Stonehenge and Avebury. The so-called Aubrey Stones are named after him, and as far back as 1666 he reported finding cavities within the earthen bank. Aubrey's theory was that Stonehenge may well have been a Druid temple. As far as is known, however, there is no evidence of Druid activity until at least ten or twelve centuries after Stonehenge was finished. Unless Druid dating is very much in error, it does not seem possible that they were responsible for building it. From what is known of Druidic practices and preferences it is almost equally unlikely that they ever assembled or worshipped there. Druids are much more likely to carry out their rituals and ceremonies in forest glades — especially near running water.

Although Aubrey's Druid theory is open to serious challenge, the association of Stonehenge with Druidism has had a very powerful influence on popular ideas about Stonehenge, and it is very difficult to disentangle the two concepts. Perhaps because of its Druidic connections the so-called Slaughter Stone has also tended to be misunderstood and misinterpreted. The reddish stains are apparently due to deposits of iron ore rather than to its once having been used for human sacrifice. According to many of the legends and traditions, however, human sacrifices *were* a frequent part of the rituals conducted at Stonehenge in the remote past, and the unhappy, restless spirits of those who died suddenly and violently on the Slaughter Stone are said still to linger in that awesome place.

Medieval myths and legends, undoubtedly encouraged by the least intelligent and most judgmental representatives of the Church, suggested that the stones were sinners who had danced on the Sabbath and had been petrified for their irreverence. It was also believed that the Devil had flown the stones in to mark the graves of the British nobles whom the Jutish invader Hengist had slain in a great fifth-century battle on the site. Some Mediterranean legends refer to a mysterious island in the west (which by a stretch of the imagination might be Britain) where a great temple in the form of a circle had been raised to Apollo the sun god.

Jason and the Argonauts, for example, were believed by some scholars to have voyaged past Gibraltar (their Pillars of Herakles, or Hercules) and to have visited Britain. Was it one of the Argonauts who brought that information back to Greece? Among the treasures and artifacts found in and around the Stonehenge site were pieces that might well have come from the eastern Mediterranean, and this gives further support to the theory that Jason and the Argonauts, or some other Greek explorers, might have reached Salisbury Plain.

Stonehenge. Drawing by Theo Fanthorpe.

The stones were also reported to have possessed mysterious healing powers. A ritual was enacted during which fresh spring water was poured over them, collected again, and used to cure sickness and injuries. Water was poured over the stones for a totally different reason when, during Cromwell's period, the Puritans had such a fanatical dislike of anything they considered to be pagan that they lit fires beneath the stones and then drenched them with water in the hope that they would split and crack.

Dr. George T. Meaden put forward a theory that Stonehenge had been built as a fertility temple: part of the monument, according to his ideas, represented the womb of the mother goddess, and the shadow of the Heel Stone represented the sky god copulating with her.

An intriguing idea put forward by archaeologist Brian Davison centres on the possibility that when the Beaker People arrived, they replaced the rotting timbers of an earlier sacred wooden building with the stones that are there today. According to this concept, the "repair work" has so far outlasted the original by four millennia.

Because the stones were credited with strange powers, many early visitors wanted pieces to take home as souvenirs, and the Amesbury blacksmith did a brisk trade in hiring out heavy hammers to visitors. There were also legends of vast treasures being hidden beneath the massive uprights of the sarsen trilithons, and several of these were weakened and damaged by ruthless digging.

The art and science of dowsing is a very interesting phenomenon, and one that would undoubtedly merit far more scientific study than it has yet been accorded. There are masses of reliable evidence attesting to the reality of dowsing, and Stonehenge shows strong, positive results when dowsed. Unfortunately, the bigoted and religiously obsessed Martin Luther didn't understand dowsing, and promptly condemned it as satanic — although it has nothing whatsoever to do with devil worship or black magic. The majority of people can dowse, although their ability — like eyesight, hearing, or the sense of smell — varies considerably from one person to another. Walking around Stonehenge with dowsing rods enables most people to find alignments centred on the openings between the stones. This raises vast questions about the nature of so-called Earth energy. It does not appear to be recognizably magnetic because copper, wood, and crystal pendulums react just as well as ferrous metals in the hands of experienced dowsers. Some of the best dowsers, in fact, do not use anything other than their hands and bodies. Is it possible that some strange form of energy beneath the earth's surface is transmitted through a sensitive human body in a way we are as yet unable to measure scientifically? Other researchers have suggested that the very strong dowsing responses reported from Stonehenge may be connected with curious properties present in quartz and flint in the area. Certainly, there is a strange atmosphere at Grimes Graves in Breckland, East Anglia, which was originally a neolithic flint mine. Intrepid pioneering flint miners cut their way through narrow, perilous tunnels in the chalk — risking life and limb to obtain the flints from which vital scrapers, arrowheads, axe-heads and spear-points were knapped. The very title "Grimes Graves" that was applied to this ancient site in medieval times is a clear indication that in popular superstition these Stone Age mines were associated with the Devil — or with some pre-Christian pagan deity. Some historians have suggested that the name is derived from Grimma — an old Saxon god associated with war and death.

It is believed that dowsing in the West Country — including the Stonehenge site — goes back as far as the fourteenth, century when German dowsers were brought to Britain in an effort to locate lost tin mines.

Carnac in Brittany with its huge avenues of stones arranged in straight lines is another mysterious site as far as the dowsing of earth energy is concerned.

Did our neolithic ancestors, who lived far closer to nature than we do now, have the ability to exercise the same kind of gifts as the Australian Aborigines? If they did, and if they were aware of the earth energy concentrated immediately below the site of Stonehenge, does that suggest at least a partial explanation for the tremendous effort that went into transporting and erecting the ponderous stones? Would it have seemed reasonable to people who understood more than we do today about the nature of this strange earth-power to have located their most important ceremonial centre over the spot where the earth energy was at its zenith?

A great deal of work has already been undertaken at Stonehenge by archaeologists, historians, and experts in esoteric research. Much has already been discovered by scholars and academic investigators, but the age and mystery of Stonehenge still lower a veil over many as yet unknown truths associated with this intriguing and arcane site.

Chapter 2
The Mystery of the Woodhenges

It is mystery enough that the great stone circles at sites like Avebury and Stonehenge have stood the march of time as well as they have. It is rather stranger that the so-called woodhenges — many of which predate their stone reflections — should still be available for archaeologists and other researchers to study today. Stanton Drew lies a little to the south of Bristol. The standing stones of Stanton have been well known for a long time. The advent of sophisticated magnetometers as archaeological accessories, however, has revealed the remains of a vast wooden structure below the soil at Stanton Drew, a structure that goes back a thousand years before Stonehenge and is almost twice as big. Archaeological teams working with the latest technology picked up weak signals that pointed to nine or ten vast concentric wooden circles a hundred yards in diameter.

When that ancient Woodhenge was constructed at Stanton Drew, very significant changes were taking place in Britain's cultural history. The population, estimated at under a million, was beginning to organize itself into large extended families, clans, and tribes. The British Isles had only relatively recently become isolated from continental Europe and these agricultural Britons were talking to each other in a proto-Celtic tongue. Ideas about the purpose of structures that were made by cultures very different from our own thousand of years in the past must always be highly speculative. It seems reasonable to assume, however, that those archaeologists and anthropologists who have come forward with theories that the great Woodhenge of Stanton Drew was a religious centre, a place where those who believed in the supernatural and the paranormal features of their world would be likely to gather, are probably working along the right lines.

Like those Greeks who frequently visited Delphi and other oracular shrines, the early inhabitants of the Stanton Drew area — and pilgrims visiting it — would have been anxious to know the future. Were flocks and herds going to prosper? Would rain come to save parched crops when it was most desperately needed? Where was the game hiding in the great forests? And where were the savage predators whom the huntsmen would be wise to avoid? Would neighbouring tribes come in war or in peace, and if in war, would we defeat them or would they defeat us? Would those who had been abducted by another tribe, or carried away as prisoners after a battle, be used as slaves or offered for sacrifice in their temple? It seems highly likely that, like the priests of Delphi, the priests of Stanton Drew grew rich from the gifts of those for whom they prophesied. If, like the priests of Delphi, the oracles of Stanton Drew became expert in ambiguity and became shrewd and perceptive about what was probably going to happen and what was not, their forecasts and divinations would be right more often than they were wrong — even without the preternatural assistance they claimed they had.

Wood was easier to handle than stone, less dense, and more workable. Why then did these ancient woodhenges give way to the monoliths and trilithons of the later sacred sites? (Perhaps it ought to be mentioned that as Christianity spread the original wattle and daub chapels were replaced by larger stone churches and even cathedrals — maybe there is a parallel here?)

Some experts have suggested that the great Woodhenge at Stanton Drew would have taken as much mature oak as twenty acres of forest could produce. (Compare three thousand oak trees for one Tudor ship.) Were our neolithic ancestors five thousand years ago doing to the great trees of the British Isles what the South American farmers are doing in our own time to the great rain forests? It is ironic to think, with all our modern concern about conservation and the ecology, that an environmental deforestation crisis struck at the technological aspirations of neolithic Britain. Is it possible that this deforestation crisis *forced* those early temple builders to seek stone substitutes simply because they were running out of suitable timber?

Woodhenge at Hunstanton, Norfolk, England, drawn by Theo Fanthorpe.

The Stanton Drew discoveries were exciting enough on their own, but when reinforced by the work being done at Milfield Henge south of Edinburgh and northeast of Carlisle, the mystery of the woodhenges becomes even deeper.

Just as the amazing discovery at Stanton Drew was due largely to skilful work with the latest and most sensitive magnetometers, so the Milfield discoveries began with the archaeologists' great friend and ally: aerial reconnaissance. When strange crop patterns were revealed from the air in this area of Northumberland, teams on site began to dig and came up with the remains of a fire that had been dead for millennia — and had been used by those who lit it to roast their hazelnuts. When fuel from that fire and the shells of the nuts themselves were subjected to radiocarbon dating, the results suggested that the great Henge of Milfield and its timbers were between six and seven thousand years old.

The vast earthworks alone on which the henge stood were well over a hundred metres across and would, in their heyday, have been conspicuous from numerous vantage points in the Cheviot Hills. The henge builders had only stone tools and shoulder blade shovels with which to carry out their enormous task. Archaeologists and anthropologists working in the area have come up with theories that when the Milfield Henge was being constructed, the neolithic hunter-gatherers had no concept parallel to the modern one of land ownership. Tribes tended to hunt in their particular territories, but boundary stones and boundary markers as such were largely unknown. On the hazy and uncertain borders between the hunting grounds of two or more rival tribes there was every likelihood that meetings between parties of hunters were likely to be aggressive, confrontational, violent, and lethal.

Some anthropologists believe that in the early days of the Stone Age, hunter-gatherers, the human self-concept, the basic realization of who and what an *individual* was, and who and what that individual's tribe and other tribes *meant*, was far from clear. The earliest people of all may not have seen themselves as being qualitatively different from the animals they hunted through the forests. When technology changed and the economy shifted from hunting and gathering to primitive agriculture, a change in the self-concept of early humans may have accompanied it. It has been suggested that once the idea that they controlled the land became part of the consciousness of our earliest ancestors, they began to construct their henges partly as symbols of their new control and status, their new dominance over nature.

The Milfield Henge and the many other fascinating ancient sites in the area around Edinburgh and Carlisle have produced evidence that human sacrifice may well have gone on there. Further south in a woodhenge near the great Stonehenge in Wiltshire, the skull of a child was discovered close to the entrance. The bone had been split by a blow from a flint axe.

One of the most recent and exciting new henge discoveries comes from the Norfolk coast close to the shore near Holme-next-the-Sea. This ancient wooden structure lay undisturbed and unsuspected for millennia, buried by the sand and peat on that part of the Norfolk coast. Changes in the coastline and the constant movement of the tides have finally revealed it. East Anglian archaeologists regard it as a find of the greatest possible importance and even rank it alongside Stonehenge itself. The Norfolk structure at Holme is thought to have been a religious centre, or altar of some kind, belonging to the early Bronze Age. The Woodhenge at Holme is less than ten metres in diameter and just over fifty posts suffice to encircle a large central tree trunk — which gives the impression that it was originally intended as some kind of altar or shrine. This little woodhenge may well have been constructed as a religious centre, the main purpose of which was to send the spirits of the dead to the afterlife by speeding up the decay of their mortal bodies. This is a funeral custom still practised by some Eastern peoples and is not unknown in Tibet.

It is also interesting to note that the little woodhenge at Holme, which has already been called Seahenge by some of the researchers who are working on it, is very close to one end of the Peddar's Way. The other end of the Peddar's Way goes all the way to Avebury in Wiltshire via the Ridgeway Path and the Icknield Way — a route that may well be one that was travelled by Queen Bodacea and her Iceni warriors. Ley-line experts are already studying the new Holme Seahenge to see how it fits with other locations of the same age. Whoever built these fascinating woodhenges had mysterious purposes and religious rituals that were meaningful to them. The more such sights we are able to uncover and explore, the closer we shall get to the heart of these prehistoric mysteries.

Chapter 3
The Mystery of the Avebury Circles

One of the largest henges in Britain is to be found at Avebury in Wiltshire. In all probability the Avebury circles were constructed at approximately the same time as the earliest phases of Stonehenge — but unlike Stonehenge the Avebury sarsen stones have not been dressed. They remain in their natural state. Windmill Hill would seem to be one of the earliest parts of the Avebury works and may well have been inhabited as much as six thousand years ago. It is arguably either mesolithic or early neolithic in origin. From about the same date comes the West Kennet long barrow, which is among the biggest and the least damaged early chamber tombs in the British Isles. There is evidence to suggest that this ancient sepulchre was in constant use for a millennium.

Silbury Hill has been subject to careful, scholarly excavation for many years, but, as will be suggested later, its precise purpose still remains a complete mystery. Some researchers have suggested that the reason the hill has defied all attempts to explain its purpose is that its mystery was centred in some curious structure of unknown purpose at its *summit* and not *inside* it.

An avenue of standing stones at West Kennet might well have been created to form a ceremonial route intended to connect the Avebury circles themselves with a mysterious area referred to as the Sanctuary, which, while being extremely ancient, does not appear to go back quite as far as the very early settlements that have left their traces on Windmill Hill.

Roman remains discovered in the great ditch surrounding the henge would suggest that Romans knew of the site and visited it as something of a tourist attraction — or simply as an inexplicable oddity during the Romano-British period.

From about AD 550 to AD 650 there is interesting evidence suggesting that a Saxon settlement had been constructed partly inside and partly outside the original henge. Beneath the present visitors' car park, inside the henge itself, a long house, or *grubenhaus*, seems to have been constructed in Saxon times.

The location of this Saxon settlement may have been the result — at least in part — of the Saxon preference for avoiding the dense and sinister forest that existed where the area know as the Weald is today. It would have been natural for the Saxons, therefore, to have proceeded down the Vale of the White Horse — particularly as a white horse was one of their traditional symbols — a symbol that returned to Britain many centuries later as part of the Hanoverian coat of arms.

The Saxons themselves referred to this semi-fortified settlement at Avebury as *Weala-dic*, which means "the British moat." Some Assize Rolls dating from the end of the thirteenth century actually make reference to it. Centuries before that

Co-author Patricia Fanthorpe at Avebury Ring.

reference was made, however, the Saxons had built a church there.

At the start of the twelfth century, the Benedictines had put up a priory in the area, followed a few years later by an oratory. It would seem that a Christian revival at the end of the twelfth century was synchronized with a successful suppression of the lingering pagan mysteries and ancient magical beliefs associated with Avebury since its foundation.

There is evidence that a great deal of stone-felling took place at about this time. A local barber-surgeon was crushed when one of the stones fell, and this too would seem to link with the theory that from 1170 to 1240 there was a general movement away from the original, esoteric, pagan purposes of the stones.

Strange names linger in the district: the Devil's Chair, the Devil's Branding Irons, the Devil's Den, and the Devil's Quoits refer, respectively, to the portal stones, the cove, the Clatford tomb, and the cove at Beckhampton.

Just as he had been involved with exploring Stonehenge, the indefatigable John Aubrey investigated Avebury — which he had discovered on a hunting trip in 1649. He records that he was "wonderfully surprised at the sight of those vast stones" he had never heard of before. Aubrey showed King Charles II around the site in 1663, but ignored the royal command to dig there.

Another early scholar to investigate Avebury was the brilliant but notoriously eccentric Reverend Dr. William Stukeley, who described it in glowing terms as "the most august work at this day upon the globe of the earth." A group of friends, including Stukeley, founded an organization they called the Society of Roman Knights. The object of their society was to preserve archaeological remains, especially Roman ones, from "time, Goths, and barbarians." Stukeley and his colleagues in this organization named themselves after real or imaginary heroes of the past.

Stukeley himself chose the title of Chyndonax, a figure who was alleged to have been a quasi-apocryphal French Druid high priest. Stukeley's obsession with Druidism and mystical religion in general led him to conclude that an unbroken tradition connected Old Testament patriarchs, ancient Druids, and the eighteenth-century Anglican Church in which he was a priest — and a source of embarrassment.

The eighteenth-century architect John Wood, who distinguished himself by his superb reconstruction of Bath, was also fascinated by

Avebury and Stonehenge, which he believed to be a temple to the moon goddess, Diana.

Sir Richard Colt Hoare believed that jewellery he had found in a neighbouring long barrow was Mycenaean, and this would have given additional credibility to theories connecting Avebury and Stonehenge with the Olympic pantheon, and provided interesting connections with ancient and highly cultured Mediterranean peoples.

It is one of the great tragedies of history that local builders destroyed many of the stones by building straw fires around them and pouring water over the hot stones to crack them. A modified version of this technique was perfected by "Stone Killer" Robinson, a very determined local farmer, who was systematically smashing the great stones even while Stukeley was studying and admiring them. Robinson and his gang of labourers would build a fire in a pit, drag a stone into it, and pour water on it from above once it was sufficiently hot. They then finished off their iconoclastic work with heavy hammers.

Most of the early scholars, like Stukeley, thought of Avebury as a temple, a burial ground, a Druidic structure, or an astronomical calendar.

Co-author Lionel Fanthorpe at Avebury Ring.

The Mystery of the Avebury Circles

Harold Grey, the archaeologist, visited Avebury before World War I, and his deep trenches revealed that the site was either late mesolithic or early neolithic. It seemed to him to have been created by a workforce using antler picks. Some thirty years later Alexander Keiller made further explorations and did his best to restore the avenue.

Much of the village of Avebury was built within the stone circle itself and a number of walls in the cottages there incorporated stones from the mysterious old circle. Over the years, several investigators have reported curious events of a poltergeistic nature as having taken place in these particular cottages. It is certainly possible that stone and other natural materials may be capable of recording events in much the same way as camera film, discs, CDs, or video tapes are able to receive imprints. Just as the relevant equipment is necessary to replay or view such film or video tape, so it may be that a particularly sensitive type of mind is required to perceive the records absorbed by the stones. The violent breaking up of some of the stones by Robinson and others may have caused their stored records to be released in a fragmentary form; thus creating the reported paranormal disturbances.

There are parallel accounts of strange phenomena being reported from a farmhouse in Baldwin on the Isle of Man. A stone from the ancient chapel of St. Luke had been brought into the house. Reports included sounds like a bleating calf and something else that sounded like a pile of stones being tipped out of a cart. The account concludes by saying that the stone was taken back to St. Luke's chapel and the phenomena ceased.

Co-author Lionel Fanthorpe was a pupil in 1945 at Langley Park School in Norfolk, where there is a prophecy that if a certain stone cross was ever taken from the ruins of Langley Abbey, there would be a fire in Langley Hall, which had been for centuries the property of the Beauchamp family before it became a school. Sure enough, one of the Beauchamps made light of the prophecy and gave orders for the cross to be removed and re-erected in Langley Park. That same day, smoke was seen pouring from the hall, but the fire was confined to one of the turrets and was extinguished before any major damage was done to the structure.

Stukeley and other pioneer investigators believed that they could trace a snakelike design leading into and away from the central circle of Avebury. It was thought that the stone patterns could have represented different aspects of the ancient earth goddess: as virgin, and later, as expectant mother. It was suggested by these researchers that the sarsens forming the Kennet avenue had been intended as the processional route along which the women would travel when attending the spring festivities associated with this ancient fertility goddess. If this view is correct, the Beckhampton avenue would have been the processional route for the men approaching from the opposite direction.

Very close to the Avebury Circle, and rich in mysteries of its own, stands mysterious Silbury Hill. As large as some of the Egyptian pyramids, it stands almost forty metres high and is the largest artificial mound in Europe. Radio carbon dating indicates that the earliest work was carried out there almost five thousand years ago.

The Duke of Northumberland and Colonel Drax were the first modern investigators in 1776, and they hired skilled Cornish tin miners to dig a shaft from the summit down to ground level. Almost a century later, the engineer Henry Blandford created a tunnel a metre wide and two metres high. To his great disappointment, no burial chambers nor remains were encountered within the hill.

Silbury Hill near Avebury Ring.

In 1867 the Wiltshire Archaeological Society explored the eastern side in an attempt to date the mount relative to the Roman road — the modern A4. Their discoveries proved conclusively that Silbury Hill was considerably *older* than the Roman occupation of Britain. The Roman road builders had lined up their track on the hill, but the actual construction had steered carefully around it.

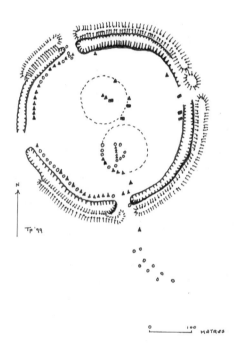

Plan of Avebury. Drawing by Theo Fanthorpe.

In 1922 Sir Flinders Petrie, the well-known Egyptologist, had searched the base of the mound for a hidden entrance; but he found nothing.

The excavations of 1968 and 1969, supported by Cardiff University and the BBC, were led by Professor Richard Atkinson. They tunnelled right to the centre of the hill and found that the building had been carried out in three distinct phases. What may conveniently be referred to as Silbury 1 lies in the middle of the mound and is only some thirty-six or thirty-seven metres in diameter. It reached a height of barely twenty feet. It seems to have been built mainly of mud and gravel interspersed with strata of soil and turf. It is this turf that has proved most interesting.

The ants preserved in it approximately five thousand years ago had their summer flight wings on, indicating that the turf on which they had settled had most probably been incorporated into the structure of Silbury Hill in August or early September. Did this indicate that the builders had got their harvest in before constructing Silbury 1?

Within a century or so Silbury 2, a very much, much bigger enterprise, was constructed to encompass Silbury 1. An ambitious ditch — over forty feet wide and half that depth — was dug as an encirclement, and most of Silbury 2 was constructed from the material taken from that ditch. Silbury 2 reached a height of over forty feet and comprised about thirty thousand cubic metres of material, which is roughly a million cubic feet.

Artist's Impression of Avebury Ring. Drawing by Theo Fanthorpe.

Before Silbury 2 was completed, however, it seems as if the designers changed their plans and launched into Silbury 3. The first great ditch was filled in and a larger one was dug farther out. Almost two hundred thousand cubic metres of material — over six million cubic feet — were involved in this work. There was nothing haphazard about the construction, which involved a very complicated network of stress-bearing walls to reinforce the entire hill. The outer walls sloped at a consistent angle of sixty degrees, which contributed significantly to the hill's stability. It is undeniable that those who built the hill had considerable civil engineering knowledge and, in addition, were well versed in soil mechanics. The hill also provides evidence that the intelligence and engineering skill of its builders were allied to a well-organized and enormous workforce — a well-disciplined workforce. Their task must have been very labour-intensive and a work-study analysis suggests that, given the tools and technology of the day, something close to twenty million worker-hours must have been needed. *It would have occupied approximately a thousand workers for nine or ten years.*

Was it built as a cenotaph or tribal marker of some kind?

A very ancient but totally unsupported legend suggests that King Sel (Sil or Zel) was buried there with his horse and that the entire structure was raised in the time that it takes to boil "a posset of milk." A variation of the legend suggested that either Sel and his horse were covered in gold leaf before being interred, or that life-sized golden statues of monarch and mount were buried alongside their bones.

It is possible that the name Sel is a derivation of Sol and that Avebury is some form of temple or huge astronomical device associated with the sun god. The association between gold and sunlight is a strong one and the idea that a sun king or sun god lies buried within the mound could be yet another reference to the idea of a sun god who begins to fight his way back to life and power after the winter solstice (the shortest day of the year) has passed.

As with Stonehenge itself, the true origins of the Avebury stones and Silbury Hill are buried deep in the sands of time and shrouded in mystery.

Chapter 4
The Hörselloch in Thuringia

The modern state of Thuringia was recreated shortly before the 1990 reunification of Germany. It is situated in the southwest of former East Germany and has an area of just over sixteen thousand square kilometres. Erfurt is its capital city. The River Werra on the west of Thuringia is a head stream of the Weser, famous for its role in the legend of the Pied Piper of Hamelin. In the legend, it was to this great river that the doomed rats were lured. Thuringia is famous for its magnificent forests and the scenic beauty of the Harz mountains.

The land traces its history to late Roman times. Early Germanic Thuringians seem to have been in the area after AD 300, but succumbed to the Huns a century or so later. Defeated by Theodoric I and Chlothar I in the early sixth century, Thuringia was reduced to a small area including the Harz mountains and the Thuringian forest, at which time Frankish dukes were placed in charge.

Converted to Christianity by Boniface during the eighth century, the Thuringians successfully halted a Magyar invasion and were afterwards controlled by the Ludowing family. In the eleventh and twelfth centuries they were ruled by landgraves.

This beautiful, romantic land of rivers, forests, and mountains contains the mysterious Hörselberg mountain, which rises like a huge stone sarcophagus. High up the precipitous northwest side of this mountain, a sinister cavern — the Hörselloch — is situated. The explorer standing in the mouth of this cavern hears the muffled roar of water from far below as a powerful subterranean stream rushes along its hidden bed.

A traveller named Bechstein wrote of his experiences there in 1835: "I stood alone on the ridge of the mountain, after having sought the chasm in vain. I heard a mighty rush like that of falling water beneath my feet and after scrambling down the scarp found myself — how I never knew — in front of the cave."

In olden times, according to the ancient Thuringian chronicles, bitter moans and cries were heard emerging from this cavern. Wild shrieks and bursts of diabolical laughter allegedly rang out from it at night. Not surprisingly, this terrified the local inhabitants, who became convinced that the Hörselloch was one of the gateways to Purgatory — or even to Hell itself. One suggestion for the origin of the name was *Hore die Seele*, meaning "hark the souls."

The pre-Christian legend, however, concerns Venus, goddess of physical love, and the noises emerging from the Hörselloch were thought to have been cries of ecstasy and sexual delight rather than shrieks of pain and dismay. In these earlier days, there were numerous witnesses who believed that they had seen the goddess and her beautiful consorts beckoning to them from the mouth of the cave. Such witnesses also believed that they had heard the sounds of exquisite music and singing above the thunder of the invisible subterranean river.

Just as the mythical sirens had lured sailors to their deaths on the rocks, so these handmaids of the goddess Venus had lured their victims into the depths of the Thuringian cavern — never to be seen again.

Another strange mystery linked to the Hörselberg concerns an entry in the ancient Thuringian chronicles. One day in 1398, at noon, three great fires, or lights, appeared suddenly in the air: these three ran together into one great globe of flame, separated again, and sank at last into the Hörselberg. The many reports of UFOs that have mainly been made over the past half century are by no means an exclusively modern phenomenon. Several ancient religious texts from all over the world contain references to what modern observers would suggest were possibly UFOs, and after so many centuries it is not possible to say with any certainty whether the mysterious Hörselberg lights were a natural phenomenon or something paranormal.

It is, however, the story of Tannhäuser that is the greatest of the mysteries associated with the Hörselloch. Tannhäuser was a thirteenth-century German poet, a *minnesinger* who seems actually to have lived the romantic, adventurous life encapsulated in his songs and poems. Born somewhere around the beginning of the thirteenth century, he participated in the 1228 Crusade and little more is heard of him after the year 1270. During the course of his many travels Tannhäuser was said to have been riding past the Hörselloch when he saw an incomparably beautiful and irresistibly alluring woman wearing a shimmering white tunic. She was escorted by a retinue of almost equally lovely young female attendants. The sounds of music and singing filled the air and Tannhäuser realized that he was in the presence of the goddess Venus and her nubile entourage. Overwhelmed with desire for her, Tannhäuser dismounted, left his horse on the mountain side, and followed the beckoning goddess into her cavern. There, concealed within the heart of the great rock, was her exquisite palace.

According to the legend, Tannhäuser spent seven deliriously exciting years with Venus and her nymphs before deciding that he was — notionally, at least — a *Christian* adventurer and ought not, perhaps, to be indulging quite so enthusiastically in the uninhibited delights of Venus' carnal court. Climbing from the Hörselloch and running to the little church in the nearest village, he made his confession to the priest and begged for absolution. The simple village pastor, however, was so shocked and horrified by the details related by Tannhäuser that he decided that it was not within his aegis to pronounce absolution for such serious offences. The hapless *minnesinger* was passed further and further up the pompous and self-righteous ecclesiastical hierarchy until he was finally referred to Pope Urban IV himself. Sadly, the pontiff reacted in much the same way as the village priest and exclaimed: "Such terrible sin is beyond all hope of forgiveness." To emphasize his point, he raised the polished wooden staff of office and said: "This staff in my hand will grow green and blossom again before God will pardon such a hopeless sinner such as you." Understandably filled with despair, Tannhäuser made his way back to the Hörselloch and the warmly welcoming arms of the nubile goddess and her sensuous companions.

Three days after Tannhäuser had left, *Urban's papal staff burst into flower!* Vatican messengers were despatched immediately to recall the penitent and give him the good news — but they were too late. By the time they reached Thuringia, Tannhäuser had returned with Venus to her palace of pleasure, where, according to the legend, he waits with his sensuous pagan girls until the end of the world.

41

It is interesting to note that there are other German mountains about which the same story is told. One is in Swabia, near Waldsee, and another is close to Ufhausen, not far from Freiburg. In Saxony there is another Venusberg close to Wolkenstein.

Paracelsus (1493–1541), who combined the roles of alchemist, physician, and magician, maintained that there was yet another Venusberg in Italy, inhabited either by the goddess herself or by a sibyl. Whoever she was, the supernatural inhabitant turned into a serpent every week. Geiler von Keysersperg, a strange old fifteenth-century preacher, spoke of witches convening on this Italian Venusberg, although he does not give its exact whereabouts.

The root of the story exists almost everywhere. There are versions in Greece, Albania, France, Denmark, Norway, Sweden, Iceland, Scotland, and Wales. In one Norse version Helgi, son of Thorir, is cruising up to Lapland when he meets a party of women in red dresses riding on red horses. One was particularly beautiful and appeared to be in command of the others. These were troll women and Helgi was taken to their mysterious home in Gloesisvellir.

The Scotch version speaks of Thomas of Ercildoune who is entranced by a strange elfin lady under Eildon Tree. She led him to a subterranean land where, like Tannhäuser, he remained with her for seven years.

In the Swedish version a young man on his way to be married was lured into an underground kingdom by an elfish maiden. Believing that he had been with her for only an hour, he found on returning to the surface that forty years had passed on earth: his family and friends had either died or forgotten him.

In terms of analyzing folklore there are three clear elements to this ubiquitous story:

1. A man or woman is enticed into the abode of strange underground beings, who wish to mate with him or her.
2. He or she eventually returns to the surface of the earth.
3. He or she goes back again to the underground realm.

What *really* lies hidden in the mysterious depths of the Thuringian Hörselloch?

Chapter Five
Glastonbury and Its Riddles

What may be termed the best known of the Glastonbury legends is the Christian tradition centred on the life and work of Joseph of Arimathea. Thought by many to have been Christ's uncle — or at least a close relative — it was Joseph who gave his own new garden tomb to receive Jesus' body after the crucifixion, and, again according to this legend, it was Joseph who came to Britain very shortly afterwards. The story tells how the apostle Philip, who had been spreading the Gospel to the people of Gaul, had asked Joseph to take the faith to the Britons just across the Channel. Bringing with him the Holy Grail, the chalice used at the Last Supper, Joseph landed somewhere on the Somerset coast and moved eastwards towards Glastonbury Tor — an ancient site of great religious significance for many centuries before the Christian era. Joseph had used the Grail, which Pilate allowed him to have, to collect some of Christ's blood, and this, according to the legend, had remained fresh and uncorrupted throughout all of Joseph's long journeys.

Exhausted from their travels, Joseph and his companions stopped to rest on a stretch of sloping ground known ever afterwards as Wearyall Hill. Stopping to pray at the foot of the Tor, Joseph drove his staff into the ground, where it miraculously took root and budded as a sign from heaven that he had reached his destination. Joseph accordingly proclaimed that the site of this botanical miracle should be consecrated to the worship of Christ forever. He further decided that twelve of the company — echoing the number of the disciples — should found a hermit community at the place to make certain that worship continued there. In accordance with Joseph's command, the "Vetusta Ecclesia" or "ancient church" was constructed there. As this was the first Christian church to be built in Britain, the legend maintained that Christ himself appeared and dedicated it to the Virgin Mary. In another version of the legend, Joseph's exhausted companions discovered to their joy and amazement that the church had already been built for them — not by human hands, but by Christ the carpenter himself.

According to such evidence as exists, it was a plain and simple little church of boughs, made from traditional wattle and daub on a timber frame, and so was felt to be totally appropriate for the Lord, who had himself been cradled in a manager and whose incarnation had been spent among the poor and underprivileged. Whatever its real origin, this simple structure, which may well have dated from the first century, became a veritable holy of holies at Glastonbury and was regarded as the most sacred spot in all of Britain. For centuries the monks tended it, renovated it, and restored it as necessary until a disastrous fire destroyed it in 1184.

The famous Glastonbury thorn that had sprung from Saint Joseph's rooted staff was said to have flowered every year at Christmas and Easter until a fanatical Puritan cut it down and burnt it during the seventeenth century. Graftings of the tree continue to flower today just as the original had done.

At the foot of Glastonbury Tor stands Chalice Well, surrounded by its gardens, and many believe that this is the precise spot in which Saint Joseph buried the Holy Grail to keep it safe.

This ancient and mysterious well has a flow in excess of one hundred thousand litres a day and the water from it is rich in iron. There are two chambers in the well built of ponderous stones. An opening in the western wall of the shaft gives access to the inner structure. The shaft itself, roughly a square metre, still shows the marks of the masons who originally cut it. The whole structure is less than four metres deep. The lower two metres do not look as if they have been disturbed at all over the long centuries since the well was first constructed. Archaeologists who have examined the well over the years have put forward various interesting theories about its possible history. The corners of the structure were clearly bonded and it is possible to discern the remains of the original mortar between the great stones.

One theory is that the present well was constructed sometime in the late twelfth century, reusing the stones salvaged from the ruins of the abbey fire — and another confirmatory archaeological find provides evidence that when extensions were made to the monastery round about 1220, a water supply from the Chalice Well direction seems to have been added.

The inner chamber appears to be a rather more recent mystery. It was possibly added in the middle of the eighteenth century as a sedimentation tank, the idea being to improve the water supply to the pilgrims' bathing pool, which then stood in the gardens below. It is also possible that this hypothetical sedimentation tank was intended to improve the quality of the water going down to the pump room in Glastonbury town.

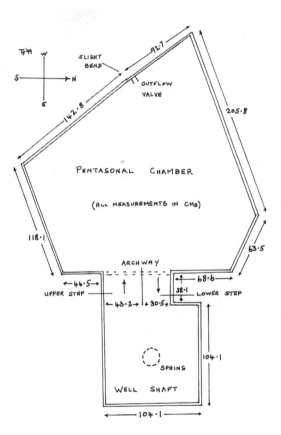

Plan of Chalice Well, Glastonbury. Drawing by Theo Fanthorpe.

As the diagram shows, the irregular pentagon of the well chamber bears an uncanny resemblance to designs favoured by ancient Egyptians, which were not, apparently, unknown to early Christian architects as well.

In 1961 some important excavations were carried out at the Chalice Well site by P.A. Rahtz. He discovered that the external stones of the chamber had been finished very precisely as though they had been intended to be visible. Is it possible, therefore, that the original "well" was once an *external* covering standing *above* a spring that broke through the earth at ground level? Did movements of the land over the centuries since its erection bring the top of the former stone shrine covering the spring down to a new ground level so that the former cover became the sides of a well? There is certainly a great deal of sense in Rahtz's theory. Of equal interest was the discovery of the stump of what had once been a great yew tree a few metres to the east of the well and four metres below the present surface of the gardens. The stump and tap root were in a layer of clay, and the discoverers were sure that it was still in the spot where it had once grown. Subsequent tests in a university laboratory suggested that the tree had flourished during the Roman occupation of Britain. The existence of a Roman yew tree gives support to Rahtz's theory and gives rise to the conjecture that an avenue of such trees may once have marked the approach to a shrine of great importance.

Certainly, the tomb of Arques close to Rennes-le-Château in southwestern France was also approached via an avenue of trees. The mystery of that curious tomb has never been solved either. It could be of very great age and significance. It could be a relatively recent addition. What is most likely is that an extremely ancient and significant site at Arques was disguised or embellished by new work not much more than a century old. This provides further interesting parallels with the Glastonbury well. It seems to be the case in the Chalice Gardens that recent work has modified an extremely old and interesting site. The wrought-iron design of the present well lid, for example, was the work of Frederick Bligh Bond, the Glastonbury archaeologist, almost a hundred years ago. Bond's design is linked to a thirteenth-century original that incorporates the legend of the sacred lance, symbolizing a balance between the invisible and visible worlds — which Bond believed to be inextricably interlocked with each other. It can also be interpreted as the mystical eastern *yin* and *yang:* the symbol of the juxtaposition of the conscious and unconscious, or the male and female principles in nature and in the cosmos itself.

Dr. John Dee, magician, mathematician and astrologer, recorded in 1582 that he had discovered the *elixir vitae* and that it was located in Glastonbury. Like Paracelsus, Nostradamus, Albertus Magnus, and others whose researches took them through the strange territory between magic and science, John Dee was capable of making intriguing statements and then lapsing into mysterious silence when intrigued listeners longed to know more.

The waters from the Glastonbury Chalice Well have certainly been credited with miraculous healing powers for centuries. Could this have been the trigger for Dr. Dee's tantalizing claim? Two hundred years after the worthy Elizabethan doctor, Matthew Chancellor, who was a resident of North Wootton, testified that he had had a strange dream directing him to drink a glassful of healing water from the Chalice Well on seven Sunday mornings in succession. In the dream he became aware that if he followed this strange prescription, his asthma would be cured. Matthew carried out the dream instructions and the asthma, according to his account, vanished.

Glastonbury Tor historic notice.

Once his story was duly published and circulated in the middle of the eighteenth century, enormous crowds were attracted to Glastonbury and records suggest that in May of 1751 over ten thousand people visited the town. The healings and cures attributed to the miraculous water from the Chalice Well and the Pump Room were duly sworn before magistrates and officially recorded, and according to these records such serious conditions as deafness, blindness, and severe ulceration all yielded to the miraculous healing power of the water.

Interesting medieval documents refer to the area of the present Chalice Well and its gardens, but the thirteenth-century spelling had varied from "Chalcselle" to "Chalkwell" by 1306. There is also a Chilkwell Street close to the gardens.

The history of the Chalice Well and its area also links in with the famous old Pasturel family who were bakers to the abbey, and in the early twelfth century Hugh Pasturel was given land on which he was permitted to build a house for the perpetual possession of his family. This Pasturel property was recorded as being near Chalkwell. Towards the end of the twelfth century there are records of one John, son of Matthew the baker, being married to Muriel de Lavandria, who came from a family of launderers with property close to the well. This documentation also refers to a wullhouse, which may mean that fleeces were washed in that area.

One of the greatest problems for scholars and researchers in connection with Glastonbury, its Grail legends, and the famous traditions of King Arthur has always been that the Christian version, relating the voyage of Joseph of Arimathea, has become intertwined with a far, far older tradition of another grail or graal that, in its original form, had no bearing of any kind on the Christian saintly tradition. This original graal was perhaps the pagan cornucopia, a so-called cup of plenty, or perhaps it was even linked with the ancient cauldron legends of pagan days. It certainly seems to have been connected with magical powers of life, death, and healing.

The Freudian symbols of a lance and cup also featured prominently in these very early pagan versions. A secret had to be discovered, and a prize of incalculable worth was there for the winning. The cup also had the power to hide itself from those who were not considered worthy of the search. Symbols and characters involved in this ancient graal tradition were inevitably a warrior, a maiden, a wounded king, and a hermit or wise man. The two major tasks of the quest were to heal the king of his wounds or his sickness and to restore him to youth and health. This would seem to have powerful overtones of the old fertility cults of the king who died in the winter to rise again in the spring. It is certain that the old graal ritual and traditions had much to do with the fertility of the land. The mysterious ancient *Red Book of Hergest*, which has Welsh origins, refers to a character named Peredur, who seems to be the chief healer. According to the different accounts, he restores the king by giving him healing herbs, by virtue of asking the right question concerning the origin of the graal, and occasionally even by discovering the graal. What is particularly significant is that the restoration of fertility to the land is brought about when the rivers return to their channels and here the ancient Welsh records bear a curious parallel to ancient India Vedas. These also refer to the freeing of the waters by the hero.

One of the strange shadowy figures of early history who seemed to have been instrumental in bringing together some of the ancient pagan graal traditions with the later Christian stories of Joseph of Arimathea was the mysterious Maelgwn — a name sometimes transliterated as Melkin. Little is known of this magician or wise man, save that he came from a time before Merlin.

This tree is a descendant of the famous Glastonbury Thorn said to have been planted by Joseph of Arimathea.

A fifth-century manuscript that he is alleged to have written and that was supposedly in the abbey library as late as the sixteenth century contains a strange prophecy Melkin made. It also contains a reference to the body of Joseph of Arimathea, whom Melkin calls Joseph of Marmore from Arimathea. Melkin also refers to Glastonbury as the Isle of Avalon. According to Melkin's prophecy, when Joseph's tomb is opened his body will be found intact, as will the "sacred cruets" he brought with him from Palestine. Melkin's strange words also fit in with the "freeing-of-the-waters" ritual because his prophecy goes on to say that from the moment the body of Joseph and the sacred treasure beside it are discovered there will never again be any scarcity of dew or rain. It might be suggested that Melkin's writings — if they are genuine — provide a link between some kind of ancient pagan spring ritual in which the restoration of water to the land was a central ingredient and the Joseph of Arimathea stories that so intrigued medieval Christendom.

Co-author Lionel Fanthorpe on the summit of Glastonbury Tor.

The mysteries of Glastonbury could fairly be described as approaching the unfathomable. There are even Hindu experts who believe that the legendary Shambala — one of the most sacred locations in ancient Hinduism — was here at Glastonbury.

Geraldus Cambrensis noted that it was the burial place of King Arthur, and in 1191 a coffin containing a male and female skeleton was discovered inscribed: "Here lies Arthur the once and future king." Whether this 1191 discovery was a commercial rather than a historical fact, it was undoubtedly true that Glastonbury Abbey's association with King Arthur brought immense wealth and power to the foundation. Poor old Richard Whyting, Glastonbury's last abbot, was executed in 1539 by Henry VIII's commissioners and for the best part of four hundred years Glastonbury Abbey was a sadly neglected ruin. Following the purchase of those ruins in 1907 by the Anglican Church, Frederick Bligh Bond was appointed to take charge of the exploration and restoration of the neglected and overgrown stones. Bond was an architectural genius and an acknowledged expert on all things Gothic. As a young man he had been powerfully influenced by Katherine Crowe's famous bestseller *The Night Side of Nature*. Her examination of occult mysteries and strange powers fascinated Bond.

The hapless Abbot Whyting had had a predecessor named Bere who had been very enthusiastic about the Joseph of Arimathea tradition. Bere was alleged to have constructed two chapels known as the Edgar Chapel and the Loretto Chapel. As far as was known, however, Henry VIII's wrecking crew had destroyed Bere's works. Bond believed passionately in the existence of these works and made it one of his highest priorities to locate them. As with almost all archaeological explorations, Bond's work was inadequately funded. What made Frederick's problem worse was the existence of a rival named Caroe who was doing his damnedest to find anything worth finding before Bond did.

It was then that Frederick decided to place his trust in Katherine Crowe's occult theories. Bond had a psychic friend named John Alleyne Bartlett, who had a reputation for being able to create automatic scripts. Almost a decade before the First World War, the two men sat in Bond's Bristol office and began their strange, psychic experiments. Their work did not begin particularly auspiciously. The first piece of automatic writing that came through Bartlett said simply that whoever or whatever was communicating with him had not been in favour of the monks or their work and — not surprisingly — was having difficulty in locating a monk willing or able to help him!

Bartlett and Bond continued their psychic experiment: the next thing to appear was a rough sketch of the abbey with a further rectangle protruding through the eastern end. The sketch was signed Gulielmus Monachus, which could be translated as William the Monk. Further drawings followed and the supposed builder of the chapels revealed in the sketches was alleged to be Abbot Richard Bere.

Their psychic informant — whoever or whatever it was — also told them that, unfortunate, Abbot Whyting had added to his predecessor's work. Another of their monastic informants gave his name and title as John Bryant, stonemason. Was such information coming from the subconscious minds of Bond and Bartlett — perhaps in touch with some kind of Jungian racial memory? Whether they were giving semitangible form to their own theories about the locations of the chapels or whether they were genuinely in contact with some kind of psychic entities are matters of conjecture. When money for the digging became available in 1908 and in 1909, Bond very soon began uncovering solid archaeological evidence for the large chapel situated to the east of the abbey. Strangest of all was the discovery of two towers, which the psychic informant calling himself Bryant the stonemason had referred to in his strange communications.

Bond was in considerable doubt and anxiety about what he should say to his Church of England employers. Brittle, pietistic, self-righteous, and narrowly traditionalist, they were terrified of anything connected with spiritualism in particular, and paranormal phenomena in general — and they were highly critical of researchers, such as Bond and Bartlett, who were not afraid. For an open-minded and highly intelligent researcher like Bond, it was very difficult *not* to publish the amazing source of the information that had led him to his astounding discoveries.

If they *were* genuine psychic entities who were communicating with him, Bond's informants referred to themselves as the Company of Avalon — and Glastonbury had always been known as Avalon in the remote past. When asked to described themselves these communicators had merely called themselves "the watchers from the other side" — which would have appealed to the narrow-minded Church authorities as much as an invitation to follow the lemmings over the nearest cliff. To make matters more complicated for Bond, the information his mysterious messages contained included one unexpected detail after another, each of which was subsequently confirmed by the excavating work. He was told of azure windows that did not seem probable. The common stained glass of the time was white or gold — but blue fragments were found in the Edgar Chapel. Bond was told that the roof had been painted in crimson and gold — fragments bearing gold and crimson paint were duly unearthed. Reinforced by success after success, Frederick decided that he would publish the true source of his information. Bond was very suspicious indeed of Caroe and Dean Robinson, and there are Glastonbury chroniclers who, with some justification, have suggested that Bond might have been mildly paranoid. Yet there can be little doubt that Caroe and Robinson and their allies would have been very happy to have seen the back of him.

Frederick's undeniable success, however, made him virtually unassailable. Among his other discoveries was a very tall skeleton: no coffin enclosed it, and a second skull lay between its knees. The

Glastonbury Tor.

mysterious communicators from the Company of Avalon informed Bond that this was the skeleton of Radulphus, who had been treasurer centuries ago. The era of Radulphus had apparently been a time for warrior monks and the exceptionally tall treasurer had killed an opponent named Eawulf in single combat. It had not been by any means a bloodless victory, and several of the treasurer's bones had been broken by Eawulf's axe before the fight ended. According to the psychic information that came through to Bond, Radulphus had made a remarkable recovery from the duel and had lived on to be over a hundred years old.

When the monks were digging the grave for their giant treasurer, they discovered that Eawulf had been interred in that exact place many years before — so Radulphus' long-defeated enemy was placed in the grave with him.

It further transpired that during the rule of Thurstan, a Norman abbot, Eawulf had been a Saxon earl. Like Thurstan, the abbot, Radulphus — otherwise known as Ralph — had also been of Norman stock. According to the remainder of the saga that Gulielmus told concerning Ralph the Norman and Eawulf the Saxon, Eawulf had been the Saxon earl of Edgarley. He was greatly angered because Norman soldiers had killed some of the Saxon monks then at Glastonbury Abbey. Leading the fight against these Norman soldiers, Eawulf was killed by the doughty treasurer, Ralph. Pathological examination of Ralph's giant skeleton showed that a fractured right forearm had healed many years before the giant's death. A man in combat with a Saxon axe wielder might very well have brought up his right arm to defend himself, and although successful in warding off the axe-blade, the shaft might well have fractured the defending bone.

Sadly, all of Bond's honesty and effort met with scant reward. The vindictive, narrow-minded traditionalists of the Anglican hierarchy reduced Bond in 1921 to a mere cataloguer and cleaner at a salary of ten pounds a month, and a year later he was told he was no longer responsible for the excavations and that the committee they had appointed to be responsible for the excavations was also dissolved.

Another great mystery centred around the Glastonbury area is the Glastonbury Zodiac. This covers an area of some fifteen or sixteen kilometres in diameter. Researcher Katherine Maltwood made the alleged discoveries of the Glastonbury Zodiac, which she named the "Temple of the Stars" during the early 1930s. She tells how she was led to these strange landscape figures through reading an anonymous medieval story entitled "Perlesvaus or the High History of the Holy Grail." A mysterious document alleged to have come from the Abbey in ancient times was said to have provided the basis for the Perlesvaus story. Is it remotely possible that the same mysterious psychic informants who gave Bond his information were hovering somewhere in the background when Katherine Maltwood made her discoveries?

So spectacular a theory as that of the Ground Zodiac or Star Temple at Glastonbury inevitably attracts its share of healthy criticism and questioning. It is the life work of any exciting theory to attract criticism and, like wrought iron, to be improved by the blows directed against it. Only the very best theories — be they psychic or physical — can survive this process. When the iron on the anvil protests that it does not wish to be beaten we may suspect that it is not really iron at all. Critics of the Maltwood discoveries have pointed out that the figures of the Glastonbury Zodiac are not readily apparent unless the observer has been told in advance that they are there and where to look for them. Some surprisingly recent features have been used in some of the figures to assist in the production of their outlines. This generates some serious doubts about them. On the other hand, these contemporary features may well have been erected on ancient sites: even the most recent roads occasionally follow ancient track ways. The history of agricultural fields and ancient pastures may go back for more centuries than contemporary farmers realize. Rorschach's famous ink blot test stimulates the subject being tested to see shapes, faces, and other signs and symbols in the random patterns that appear on folded paper upon which coloured pigment has been dropped. If five or six subjects all see the *same* face, animal, or submarine creature in the *same* Rorschach ink blot, then it could be suggested that that particular blot really *does* resemble the shape that the subjects are reporting, and that the experience is not confined to the imaginations and general creativity of the observers.

Psychology teaches that the human mind abhors meaningless chaos and will always try to make patterns from random collections of sounds and shapes. While admitting the possibility that the Glastonbury landscape is neither more nor less mysterious than any other, that it is, perhaps, merely a gigantic Rorschachian ink blot —

it is nevertheless impressive, and once the features of the landscape are superimposed on a map it has to be agreed that there is possible mileage in Katherine Maltwood's interesting theories.

Strange support for them comes from long before her time from no less a pen than that of Nostradamus. In Century VI, Quatrain XXII the words can be broadly translated as "In the country of the vast heavenly temple a false peace leads to the death of a nephew in London." Some researchers have argued that the vast heavenly temple to which Nostradamus refers in this strange quatrain is the ground zodiac at Glastonbury, and the events may well be referring to the execution in 1685 of the unhappy young Duke of Monmouth who rebelled against his uncle, James II. Monmouth's army was certainly in the Glastonbury area. It might also be argued that the peace that followed was an extremely short, false, and temporary one prior to the revolution of 1688 and the arrival of William of Orange. Mystic and unsolved mystery researcher Elizabeth van Buren has spent many years working with her psychic talents on the riddles centering upon Rennes-le-Château in France — and Elizabeth is convinced of the existence of a ground zodiac there very similar to the one alleged to surround Glastonbury. It is interesting to note that in her fascinating little publication *The Dragon of Rennes-le-Château* (1998), Elizabeth also refers to the prophecies of Nostradamus in connection with a mysterious ground zodiac. In Century XI, Quatrain XIX, Nostradamus wrote: "Long hidden underneath the olive tree the crocodile of earth has lain. That which was dead will return to life."

In the course of her own researches into the Rennes mysteries Elizabeth associates this crocodile in Nostradamus' prophecies with the winged dragon of Rennes-le-Château.

A final comment on the Glastonbury mysteries must refer to the myths and legends surrounding King Arthur. Today's Glastonbury was the mysterious Isle of Avalon of bygone times where, according to the chroniclers, the desperately wounded Arthur was brought for healing and rest. Despite the 1191 discovery of what was alleged to be the grave of Arthur and Guinevere by Glastonbury Abbey, does the once and future king still sleep in his mysterious cave waiting to reassume his royal mantle? There is at least one fascinating and impressive man in Britain today who sincerely believes himself to be Arthur's reincarnation. His story is included in the chapter on Tintagel.

Chapter 6
The Mystery of the Margate Shell Grotto

In 1835 a strange discovery was made accidentally in the seaside resort of Margate. Situated on Grotto Hill, which lies between Kings Street and North Down Road, the shell grotto is unique. Its two thousand square feet of winding subterranean passages are covered with exquisite mosaic designs created from literally millions of shells. The mystery of the grotto is: *who* did this unusual and time-consuming work, and *why*? As researchers puzzle over massive undertakings like the trilithons of Stonehenge and the vast pyramids of Egypt and South America, so these remarkable shell mosaics also impress the observer with the amount of time and energy — not to say determination — which must have gone into making them. This is their small but particular miracle. We do not find ourselves asking *how* it was done as we do when we survey the pyramids or the great trilithons on the Marlborough Plain. It is evident that a team of artists and their assistants could have stuck the mosaic shells in place without too much difficulty. The intriguing question is *why* they did it. What is the *purpose* of the shell grotto? Many of the signs and symbols down there in the grotto relate to everyday life on earth, and those who have studied the designs in detail believe that they probably represent some simplistic form of pagan worship. The land — and the sun that brings it life — are clearly there to be seen, as are the ideas of fertility and the miracle of the continuation and regeneration of life. Yet over and above the meaning of the patterns into which the shells are arranged is the meaning of the shells themselves.

From time immemorial human beings have regarded the sea as a source of awe and mystery, and almost every ancient mythology contains numerous references to gods and demigods, monsters, mer-beings, and mysterious aquatic creatures that have come from the sea and returned mysteriously to it, to hide from mortal sight in the darkness of its unknown depths.

It is possible, therefore, that those who constructed the mysterious shell grotto in Margate some two thousand years ago or more chose to decorate it with shells as a tribute to those vast and esoteric powers which they associated with the sea.

In the belief system of the ancient Romans, all stretches of water, rivers, springs, ponds, and pools had their own deity. One of the nymphs, variously known as Juturna or Diuturna, had come originally from Latium, and had been rewarded by Jupiter in return for her love for him. The king of the gods had given her power over all still waters and rivers. On the eleventh of January each year, she was worshipped and honoured during a feast known as the Juturnalia. Responsibility for these ceremonies was in the hands of the Fontani, the guild of skilled workmen, who were responsible for fountains, aqueducts, and similar structures. The Roman water god, Neptunus, may originally have been conceived of as a defender against drought and it is interesting to note that during the Neptunalia, held on the twenty-third July, huts of branches would be built as shelters against the sun to prevent water from evaporating too quickly in the heat.

For the Romans, almost all of the nymphs in their pantheon were connected with water divinities in one way or another. Being minor players on the divine chess board, nymphs tended to be associated with Jupiter, Ceres, or Diana — rather like personal assistants associated with top managers in a large organization.

The whole nymph cult seems to have begun in Latium, and springs dedicated to them were uncovered there near the Capena Gate. One of the best known of these nymph cult shrines was a fountain dedicated to Egeria. She was the nymph whom Numa the king came to consult by night. In Ovid's version of the story, she and the king eventually married, and after the death of her mortal husband she withdrew to the wooded valley of Aricia, where the goddess Diana transformed Egeria into a beautiful fountain.

One of the nymph's major prophetic functions had been to foretell the life and adventures of new-born babes who were brought to her shrine. Other prophetic nymphs included a group known as the Camenae. One of them, Antevorta was more of an historian than a prophetess, for her province was the past. Her companion Postvorta was the one who had the priceless and coveted knowledge of the future.

The leading member of the Camenae, however, was Carmenta, who came originally from Arcadia. While living there she had produced a son, Evander, whose father was the god Mercury. This boy left Arcadia and journeyed to Italy, where he was regarded as the founder of Pallantium. His mother Carmenta came with him and changed the fifteen Greek letters Evander had brought into Roman letters. According to this tradition, Carmenta herself was far from being immortal and died at the age of 110. It was only after her death that she was accorded divine honours in the Roman style.

If the shell grotto at Margate was the result of work by Roman legionaries during their occupation of Britain, it seems reasonable to suggest that followers of one or more of the nymph cults could have been responsible for constructing it. In times of peace, with a reasonably flexible and tolerant commander in charge of the Roman garrison in the area, there would have been ample time for off-duty soldiers to have dug and decorated the shell grotto. What raw materials more natural than seashells could be used for decorations raised with the intention of honouring water divinities?

Returning to the idea of Neptunalia celebrated on July twenty-third, the idea of building huts of branches as protection against the sun could well have been extended to the idea of digging a subterranean shelter, which would have been far more effective in keeping out the sun and preserving moisture than would a structure of branches raised above the ground.

If it could be assumed that there were Fontani among the Romano-British, skilled builders of aqueducts, fountains, and other waterways, is it possible that a small group of them working in the Margate area could have dug the subterranean grotto and decorated it with seashells in honour of Juturna (Diuturna)?

An army and its accompanying artisans in times of peace are more likely to be troublesome when underemployed than when happily occupied. If a liberal commander had been asked for permission by a group of his men to create a structure similar to the shell grotto, he would very probably have leapt at the opportunity.

The Greco-Roman goddess Aphrodite/Venus is the one who

seems to be most closely connected with shells. There are different versions of the story of the birth of Aphrodite, or Venus. Homer describes her as the daughter of Zeus and Dione — who seems to have been a somewhat indeterminate divinity related to Oceanus and Tethys. Scholars of mythology know very little about her other than that she was closely associated with the Dodona cult of Zeus. A much more popular version than the rather vague Homeric tradition was the one that suggested that Aphrodite had been born from the white foam which floated upon the surface of the ocean following the injury done to Uranus by his ruthless and audacious son Cronus.

Zephyrus, the West Wind, had carried the foam-born Aphrodite along the coasts of Cythera and brought her at last to Cyprus. The Horae welcomed her here, dressed her in beautiful robes and scintillating jewels, and led her to meet the pantheon of the gods. The immortals themselves were overwhelmed with love and admiration for the beautiful newcomer and each of the male gods wished to take her as his wife. There was something deliciously sensuous and responsive about the lovable Aphrodite/Venus, which neither the haughty Hera nor the severe Athene were ever able to equal. Aphrodite had a warmth and seductiveness the two sterner, more distant goddesses could not hope to match.

In Greco-Roman mythology, therefore, Aphrodite/Venus was inseparably associated with the sea. As goddess of love she would be particularly popular with Roman soldiers. And the possibility that the Shell Grotto at Margate was intended in *her* honour must remain a strong contender among the theories of its origin.

But Aphrodite/Venus was by no means the only sea divinity who could have inspired the builders of that ancient, sacred grotto.

Pontus, son of Gaea, is another contender. As Greek gods go, Pontus was rather lacking in distinctive attributes, and was perhaps not much more than a simple personification of the sea itself. Long before the Greeks came on the scene, the ancient Chaldeans had imagined a vast river encircling the universe like a girdle, and this was a concept they later shared with the earliest of the Greeks. In a rather curious way, which hydrologists would be at some pains to explain, this mysterious girdle of water never actually *mingled* with the sea, although it *embraced* it. Sometimes referred to as a river-ocean, this girdle-god, Oceanus, had neither a source nor an outlet, but managed to be the parent of every well, every spring, all of the sea and oceans, as well as all of the rivers. In the primitive mytho-geography of that strange dawn of time all of the lands of the fabled races bordered the shores of Oceanus. There were the Ethiopians, the mist-encircled Cimmerians, and the tiny pigmies. Understood in this early mythology to be the offspring of Gaea and Uranus, the Titan Oceanus was really more of an elemental force than a god in the later sense — and his main contribution to this early understanding of the universe was that he was among those who were responsible for the formation of the world.

To Homer, he was the essence of all that was: in a sense this parallels the idea of the four elements — earth, air, fire, and water — from which all things were once thought to have been made. In Homer's view Oceanus was second to none but great Zeus himself.

Mysterious Shell Grotto in Margate, England. Is it a two-thousand-year-old temple to the goddess Aphrodite? Drawing by Theo Fanthorpe.

In the theological family tree of the Titans, Oceanus was married to his sister Tethys and their six thousand offspring were the Oceanids — along with three thousand rivers. There is a variation of the story suggesting that Tethys and Oceanus guarded Hera during her infancy and kept her safe in their mysterious stronghold far to the west of the world.

As in all other spheres, however, the Olympians eventually triumphed over the Titans and took charge of the waters that had once been the province of Oceanus and Tethys. These waters were passed into the care of Poseidon, or Neptune, while Oceanus went off to spend his dotage in the most distant corner of what had once been his very considerable aquatic empire.

The Greeks were a great seafaring and trading people, which makes it highly likely that Greek merchants were not unknown in the area now occupied by the mysterious Margate shell grotto. Being citizens of a maritime nation, these ancient Greeks gave a very senior position in the divine hierarchy to the god Poseidon, so that some other, older sea gods were relegated to less important supporting roles.

These secondary Greek divinities of the waters, however, are nevertheless worth more than a lingering glance in connection with the shell grotto — *because it is more than possible that Greek travellers brought their various cults with them in the course of their trading visits to Britain.* Nereus is therefore another contender for over-lordship of the Margate grotto. He was the son of Gaea and Pontus and predated Poseidon by millennia. Nereus was born during the very earliest mythological period and because of this was often depicted as an elderly, white-bearded god. There were even times when the title "Old Man of the Sea" was conferred upon him. In character, however, he was very different indeed from the Arabian tale's depiction of "The Old Man of the Sea," who was an almost lethal trial to Sinbad the Sailor. Far from being like the greedy and murderous parasite of the Arabian adventure tale, Nereus was benign, helpful, and just.

Along with his equally kind-hearted wife Doris, Nereus dwelt somewhere in the deepest fathoms of the Aegean, but came up periodically to assist and advise sailors in difficulties. Nereus was reputed to be a god of prophecy, and gods who were also oracles were very much in favour with sailors and soldiers. It is, therefore, possible that the Margate shell grotto, like the shrine of the oracle at Delphi, was a place where worshippers and enquirers came to have their future divined by Nereus. Some of his prophecies were particularly grim and unwelcome despite his kindness and benign nature. Paris, the ill-fated prince of Troy, encountered Nereus emerging from the Aegaean and heard from the prophetic water divinity that his beloved city of Troy would soon be destroyed.

Many of the members of the Greek pantheon were exceptionally prolific, and Doris and Nereus were no exception. They were the parents of some fifty daughters known as the Nereids, who were beautiful golden-haired girls and lived with their parents in the depths of the Aegean. They were great friends and close companions of the Tritons, and could frequently be seen by observant Greek sailors of the time laughing and playing together on the wave crests.

Galatea is perhaps the Nereid most likely to have a connection with the Margate shell grotto. According to the myth, she was courted by Polyphemus, the great Cyclops, but was at the time in love with a young Scilian herdsman by the name of Acis. As with all such star-crossed lovers, tragedy was not far away.

The angry and jealous Polyphemus surprised Galatea and Acis as they talked together in a grotto. The enraged Cyclops seized an enormous boulder and used it to crush the young herdsman. Using her divine influence, however, Galatea was able to arrange for Acis to be changed into a river rather than to die. It is the grotto connection that is of particular interest to us here. Was it to Galatea and Acis that the shell grotto in all its intriguing beauty was dedicated?

Proteus is the central figure in yet another mysterious old sea-god legend. Son of Tethys and Oceanus, Proteus had the job of guarding the seal herd that belonged to Poseidon. He was principally another of the oracle gods whose wisdom was much sought after by Greeks and Romans. Because his seal-herding duties were exacting and exhausting, Proteus got into the habit of resting on the shore with his flock around him. In the ancient mythological tradition, if you could catch him in this resting state, Proteus would be forced to foretell your future. He saw accurately, according to the legend, and he always spoke the truth. He was, however, a very reluctant prophet and the enquirer had to catch him first. Proteus was an expert shape-shifter who could become anything he wanted in order to escape capture, and it was a bold-hearted enquirer indeed who would continue gripping fiercely on to a tree, a dragon, a panther, a lion, searing fire, or swirling water — all of which, of course, were really Proteus. Provided that the enquirer had sufficient courage not to be terrified by this shape-shifting technique, Proteus would sooner or later accept defeat and answer the enquirer's question.

Because of the popularity of oracles and prophecies in classical times, it is again possible to suggest that the shell grotto had originally been constructed as a shrine to Proteus.

An evil and dangerous sea deity whom the grotto builders *might* have sought to placate was Phorcys. He was yet another son of Pontus and Gaea. Having married his sister, Ceto, Phorcys became the father of the Gorgons and a dragon named Ladon. An affair with Hecate led to the birth of Scylla — a particularly terrifying antagonist for any sailor unfortunate enough to draw too near.

If his dangerous offspring are anything to judge by, Phorcys was most probably intended by the Greeks to personify the sea in its most evil and treacherous moods.

The Tritons were yet another group of strange marine beings. Coming closer in appearance to the medieval myth of mermen then to anything else, the Tritons are described as being part man and part fish, armed with sharp teeth and claws, and possessing scaly bodies. Noisy and mischievous Tritons tended to blow conch shells; a few even had horse's legs as well as fish tails and were known accordingly as centaur-tritons. In Tanagra there was a tradition concerning a Triton who had left the sea and ravaged the country roundabout. He was eventually disposed of when a vase of wine was left on the beach. As soon as the Triton was helplessly drunk, the boldest of the fishermen decapitated him and placed a statue commemorating the deed in the Temple of Dionysus. The Triton's characteristic mischief and noise gave way to friendship and benevolence in the case of the Argonauts. When their ship was driven up and beached on the Libyan coast, it was a Triton who helped them. Like Nereus and Proteus, this Triton had the gift of prophecy, and it is this prophetic element that *may* have led some of his followers to create a shell temple at Margate in his honour as a place from which he might be persuaded to divulge the future to enquirers.

These are only a representative sample of the possibilities that may, perhaps, explain the creation and purpose of the shell grotto at

The Mystery of the Margate Shell Grotto

Margate. The mystery may never be definitively unravelled, but the possibility that it is connected with the worship of some Greek or Roman sea god is one that cannot be ignored.

Note: The authors would like to express their appreciation to Steve Jones of Fairwater in Cardiff, who first brought the Shell Grotto mystery to their attention.

Chapter 7
The Legend of Glamis

There are some strange locations — Bowden House near Totnes, for example — that seem to have more than their fair share of ghosts, monsters, and legends. Many such buildings and allegedly haunted sites have had centuries, if not millennia, in which to acquire such reputations. And Glamis is no exception. In essence, the central story of Glamis maintains that since very early times the lord of the castle, his trusted bailiff, and the lord's eldest son, on attaining his twenty-first birthday, are the only ones who share the secret of a sinister hidden room. Amplification of this basic story suggests that this hidden room contains — or once contained and for a very long period — a monster dangerous and terrifying that none who had ever seen it were prepared to speak of what they knew.

The location of Glamis is in the impressive vale of Strathmore, which is part of Tayside in Scotland, and for many centuries the Earls of Strathmore made Glamis their ancestral home. What stood on that beautiful Tayside site during the time of the Picts and the earliest inhabitants of Scotland is now unknown, but it is possible that long before the first modern fortification occupied the site of Glamis there were strange and sinister pagan settlements on the site.

Shakespeare's nimble mind certainly associated it with regicide, and apart from his tale of the brutal and undeserved murder of kindly old King Duncan, there is a well-documented account of the murder of King Malcolm II who was butchered there by Scots rebels armed with their traditional claymores, the deadly Scottish broadswords with which the fierce clansmen fought so well. According to the historical records, Malcolm II was murdered in the year 1034, just thirty-two years before William the Norman arrived at Hastings. So savagely was the unfortunate Malcolm II hacked by his killers that almost all the blood drained from his dying body into the floor boards of the room in Glamis that is still known as King Malcolm's Room.

Guides will still point out the mark on the floor that is supposedly the indelible blood stain. Other records indicate that because the mark was impossible to remove, an entire new floor was laid over the old one. Whether something sinister and supernatural has succeeded in making its way up through this second layer of flooring is a matter for considerable debate!

The regicides gained nothing from their brutal attack on the king, for as they attempted to escape across a frozen loch, the ice gave way beneath them and they drowned in the deep, dark water below. The Earls of Strathmore and Kinghorne acquired Glamis as the gift of King Robert II, whose daughter married Sir John Lyon in 1372. Prior to that wedding the Lyons had lived at Forteviot, where a prominent heirloom took the form of a great chalice. Many of the medieval Lyons believed that it held their luck, or the family's good fortune, and there was a tradition in that ancient and noble family to the effect that the cup must never be moved; if it was, their luck would be spilled. Young Sir John, however, decided to ignore the curse and take the cup with him to his magnificent new home at Glamis. Eleven years later, in 1383, the unfortunate Sir John died as the result of a duel.

In 1573, the very worst kind of bad luck struck Glamis again. John Lyon, who was then Lord, had a jealous relative named William. This devious and treacherous character concocted a great web of lies accusing John Lyon, his wife, Joan (or Janet) Douglas, their son, and a harmless old priest with whom they were acquainted, of planning to poison King James V. Bold and courageous to the last, John Lyon tried to escape from Edinburgh Castle and fell to his death in the attempt. Indomitable Janet Douglas was burnt at the stake in front of a jubilant crowd who were convinced that the innocent woman was a poisoner meeting her just deserts. Their son's execution was postponed until the lad reached his twenty-first birthday.

In the meantime Glamis reverted to the Crown. Far, far too late to save John and Janet, William confessed that his accusations were all false. The property was returned to the son, whose youth had saved him from execution.

One of the many spectres reported from Glamis is that of a lady in grey: it is believed to be the spectre of Janet Douglas.

The third Earl of Strathmore was Patrick and it was around him that many of the strangest of the Glamis legends began to accumulate. Although many colourful tales were told of his drinking, gambling, and womanizing, Patrick was by no means entirely bad, and, from what little is known of him, his understandable human excesses seem to have been more than offset by his kindness and generosity to those of his impoverished tenants who were most in need of his help. Certainly it was Patrick who built a group of dwellings on the estate for the use of workers who had been forced to relinquish their former jobs by reason of age and infirmity. That kind of generosity and concern were all too rare during the seventeenth century. Those retirement dwellings known as Kirkwynd Cottages were handed over to the National Trust during the 1950s by the sixteenth earl. Despite Patrick's generosity, two very strange stories clung persistently to him. It is said that as an insatiable gambler with no fear of the risks he was taking, Patrick dared to play cards against the devil with his soul as the price — *and he lost.* It is a story which is parallelled by the tale of the vessel *Flying Dutchman* where the reckless skipper played dice with Satan using his ship, his crew, and his own soul as the stake. Like Patrick, Third Earl of Strathmore, the daring Dutch seaman lost and the *Flying Dutchman* allegedly tries in vain to round Cape Horn — *forever.*

Visitors to Glamis maintain that they have heard the ghost of Patrick and his friend, the Earl of Crawford, playing cards with Satan late at night.

The second story that clings to Patrick is that one of his children was born hideously deformed and was therefore, according to the standards of the day, kept hidden from sight deep in a secret chamber within the castle. One famous picture of the third earl, still on view in Glamis, shows him wearing bronze armour that looks as though it belonged to ancient Greek or Roman times. His left hand points to a landscape that includes Glamis. In the picture with him, on his left side, is a child — a very strange-looking child

— who is wearing green, almost as though to suggest that he was some kind of faerie or changeling.

There were two strange children who appeared out of the wolf pits in the Suffolk village of Woolpit during the turbulent reign of King Stephen, which was ruined by his constant battles against the Empress Matilda. These two strange children, a boy and a girl, spoke no known language and were not only clad in green but had green skin and hair as well. The boy died within a short while, but the girl survived, grew up, lost her green colouring, was criticized for her promiscuity, and ended up married to a man from King's Lynn in Norfolk. Who the green children of Woolpit really were, or from whence they came, no one knows. Green, nevertheless, seems to have been a colour associated with nature, wild mysteries, and the paranormal.

Was the artist who painted Strathmore's picture containing the strange, sad, little green-clad child trying to symbolize something mysterious by that green tunic?

There is another mysterious figure to the Earl's right in the same painting: it, too, is depicted as wearing armour from the Greek or Roman period, — but this figure is also shown as having some kind of physical problems. The left arm, especially, looks *wrong*. What is the artist trying to show in this canvas?

One theory that sets out to explain the so-called curse of Glamis is that perhaps as long ago as the time of Patrick, the third earl, or perhaps later, in early Victorian times, or possibly on *both* occasions, a handicapped child was born into the succession. If the heir to a great estate was clearly so severely physically and mentally challenged that he would have been totally incapable of running the estate, would it not be probable that the infant would be hidden away? There would be no shortage of hiding places in a building as vast as Glamis! Many of the walls are thick enough to hold the lounge of a modern semi-detached home.

In terms of land inheritance and wealth for the heirs and posterity of the great family, here was a very serious problem indeed. If the rightful heir was too ill to be placed in charge of his property, what was to be done with him?

Patrick might have been compelled to be ruthless because of the force of circumstances and the demands of the law of inheritance, but, as was clearly revealed by his kindness and generosity to his retired tenants, there was also a warm strand of humanity running

70

through him. A gambler, a womanizer, and a heavy drinker, Patrick might also have been, but there was no way that he was capable of disposing of his poor handicapped child.

Sharing the secret only with his trusted bailiff, Patrick perhaps concealed the poor infant as best he could in some secret place deep within the castle. It is also apparent that whatever deformity had afflicted the luckless child, it was not one that had shortened his life. It might even be possible to suggest that in the consistent temperature of that hidden room and in a relatively germ-free environment, the handicapped child lived an abnormally long time. Was it Patrick's son, grandson, or even great-grandson who finally ended that faithful vigil of attending with care and kindness to the so-called monster of Glamis immured in its secret chamber?

Glamis Castle, Scotland. Drawn by Theo Fanthorpe.

Another date for the deformed child "monster" story goes back to the early 1820s. Some researchers have suggested that the then Lord and Lady Glamis had married without realizing that they were first cousins. According to *Burke's Peerage*, Lady Glamis gave birth to their first child on September 22, 1822: this was almost two years after her marriage. The boy was perfectly normal and healthy, was christened Thomas George, and lived on to become the twelfth earl; but in those days it was not usual for a first child to be born as long as two years after the parents were married. Researchers claim to have found *another register* showing that there *had* been a son born before 1822. It simply said that the boy had been born and had died on October 21, 1821. A similar register gave the date as three days before, on October 18. Might one suppose that this record had actually referred to the unfortunate deformed child who had *not* died as stated, and as his parents possibly publicized, but had lived on in the secret room to become the unhappy monster of Glamis?

In 1865, if this child had lived, it would have been between forty and fifty years old. There is an account of a workman who found a door in the labyrinthine interior of Glamis Castle and walked through it into a strange corridor. This dark passage led him on until he reached the hidden chamber where he saw the "monster." The superstitious workman was in semi-darkness and in a huge building he believed to be haunted by God alone knew what. Harmless as the unfortunate "monster" was, its appearance in flickering candlelight in such a setting drove the workman almost mad with terror. He ran screaming from the secret room and fled from the castle.

News of his accidental discovery reached Lord Strathmore, who immediately cross-examined the man under the strictest secrecy — and as a result paid for him and his family to emigrate to Australia and make a new start: the price was the workman's silence. Records held by the Society of Psychical Research contain a statement to the effect that after this episode with the workman who was sent abroad, "Lord Strathmore was a changed man: silent and moody with an anxious, scared look on his face."

In view of other strange statements that have been made about the possible nature of the secret of the sealed room of Glamis, it seems hard to believe that the enigma is no more than the concealment of a sadly handicapped child.

One of the earl's "factors" or agents, Arthur Ralston, never stayed in the castle overnight, and on one occasion when Lady Strathmore questioned him about the secret of the hidden chamber, all he would say was: "It is fortunate that you do not know and will *never* know — for if you did know you would *never* again be a happy woman." This grim comment of Ralston's is reminiscent of an episode associated with the mysterious Man in the Iron Mask who was confined for so many years in the Bastille on the orders of Louis XIV, the great Sun King of France. Monsieur de Saint Mars, who was charged with Iron Mask's safe custody at Pignerol and at St. Marguerite prior to moving to the Bastille, was said to have been visited by a fisherman while the mysterious masked prisoner was confined near the coast before being taken to the Bastille. This fisherman handed an engraved plate bearing the royal fleur de lys to Monsieur de Saint Mars and told him that it had been flung from a window of the prison. The prison governor looked sternly at his visitor and asked: "Have you read what it says on this plate?"

"No my Lord," replied the fisherman, "for, bless your Lordship, I can neither read nor write." The grim expression softened on Saint Mars' face and he reached into his purse for a gold piece, which he passed over to the fisherman.

"You are a very lucky man!" said the prison governor.

"Why, Sir, am I lucky because I have been given a gold piece?" he asked. "You are lucky because you cannot read or write. If you had known what was written on this plate, I would have been forced to kill you!" That particular Iron Mask incident may well be apocryphal, but it has a haunting ring of truth about it.

Perhaps Ralston was right and it was indeed fortunate for the then Lady Strathmore that she did *not* know the secret of the mysterious hidden room and its occupant. Another intriguing but somewhat paradoxical fact researchers unearthed about the faithful Arthur Ralston was that although it was said that he would never stay overnight in Glamis Castle, he was known at one time to take regular walks near it late at night. Is it possible he was accompanying the poor handicapped creature to get some exercise?

Glamis is so vast and rambling that it is almost impossible to measure its exact dimensions, or to count its many rooms — an architectural feature that makes the discovery of the secret chamber very difficult indeed — unless the searcher knows precisely where to look, and has been let into the dark secret. On one occasion, early in the twentieth century, a group of happy young people enjoying a weekend house party decided that they would try to locate the secret chamber by hanging towels or bed linen from every window and then going outside to see which, if any, had no linen hanging from them. This plan was put into effect and not just *one* window but as many as half a dozen were found to have no linen indicator when viewed from outside. The then Lord Strathmore returned in time to prevent the search from going any further and what had been a particularly enjoyable house party weekend petered out with much humiliation and embarrassment on the part of the guests who had abused the earl's hospitality.

Apart from the legend of the monster — whatever it may be — in its hidden chamber, and the Grey Lady who was burnt at the stake, there is a tall, thin spectre, a gaunt creature, known as "Jack the Runner," and another ghost said to be that of a coloured page-boy.

The wife of a former archbishop of York was staying at Glamis and told how she had dreamed about the spectre of a man who had the face of a corpse. Curiously, another guest had dreamed the same dream simultaneously. Heavy knocks and bangings were frequently heard, as though Lord Strathmore's builders had begun work early. Yet on many of these occasions there were no builders working in the house at all. Another legend tells how members of the Ogilvies were running from the Lindsays and begged the Lord of Glamis to provide them with protection and shelter. They were led deep into the castle dungeons, where they were locked in and left to starve to death. There are tales to the effect that the Ogilvie skeletons still lie there and that at least some of the captives had been forced into cannibalism by the desperateness of their hunger in the darkness and cold of the dungeon. Do their ghosts glide miserably along those dark, forbidding Glamis corridors?

It is highly probable that mysterious and tragic Glamis Castle holds many paranormal secrets — and not least among them the secret of the "monster" in its hidden chamber. Should the truth of that chamber and its mysterious contents ever be fully revealed, it seems likely that it will turn out to be something infinitely more terrible than a sadly deformed and harmless human child.

Chapter 8
The Ghosts of Bowden House

There is no guarantee that great age and an eventful history will fill an ancient site with psychic phenomena, but many experienced researchers into the paranormal have found a strong correlation between the length of time a site has been occupied, the number of major events connected with its past, and the reports of psychic phenomena emanating from it.

This correlation certainly holds good in the case of Bowden House just outside Totnes, Devon, England. Its earliest history goes back well before the Norman Conquest. Romans and Saxons have both left traces of their passing and there is no good reason to think that the ancient Britons and Celts were not there before them. The oldest of the residents to whom a name can be given was Vacili, whose grave marker indicated that he had lived at or near the present Bowden House about the year AD 600.

There are two possible derivations for the present word "Bowden." The first suggests that it is taken from "Boga" and "Dunne," which mean "the crest of a hill." Until Chaucer's time, however, various spellings rendered it "Bodeton." Just as the suffixes "thorpe," "by," and "toft" indicate Norse homesteads, so "ton" or "tun" serve the same purposes for the Anglo-Saxons and a "ton" would have been a farmhouse or homestead of some kind in pre-Norman times. Bodeton could then have meant that it was the farm or homestead of someone named Bode or Bude.

Scarcely twenty years after the arrival of William and his Normans, Judhel Fitz Alured founded a monastery in Totnes not far from Bowden House. There are interesting legends suggesting that one of the famous Saint Katherines, along with pious members of this local monastic community, was buried at or near Bowden. The *Oxford Dictionary of Saints* lists three famous Katherines. Katherine of Genoa, who flourished from 1447 to 1510, is too late, as is Katherine of Sienna, whose life span ran from 1333 to 1380. Katherine of Alexandria is the most famous of the three, but her history is the hardest to trace. She was alleged to have lived during the fourth century, although her cult did not begin until the ninth. According to her legend she had been born into a noble family and then persecuted for being a Christian. Declining an offer of marriage from the emperor on the grounds that she was "a bride of Christ," she successfully refuted the arguments of some fifty philosophers who had been summoned to persuade her that Christianity was an error. During the persecutions of Maxentius she was tortured on a wheel (the famous Katherine Wheel named in her honour) that broke down, injuring the callous onlookers who had come to watch her death. Her persecutors then beheaded her. According to the colourful legend, milk, rather than blood, flowed from the wound. Over the centuries she became the patron saint of girls, students, especially students of philosophy — nurses, and wheelwrights. A miracle play was performed in her honour at Dunstable as early as 1110. A mural of her dating from the start of the thirteenth century is in Winchester Cathedral in the Chapel of the Holy Sepulchre. According to legend, Saint Katherine's remains were transported by angels to Mount Sinai. It is more than likely, however, that the "angels" of the legend were perfectly ordinary human monks, as it was customary in ancient times to describe the life of a monk or nun as "angelic."

The performance of the Dunstable miracle play and the painting of the Winchester Cathedral mural may be indications that during the twelfth and thirteenth centuries the intense British interest in Saint Katherine *might* have led to her body, or at least a relic of her, being fetched from her alleged burial place on Sinai and brought to Devonshire. Certainly there is a persistent element in the legend associating Bowden House with this saint's final resting place.

By the middle of the twelfth century Bowden was already being described in the literature as an old family mansion, the property of Reginald de Brieuse, whose son, William, was a favourite of King

John. The situation changed dramatically in 1208 when William organized a rebellion against the king because of the very heavy taxes and knightly dues the impoverished John was demanding from his nobles. The rebellion, unfortunately for William, was an idea whose time had not yet come. The rebels were defeated.

In a desperate effort to keep Bowden House out of John's clutches, William passed it adroitly to his second son, who was Bishop of Hereford at the time. John, never noted for his clemency or good temper, decided that the only good Brieuse was a dead one, and executed the Bishop of Hereford, as well as the other rebels.

Bowden and Totnes castles were then handed over to Henry, son of Reginald, Earl of Cornwalls who was in turn an illegitimate offspring of Henry I. Richard the Lionheart came back from the Crusades and began restoring property to those who had lost it during John's mismanagement. By 1216, less than ten years after William de Brieuse and his son, the Bishop of Hereford, had been executed, King Henry III restored Bowden to Reginald de Brieuse, who was the unfortunate William's third son.

It was at this point that the spelling changed to Broase. By 1315 the modern spelling of Bowden had appeared, and during the century that followed, it was separated from the Manor of Totnes

Bowden House, Totnes, Devon, England: the haunted staircase.

and the castle itself. Bowden passed into the hands of the Gylles Family in 1464. The name was later spelt Giles and it remained in their keeping for almost two hundred and fifty years. During that period they were prominent as members of Parliament, jurymen, wardens of St. Mary's, Totnes, and wardens of fisheries. Remembered as a prosperous family of merchants, wool traders, and financiers, it was John Giles and his son William who expanded the ancient house into a glorious Tudor mansion almost three times larger than it is today. Warriors as well as financiers, the Giles family were honourably represented by Edward during the reign of Queen Elizabeth I when he fought against the Dutch as a member of Her Majesty's light infantry. He was duly knighted at the coronation of King James I in 1604.

The Giles family were not only prosperous merchants and fearless soldiers, there was a noble generosity about them, and there is evidence that John Giles fed as many as two hundred hungry townspeople at his own table during a period of near-famine.

Nicholas Trist was only 14 when he came into a large estate. He inherited a great fortune from his uncle, also called Nicholas, and set about the popular eighteenth-century custom of consolidating and expanding his land holdings. In 1704 he bought Bowden House, which he renovated and rebuilt, reducing its size considerably and adding the Queen Anne façades. By 1708 the astute young Nicholas Trist owned well over two thousand acres of land, numerous houses, farms, mills, orchards, and even entire villages. He became high sheriff of Devon in 1709 and mayor of Totnes ten years later. His coat of arms bore the family motto "*Nec Trist, Nec Trepide*," which translates as "never sad and never fearful." As with many similar mottos it is a Latin pun, the "*Nec Trist*" sounds remarkably like Nick Trist and could be understood as "Nick Trist is never afraid."

There are strong American connections with Bowden House as well. Nicholas Trist's grandchildren were born there and went to America as soldiers in the War of Independence. Their commissions were signed by George III and they served in the 18th Irish Light Infantry.

A member of the American branch of the family, Hore Browse Trist, became a close friend of Thomas Jefferson and another member of the family became a famous diplomat who was involved with the acquisition of nearly a million square miles of extra territory for the United States. The famous and talented American Trists are still going strong today.

Returning to the British history of Bowden House and its outstanding occupants, William Adams bought the property in 1800. He was private secretary to Pitt the Younger when the latter was prime minister. William Adams was the M.P. for Totnes in 1802.

In 1887 Bowden passed into the possession of the Singer family of sewing machine fame, and Mr. A.M. Singer bred and trained racehorses on the site. Just before the end of the nineteenth century, the Harvey family bought the property and it stayed with them for almost a hundred years.

During the Second World War the great house did its duty when two hundred British and Canadian medical orderlies were stationed there and later a great many American G.I.s (including the famous 101st Airborne) were billeted at or near Bowden in preparation for the D-Day landings of 1944.

The present owners of Bowden House and the twelve acres of grounds surrounding it are the Petersen family. They took on the restoration work with massive enthusiasm and equal taste and skill. Luxurious holiday apartments are now available there and the attractions also include a fascinating photographic museum.

Yet it is the *supernatural* aspects of Bowden House that are even more fascinating than its long history and its scenic, photographic, and architectural attractions. The paranormal phenomena reported frequently from Bowden House can be divided into five categories: sudden inexplicable drops in temperature and strange feelings of paranormal cold; the impressions, or fleeting glimpses, of things that seem to be observed out of the corner of the observer's eye; hearing orders or directions being given by something or someone invisible; the sight of an animal, or the feeling of being touched by an animal as it passes; clear and persistent apparitions — complete or partial — some in full lifelike colour, others white or semitransparent.

The Bowden phenomena can also be categorized by the different locations in which they appear. Some are encountered persistently in the grounds, others are met with in specific buildings or particular rooms.

All mysterious haunted sites, like Bowden, seem to have their own characteristic atmosphere or ethos. Whatever psychic presences may still be lingering around the Bowden site, they all seem, in the words of the Petersen family, "very amiable and friendly." One of the apparitions seen in and around the grounds is the spectre of a Grey Lady who is normally observed at twilight or during the hours of darkness. She frequently appears in the entrance drive or along the stretch of public road running parallel to the Bowden driveway.

One report dating from 1992 tells how a local visitor was using that public road alongside the Bowden drive when his car headlights picked up the apparition of the Grey Lady, whom he described as being dressed like a nun. She appeared so suddenly that the driver was unable to brake in time and his car went straight over the spectre. He stopped and leapt out looking to see whom he had killed or injured, but there was no one there. Neither was there anywhere into which the Lady could have vanished. The closest gateway was almost two hundred yards away and the tall hedges — approximately two metres high — would have made it impossible for any normal human being to have got through them swiftly into a field.

There is a well-known Victorian or Edwardian ghost story — a piece of pure imaginative fiction — concerning two friends visiting an allegedly haunted house. It was a dark, sinister place, and as far as each was aware, two very separate occurrences took place. Like the character in the traditional English pantomimes, the first of the

Bowden House: exterior view.

investigators walked up the stairs certain that the steps he heard close behind him were those of his friend, *but turned round and saw that they weren't.*

The other man thought that the stooping figure that appeared to be struggling with the key in the front door was his companion. "What's the matter," he asked innocently, "having trouble with the lock?" The *thing* in front of him then turned round and faced him.... Pure fiction, of course, but a piece of very neatly turned fiction: worthy of O. Henry or Roald Dahl at his best.

Something amazingly similar, but far less frightening, took place just outside Bowden House in the early 1990s. A visitor was standing in the entrance to Bowden House reading the notice board alongside his friend when he was quite certain that he heard footsteps coming up from behind them. Naturally assuming that someone wished to go past and enter the house, he stepped aside politely to give them room. *There was no one there.*

Another of the outdoor sightings occurred quite regularly some twenty years ago, not long after the Petersens had moved into Bowden House. This apparent visitor from another world was dressed in a red Tudor costume, complete with the traditional ruff. The figure, which seemed to prefer hot, sunny August weather, walked behind the plane tree and vanished.

A family named Ayles lived at Bowden prior to the mid-1970s and reported frequent noises of horses' hooves clattering in the inner courtyard, while on other occasions monks could be heard chanting. The Ayles' reports of the sound of horses is very reminiscent of a case we investigated for our *Fortean TV* series involving two treasure hunters using a metal detector in Boulder Field near Shrewsbury. They had already found a number of pieces of Roman cavalry harness in the vicinity, when, very late at night, they suddenly heard the thunderous hooves of what sounded like a cavalry squadron approaching them at high speed. They flung themselves sideways thinking that horses were stampeding towards them. When they regained their composure, and the sounds of the invisible horses had trembled away into silence, they found it was impossible to get back to their car because of what felt like a solid stockade right across the field. It was a field they knew well and had searched often. They knew perfectly well that no such barrier existed there. Feeling very alarmed and disoriented, they made their way along parallel to the obstacle until it finally turned a ninety-degree corner. They were then able to get past it and relocate their car. They spent the rest of what should have been a good night's search sitting in their car for protection. They drank coffee and ate sandwiches as they waited for the first light of dawn.

As soon as the sun rose they ventured back into the field. There was no sign of any horses, neither was there any indication of the stockade that had prevented their return to the car. What they did see quite clearly in the soft earth, however, were their own footprints. These had turned suddenly as if their path had been blocked, had then continued in a straight line, and had finally taken another right-angled turn before heading back in the direction of their parked car. On taking the pieces of metal they had discovered before being disturbed by the noise of the galloping horses to a friend who worked in the Shrewsbury Museum, the treasure hunters were informed that the pieces that they had found that night were indeed accoutrements from Roman cavalry harness and saddles.

A similar event involving the sound of horses and the turning wheels of a coach comes from Norfolk, in England, where there are strong traditions of a phantom coach travelling from Great Yarmouth to King's Lynn. Many of the reports of this coach refer to guests in Norfolk halls, granges, and farmhouses, waiting for friends to arrive for a party. The people inside the house hear the sound of wheels on the carriageway, go out to greet their friends, and find that there is nothing there; neither are there any marks on the snow.

George Mace, a notorious eighteenth-century poacher and petty criminal, was at one time the leader of a gang of desperados in the Watton area of Norfolk. Such was Mace's reputation that the constables and magistrates, who did their best to prevent his nefarious activities, were often heard to mutter darkly that George Mace was marked for hanging.

Their predictions were unfounded. On one of his sinister nocturnal expeditions George was reported to have been gathered up by the sinister phantom coach and carried away by it, screaming into the sinister lonely darkness of the Norfolk night. His body — unmarked, but with a look of indescribable terror on the face — was found at Breccles Hall at daybreak. It would be easy enough to suggest that the forces of law and order, tired of being unable to secure a conviction against the wily poacher, had meted out their own direct, informal justice. Another possibility is that the so-called phantom coach was on this occasion driven by a rival gang who were tired of Mace and the Watton thugs encroaching on their territory. But if neither of these two basic physical explanations held good, what had *really* happened to George Mace on that dark, bleak Norfolk night?

Mrs. Belinda Petersen, the member of the team responsible for the excellent and exciting tours of Bowden House available to visitors, records seeing a mysterious figure dressed in brown walking along the drive in the direction of the front entrance close to the point where day visitors park their cars. Naturally assuming it to be one of the resident guests, she approached the figure, which then disappeared mysteriously behind one of the kiosks. When Belinda reached the kiosk herself there was no one there and nothing to be seen, although there was no logical way in which the brown spectre could have disappeared. The sighting occurred at around six p.m. on an August evening.

Alan Payne, who has an extensive knowledge of the area, reported to the Petersens that the west end of the building had once contained some superbly carved medieval angels together with inscriptions. Unfortunately these ancient gravestones and carvings

Co-author Lionel Fanthorpe with his Harley Davidson inside Bowden House.

disappeared in the late 1940s and nothing is known of their present whereabouts. The gravestone of Vacili dating from the year 600 vanished at about this time.

While much of the important conversion, renovation, and restoration work was taking place, many of the builders — solid, dependable craftsmen — experienced glimpses of strange figures, especially during the late afternoons. One singularly frightening experience occurred to a building team who were working on a high roof. While they were in the act of fixing the roof trusses to the ceiling rafters, they spotted a human hand inching its way along the rafters. Part of the forearm was also visible, *but nothing else*. As they watched, the fingers appeared to lose their grip and fall off. This so affected one of the builders that he, himself, almost fell as a result of the shock. The hand appeared again later in the week and the effect on the roofing team was such that they left the job and had to be replaced by a fresh team.

Completion of the work on these excellent holiday units involved cladding the steps with ancient stone dug up in the grounds, and it was Chris Petersen who undertook this work. We know Chris well: he is a highly intelligent man with a calm, steady, friendly personality. He is not the type to imagine things. Yet while Chris was working on the stone cladding he felt all the time that he was being watched. The feeling became so strong that he turned round periodically to see if there was actually anyone there. But he never succeeded in catching a glimpse of any watcher.

On one occasion, when Chris was holding his mason's trowel in his left hand, a bright light suddenly appeared actually on that hand and moved slowly up his arm as far as the shoulder. For some ten seconds the whole of his arm was illuminated and spots of red, blue, and yellow light came from it. Talking to an experienced medium some weeks later, Chris was told that this light manifestation was probably an attempt by a spirit to make contact with him.

During the construction of the museum complex, builders saw the shadows of horses and several men crossing the space by the existing kitchen door. During another period of roof construction the builders noticed what they thought at first might have been a member of their team moving around among the rafters and trusses. A little later, during their tea break, they started a conversation with what looked to them like one of their team up on the roof again. The figure made no reply, and by the simple expedient of counting their teacups the builders realized that everyone was accounted for. Was the figure whom they saw on the roof the same ghost that has since been reported from the museum?

Moving inside the building, very heavy and pronounced footsteps are frequently heard above the museum complex at night. The first time that the Petersens became aware of these strange sounds, the steps were heard on surveillance equipment and Alex Smith, who was present at the time, rushed immediately to the museum to investigate. He found nothing. There was no one there. By the time the footsteps had been heard on six or seven occasions Alex no longer raced across to investigate, but listened attentively to whoever, or whatever, apparently comes from another world to patrol the museum at night. The ghost has almost become a supernumerary member of the Bowden security team.

A very striking report was made by Mr. Rolle who had been a banker in New Zealand prior to his retirement. He had rented the delightful Singer cottage while taking time to look around for a permanent retirement home in the area. He was woken in the middle of the night by a tall, powerfully built monk well over two metres tall who stood at the foot of his bed. Mr. Rolle distinctly remembers that this strange visitor wore a brown habit. The spectre appeared to be looking directly at Mr. Rolle, but there was no face — only a bright blue light inside the monk's cowl. Mr. Rolle reported that the monk remained absolutely motionless. It was not hostile or frightening in any way, but certainly strange. The experience lasted for some ten or fifteen minutes and the retired banker was wondering whether he ought to wake his wife. He decided against it, however, in case the sight upset her, and she did not normally sleep very well. He wanted her to have the benefit of the deep sleep that she was enjoying during the period that the monk was in the room and, as the harmless monastic visitor showed no signs of leaving, Mr. Rolle closed his eyes, turned over, and fell asleep.

During his researches among the many historical documents relating to Bowden House, Robert Lamb was working upstairs when he distinctly heard someone moving below. On several occasions he went downstairs to investigate the noise, thinking that perhaps a visitor had called to see him, but there was never anyone there. On one occasion he left the work that he was doing and ran across to see the Petersens in very great distress. He reported to them that he had been working in an upstairs bedroom when suddenly all of the windows started banging loudly. He examined them and found that all were tightly closed and secured — but the banging continued. Robert continued to work in the main house but was never able to say what he had seen and heard that had been so upsetting to him in Singer Cottage. Later tenants repeatedly heard footsteps but were not worried by them.

Exhibits on the wall of a haunted room in Bowden House.

The Bowden ghosts may occasionally be noisy and mischievous, but they are certainly not evil. A later tenant of Gipps Cottage reported that regularly at four o'clock in the morning, for a period of several weeks, an apparition had appeared in the entrance of the bedroom that she and her husband shared. It began as a very faint outline, but over the weeks became more real and solid until it was able to speak and actually make physical contact, shouting, "Wake up! Wake up!" On some occasions it actually pushed them.

Graham Wyley was called in to exorcise the troubled spirit of Kenneth Durell who had died at Bowden on the October 8, 1636, when he was only fifty-three years old. Durell, a married man, had been having an affair with a servant girl who had told him that she was pregnant. Unable to face the scandal in those puritanical days, the unfortunate Durell committed suicide. He worked at that time as a driver coachman and lived above the coach house. He committed suicide by jumping off the top of the building. Tragically, the girl had lied to him. She was not pregnant at all; but the truth came too late to save the coachman's life.

While Graham Wyley's investigations and exorcisms were continuing, the spirits of the servant girl and Durell's wife also appeared in the same area. Wyley's spiritual rescue work seems to have been successful, for none of those three ghosts have ever appeared in the area since. The lady who first saw Kenneth Durell's ghost moved into a house in Totnes with her husband and has since reported to the Petersen Family that the ghost occasionally visits her dreams in quite a friendly way.

This dream report was of particular interest to us during our research visits to Bowden House.

Some people dream regularly and have vivid memories of the sights and sounds together with the emotions their dreams contain. Co-author Lionel either does not dream, or hardly ever recalls doing so. After a visit to Bowden House while filming a sequence for his *Fortean TV* series, he returned to Cardiff and had a nightmare that he recalled with great vividness and in sharp detail. In this nightmare he was being confronted by an apparition about the size of Frankenstein's monster with a shadowy face and glaring, hostile, challenging eyes. Sometimes we tend to behave in dreams as we would do in waking life. Being a 210-pound trainer and martial arts instructor, Lionel's first reaction in the dream was to launch himself at his antagonist with the aggression of a Welsh international fullback intent on bringing down an opponent when the Triple Crown was at stake! He was thrown casually aside as if he had tried to charge a steam locomotive. He tried again, twice more, and was hurled away like a rag doll on each occasion. Again, acting as he would have done in a waking situation against an entity that seemed impervious to physical attack, he concentrated his mind and will on pronouncing an exorcism. No intelligible sounds would come out. It was during this period of mental and spiritual struggle against the monster in the dream that Lionel noticed that the great arms of his opponent did not end in human hands, but in what looked like fronds of black, trailing seaweed. His attempts to speak, which had resulted only in loud, unintelligible noises, woke Patricia, who shook him awake. The dream ended there and has never recurred, but if the benign and harmless ghost of poor

Kenneth Durell, the suicide coachman, could follow the residents of Singer Cottage to their new home in Totnes in their dreams, there is a possibility, however slight, that something strange followed Lionel from Bowden House that night.

Medium Graham Wyley, who had helped in the Durell case, came across another phantom in Bowden House while carrying out his work there. This one communicated to Graham that he had been killed in an accident during the eighteenth century. While out riding he had jumped a tall hedge and landed to his horror on a heavily spiked hay turner.

It is not only the Singer Cottage in which manifestations are experienced. When the Petersens moved into Bowden House in 1976 they soon discovered that the mansion house itself was a very interesting psychic site. Their friend and colleague, Alex Smith, was moving some items into the undercroft or cellar (one of the oldest parts of the structure) using an oil lamp, as there was no electric light in the cellar at the time. He was carrying a number of glass shelves on one of his journeys when he became aware of a strange voice telling him to crawl along the brick floor; not surprisingly, he ignored it. But the voice went on so insistently that he finally got down on his hands and knees and moved slowly along the floor of the passage. He was about to get to his feet again when the voice once more told him to crawl. Suddenly he noticed a small spot of bright light coming from an aperture at ground level. He reached into the hole and discovered a Georgian wine bottle. A moment or two later he discovered a second aperture containing a wineglass from the same date. Unfortunately, from any collector's point of view, both articles were damaged and almost worthless as antiques. Why had the ghost — if it was a ghost — bothered to lead anybody to them? One rather amusing possibility is that the spectre was that of a butler or footman who had been purloining the master's drink and concealing the evidence.

Further interesting reports came from Fred Selwood. Fred's father had been a footman at Bowden House before World War I. Fred remembered how he had played in the grounds occasionally during his boyhood. He also recalled, with the morbid fascination most children have for such things, that during his youth the cellar had been full of medieval instruments of torture, including an iron maiden and a rack. Some time before 1920 the collection seems to have been split up and no one knows today what became of it. Fred also recalled that there had been a mysterious secret tunnel in the cellar when he was a boy. Who constructed it, where it led, or what its purpose might have been remains one of the mysteries of the Bowden site.

The Bowden House Ghost Tour is an experience no serious investigator of the paranormal should miss. The tour begins near the old Tudor bakery, which boasts of sixteen large bread ovens. From here the tour proceeds to the great Tudor hall where an amazing poltergeist-type phenomenon occurred a while back and involved a large glass salad bowl of the oven-resistant type. A member of staff had simply picked up the bowl, which formed part of a large, tasty buffet, when it literally exploded in his hands, showering glass fragments all over the room. So complete was the destruction of the bowl that the member of staff who had been holding it was left with nothing in his hands at all. That kind of event is very difficult to explain.

The Green Bedroom is associated with reports of unearthly green lights that move around it. In 1983 a strange figure in the Georgian costume of the 1740s, complete with buckled black shoes and red jacket, was seen in the Red Drawing Room. Those who witnessed this apparition reported that it stood perfectly motionless for a period of almost three minutes. A curious feature was that the spectre — if it was a spectre — was wearing its tricorn hat indoors. Far from feeling uneasy as they saw it, the witnesses had a feeling of great happiness, excitement, and euphoria — as if some good and pleasant aura had arrived with the strange Georgian visitor. The apparition in red appeared on several occasions, and around the Christmas period he was accompanied by another spectre of similar date — but this one was wearing a green coat with his tricorn hat.

The Pink Room is alleged to be the most haunted location in the whole of Bowden House. An Australian visitor who stayed there some years ago felt rather ill in the night. Her husband was with her and she held out her hand in the darkness for him and felt his hand close affectionately and comfortingly around hers. She then went back to sleep. She woke in the morning fully recovered and suddenly realized that her husband's bed was almost ten feet away from hers.

Babs Dyment was a guest in this same Pink Room on Christmas Eve of 1988. She reported a similar strange occurrence to the other guests on Christmas Day. She had been woken during the night by the sound of chanting monks and, assuming there was a rational explanation for this, she got up, put on her dressing gown, and went to investigate the source of the music. She went back to bed and awoke again to find that someone was holding her hand. A peacock-blue light appeared hovering about five feet off the floor at the foot of her bed. It was oval in shape and not quite as large as a football. She heard the monks continuing to chant for over an hour and during all of this time she had the same feeling of great happiness and euphoria that had accompanied the red-coated spirit in Georgian costume. Since her encounter with the happy, friendly spirit in the Pink Room, Babs has reported that if she feels tired or unwell and thinks hard about her meeting with the friendly ghost — if that is what it was — she immediately begins to feel better.

The tour also takes in the main staircase, a beautiful feature made of English oak and constructed on the orders of Nicholas Trist in the early eighteenth century.

On the hot, sunny afternoon of August Bank Holiday Monday in 1988 the house was full of visitors and at least a hundred witnesses must have seen the ghost known as Little Alice, a child of roughly eight years, wearing a long blue dress with white lace. Her thin, rather sad face and deep-set blue eyes are framed by her shoulder-length hair.

The child concerned is Alice Eteson, who died tragically of tuberculosis in August of 1765 when she was only seven years old. Her father, Simon, worked in Bowden House and her mother was a seamstress. The family lived in what is now the Pink Room at the top of the stairs.

Nicholas Trist's old study or library is also included in the tour and the magnificent carved oak chimney piece there shows Holophernes and Judith. Many visitors and tour guides report having seen a spectre in this study standing close to the door. Like some of the other spectres described earlier, he appears to be Georgian and is quite short, being only five foot three or four inches tall. He wears a frock coat decorated with silver braid and seems to have been a footman at one time. It was also in this study that phantom dogs have been noted — another of the strange phenomena reported so frequently from Bowden House. Then there's the mystery of the camera and flash gun. This took place in the morning room, another port of call on the fascinating tour. Two or three flashes went off entirely of their own account and another visitor called suddenly to Chris Petersen, "Look at my video camera." Chris looked into the viewfinder and saw two distinct images side by side. There was no physical explanation for them. On other occasions visitors' cameras have mysteriously failed to work.

There are so many more reports from Bowden House of paranormal events witnessed by sensible and reliable observers over the last few years that this intriguing and very attractive location must be a strong contender for the title of "the most haunted house in Britain."

Chapter 9
Llancaiach Fawr Manor

The manor house stands in the beautiful and historically interesting Rhymney Valley. It is not known who first inhabited the site, but it is highly likely that the ancient and mysterious Celts lived here in the dawn of time. A building was erected in medieval times but the present manor is Tudor. It is certainly older than the Acts of Union that joined England and Wales, and Leyland refers to it in his itinerary in 1537. The first master of the manor was David ap Richard, who was undersheriff of Glamorgan during the sixteenth century. The Welsh "ap" meaning "son of" frequently became attached to the second part of the name so that ap Richard became Pritchard, a name that is very well known and respected throughout Wales today.

When David Pritchard's son married Ann, a daughter of Thomas Lewis, the marriage settlement contained a reference to a mansion that was then spelt "Glankayach."

Pritchard's great historic house was as much a fortress as it was a dwelling. The walls were well over a metre thick and just as Norman castles had their outer baileys, inner baileys, and keeps so that the defenders could fall back and back yet again if they had to, so Llancaiach Fawr could be defensively split in half if a serious attack was mounted against it. The east wing was the second retreat and only those who were defending it had access to the toilet tower. Llancaiach has very small windows on the ground floor and its thick, robust old doors are evidence of what life must have been like in this part of Wales during Tudor times.

Things went well for the Pritchard family and architectural modifications and improvements reflected their growing wealth during the early seventeenth century. The rear of the house was extended in 1628 so that the grand staircase could be built there; formal gardens were laid out and some rooms were panelled.

Not surprisingly, the Welsh nobles and gentry were very proud of their long and distinguished heritage: the Pritchards traced their line back to the famous Ivor Bach. The great chronicler, Gerald of Wales, had described the famous Ivor as being of short stature but high courage. Descended from the fiery Celtic nation, the fearless and emotional Welsh temperament can lead its owners more easily than the genes of some more sedate races into fighting and quarrelling — and the reigns of Elizabeth I and James I experienced their fair share of this in Glamorgan. If there was going to be a fight between rival families in those days, those involved were not very bothered about where it took place. Both Edward Pritchard and his son David, who lived during the early years of the seventeenth century, were involved in an enthusiastic brawl outside the church at Gelligaer.

The Lewis and Pritchard families were closely related, but that did not prevent William Lewis from abducting one of Edward Pritchard's daughters when she was only 14 and coercing her into

Interior of haunted Llancaiach Fawr Manor House in Wales.

marriage. The causes of these quarrels and disturbances among the seventeenth-century gentry of Glamorgan can best be understood when some words of Richard Kynwall are examined. He wrote: "His name and his fame are more important to a gentleman than his gold." Shakespeare well understood the same truth when he wrote of those who were "seeking the bubble reputation even in the cannon's mouth." The history of Llancaiach Fawr Manor and those who lived there cannot be fully understood without considering the traumatic civil war between Charles I and Cromwell.

The sinister roots of that conflict went far deeper than Charles' reign. His father, James I, was highly intelligent and well educated by the standards of the time — but he was sadly in need of spin doctors and public relations experts. He did not have the advantage of a powerful and dominating physical presence and his reliance on court favourites did nothing to help his cause in the rest of the country.

The great problem facing the Stuarts was their belief in the divine right of kings. Convinced, in the words of James I, that the monarchy was the supreme thing in the whole of the world, they did their best to put that strange fallacy into effect. The sadly misguided Archbishop Laud devoted his considerable energies to teaching his flock that questioning the royal judgement was a matter of the deepest, darkest sacrilege. The great historian Collingwood always maintained that *history is the history of ideas*. Few things are as powerful as an idea whose time has come. The particular idea that came to the House of Commons at about the same time as the idea of the divine right of kings came to the British monarchy was the thought that Parliament was the keeper of the Common Law and was the people's defence against impositions by the monarch.

The ridiculous excesses of the Puritans on one side and the High Church Anglicans on the other were making armed conflict inevitable. Charles I, who had a Catholic queen, gave the Puritans reason to believe that he was heading back towards Rome, and he, in turn, became increasingly irritated by what he regarded as Parliament's persistent interference with his royal prerogative.

Over and above the struggle for power and the religious quarrels was the great problem of money. Parliament was the tap through which money flowed, and when Charles began drilling holes in the pipe with crude instruments like his ship money scheme, further clashes of a deeper and more dangerous kind began to occur between the king and Parliament. By 1640 the king's finances were in such a mess that he had no choice but to recall a Parliament he had happily done without for nearly twelve years.

It was at this time that Colonel Edward Pritchard of Llancaiach Fawr Manor played a very significant part in the history of Wales — and of Britain as a whole. It was in Nottingham, England, rather than in Wales that hostilities were declared. On August 22, 1642, King Charles I raised his standard in that midland city and Edward Pritchard was among those who pledged his support for the king.

Interior of haunted Llancaiach Fawr Manor House in Wales.

He was rewarded by being made one of the commissioners of Array whose task it was to recruit men and find money for King Charles. As a commissioner he had the king's authority to confiscate land belonging to supporters of Parliament. It is difficult to understand, with the virtue of hindsight, why Colonel Pritchard supported Charles in the first place. Pritchard and other leading members of the Welsh aristocracy were very unhappy with the high level of taxation Charles was demanding. Gerard, who was commander-in-chief in South Wales at the time, was understandably hated by the Welsh gentry, as was Tyrell, who was the commander of the garrison in Cardiff Castle.

Pritchard and his peers wanted both Gerard and Tyrell removed, but when Charles I met the Welsh delegation at St. Fagan's, these were by no means the only complaints brought forward by Pritchard and his group. To them religious faith was far more important than taxation or membership of the hierarchy. Looking back at the situation it seems almost unbelievable that a dedicated and enthusiastic Puritan like Pritchard could ever have supported the king. The Colonel belonged to a Baptist group in Eglwysilian. As far as Pritchard and his fellow Baptists were concerned, Charles' Anglican Church was decadent, corrupt, and lamentably distant from what the Eglwysilian Baptists believed to be scriptural truth.

The arguments for changing sides became overwhelming. Pritchard left the Royalists and became a staunch Parliamentarian instead; politically, it was a shrewd move. He was made a member of the Commission for the Propagation of the Gospel, the Glamorgan Parliamentary Committee, and — most important of all — Governor of Cardiff Castle. It was in this role that Colonel Pritchard acquired military distinction by holding the castle against the siege conducted against it by Edward Carne of Ewenny and his Royalist troops. Pritchard also fought well at the Battle of St. Fagan's. Colonel Horton described him as "constant minded."

Just as many old English manor houses bear the legend "Queen Elizabeth slept here," so Llancaiach Fawr once accommodated Charles I. On August 5, 1645, Charles, in what was probably intended to be an attempt to retain Pritchard's support for the Royalists, had dinner at Llancaiach. The great feature of this mysterious old house — with its many reported hauntings — is that it has been carefully and expertly restored to the way it would have looked during Colonel Pritchard's time there. As was the way with all fortified manor houses of the time, there was in the beginning only a single entrance to Llancaiach Fawr. From the point of view of defensive strategy and tactics at times of siege, this was a vitally important issue. Visitors waiting in the entry area could be discreetly observed by loyal servants to ensure that they were not a danger to the household. The first stairway to the great hall would have faced such visitors as they came in, until the grand staircase was constructed early in the seventeenth century. In our century of central heating and running water it is not easy to imagine the difficulties confronting kitchen staff during the sixteenth and seventeenth centuries.

In the great kitchen of Llancaiach Fawr Manor the fire would have burnt continuously so that meals could be cooked and food heated at any time the family demanded it. Disposing of waste water from the kitchen was no great problem: there was an outlet in the wall. The difficulty lay in fetching the water *in*. A small passage connects the kitchen and the servants' hall and this passage leads to another staircase that gives access to the great hall above. The purpose of this was to make sure that food served to the family and their guests was hot when it reached the table above.

The servants' hall was another regular feature of houses like Llancaiach Fawr. The many who worked in such great houses would take their recreation there when their duties permitted, and it was also a place where they could carry out those parts of their work that were not tied to other rooms.

A very unusual discovery — and one with certain magical significance — was made in the fireplace in the servants' hall. A fox's paw and a lock of human hair had been hidden away in a crevice between the stones. In terms of sixteenth- and seventeenth-century "spells," this ritual could have been intended to bring good fortune to the person whose hair it was, or, conversely, to have given them a fever if the hair and fox's foot had been placed there by an enemy. The ritual could have been intended to ward off lightning, chimney fires, or witches — who were thought to have been able to enter via chimneys at that time.

The storeroom and wine cellars at Llancaiach would have been used for preserved meat, fruit, grain, ale, cider, and wine.

Another feature of the great fortified manor houses of the Llancaiach Fawr period were the stairways inside the walls. Until the grand staircase was added as a mark of increased prosperity in 1628 these narrow wall staircases would have been extremely defensible. The stairs connecting the family quarters to the wine cellar probably had two purposes. In times of peace and prosperity they would have been a convenient route for servants bringing drinks up to the family. In times of danger those same stairs would have served as a safety exit. When Glamis Castle was investigated by the guests who hung towels and linen from the windows in an attempt to locate the secret room, it was found that numerous windows at Glamis did not appear to belong to any of the rooms the guests had been able to enter — for those windows had no linen marking them. A very similar situation applies at Llancaiach Fawr

Manor and researchers have wondered whether certain rooms there were deliberately sealed for some sinister purpose. An examination of the Llancaiach Fawr windows internally and externally soon reveals that more windows can be seen from the outside of the house than can be counted by the explorer inside.

When the authors were assisting Canon Noel Boston and his son, Jonathan, to explore Lamas Manor in Norfolk as far back as the 1950s, a strange secret room was uncovered high in the roof. Our explorations revealed that this must at one time have been some kind of servants' dormitory. It was probably in use during the sixteenth and seventeenth centuries and must have been sealed up around the start of the nineteenth.

One of the darkest and most sinister sealed room stories of all time comes from Chambercombe Manor on the bleak but beautiful wild coast of north Devon. At the end of the nineteenth century the farmer then living in Chambercombe was carrying out some urgent repairs to his thatched roof. From his vantage point at the top of the ladder he saw that a window just below the thatch had been filled in at some time in the past. Mystified and intrigued he

Exterior of haunted Llancaiach Fawr Manor House in Wales.

went upstairs to calculate where that window would have been. Pacing the floor and making a swift mental calculation, he realized that a room had been concealed — *a room from which that window had once opened.*

The farmer broke through the wall of a small bedroom situated just below the thatched roof. There was a bed in the centre of the room and a skeleton — which later turned out to be that of a young woman — was lying on it. It was said that documents were later discovered indicating that a certain William Oatway had once been a resident of Chambercombe. Following a career as the perfectly honest and respectable steward of Lundy Island, Oatway reportedly took up smuggling and wrecking toward the end of the turbulent seventeenth century. The treacherous and fatal rocks of Hele Bay lay not far below Chambercombe Manor and on one inauspicious night, Oatway and his gang lured a passing ship into that deadly trap.

While he and his gang were searching the beach for valuables from the wreck they found the corpse of a young woman who had evidently been a passenger on the ill-fated ship. The body was carried up to the house and searched for valuables.

When Oatway's torchlight fell on the dead girl's face he recognized his own daughter who had been travelling to visit him from her home in Ireland. Insane with grief and remorse, Oatway sealed up the room with the girl's body on the bed and left Chambercombe Manor forever.

There may, however, be another sinister explanation for the skeleton on the bed in the sealed room at Chambercombe. William Oatway has proved an elusive quarry for historians and researchers who have tried to trace him as one of Chambercombe's owners.

Other accounts of the discovery of the skeleton towards the end of the nineteenth century have added a further grim detail. The girl's skeleton was not merely lying on the bed *but chained to it.* Rather than being the daughter of William Oatway, the wrecker and smuggler, it is more probably that she was a victim of kidnappers or white-slavers.

A similar gruesome discovery was made in 1708, when the owner of Lovel Manor in Oxfordshire was making some improvements and alterations, which included a new chimney. As the builders prepared their work, they broke through into a small chamber furnished with a table and chair — in which a gaunt skeleton was sitting as upright as the day the man had died centuries ago. Research suggested that it was none other than the missing Lord Francis Lovel, who had vanished in 1487 — as completely and as mysteriously as Benjamin Bathurst had done in Germany during the Napoleonic Wars at the beginning of the nineteenth century.

Wherever they are found — with or without skeletons inside — sealed rooms are always intriguing, and they are frequently found via entrances concealed behind old oak panels.

The panelled parlour is one of the most interesting parts of fascinating Llancaiach Fawr: the oak dates from the early seventeenth century. What is very significant is that this panelled parlour is in the most defensive area of the house. It has easy access to the vitally important toilet tower and could also be sealed efficiently from any attackers. At least two of the panels move to reveal storage places behind. The one closest to the hearth may simply have been a convenient location for the Colonel's port so that it was maintained at the temperature wine connoisseurs preferred. There is also a fascinating old story of a traditional Llancaiach miser who was said to have concealed his enormous wealth behind the carved oak panels in the parlour.

The north bedchamber of Llancaiach Fawr has an interesting architectural feature dating back to a period in the manor's history when it had become simply a tenanted farm. The upper floor was then used as a store, and a doorway was made in the external wall so that sacks of grain could be raised and lowered with a pulley as they were in some early mills. There is a tragic legend, which may go some way to explaining the origins of some of the reported ghostly sightings of Llancaiach, to the effect that a young child fell through that doorway and died as a result.

Just as at Lamas Manor in Norfolk, the attics at Llancaiach served as dormitories for the servants as well as for storage, and the one above the toilet tower provides interesting cultural evidence from the Tudor period. There is a crevice in the wall in which dried moss was kept; and dried moss was the toilet tissue of Tudor times.

Other specialist areas include the cheese room, which was kept well ventilated and apart from the kitchen. This is reminiscent of the wonderful account in Jerome K. Jerome's famous *Three Men in a Boat* in which Jerome tells of a hilarious journey he made to assist a friend by transporting two incredibly powerful cheeses from Liverpool to London. The Jerome cheeses worked miracles by emptying crowded railway carriages for him and, according to his account, when they were finally disposed of beneath the sands of a beach, the resort in question became famous for years afterwards for having a bracing, health-giving atmosphere. The cheeses in the Pritchard manor house at Llancaiach were no match for the ones in Jerome's fictional account, but it would nevertheless have been considered prudent to give them air and room in which to mature.

The great hall was undoubtedly the social centre of the entire building. Almost certainly it was in this great hall that the luckless Charles I would have dined on August 5, 1645. The steward's room contains a that which would have given the steward a discreet view into the great hall. He would have had the massive advantage of being able to see without being seen.

The sixteenth and seventeenth centuries lacked the sophisticated electronic listening and spying equipment that are so much a part of security and observation in our century — but a keen ear and a bright, inquisitive eye at this spy-hole would still have been able to discover a great deal — as the astute stewards of Llancaiach Fawr undoubtedly knew.

On one of his research visits to Llancaiach, co-author Lionel Fanthorpe carried out some investigations accompanied by another

Garden of haunted Llancaiach Fawr Manor House in Wales.

psychical research expert, Robert Snow. On this occasion both investigators were keenly aware of an unusual fragrance that persisted in an area associated with a housekeeper named Martha or Mattie who died in Llancaiach in tragic circumstances centuries ago. The great house has been reputedly haunted for many years and reports of strange paranormal events still persist.

Phantom children are reported to have been observed at play on the stairs and the figure of the mysterious housekeeper — frequently wearing a long white dress — has again often been reported by reliable witnesses visiting the house. During some restoration work a while back one of the craftsman experienced very considerable difficulty in plastering one particular area of the ceiling. Curiously enough that area lies below the great hall across which paranormal footsteps have been heard to echo on numerous occasions. Is it possible that there is a strange connection between these paranormal treads and the difficulty the craftsman had in persuading the ceiling plaster to adhere in the place to which he was directing it? Another apparition has also been reported from that area: the figure of a man reclining on a window seat.

More concrete evidence of bygone beliefs in the supernatural and the paranormal has also been unearthed. A party of workmen repairing the garden walls came across a pentagram that had been clearly and expertly carved. The pentagram is, of course, a significant feature of early magical rituals.

Some of the most reliable and compelling Llancaich evidence comes from the experience of Ed Williams. As a boy and young man he had actually been brought up in Llancaiach Fawr and in those days had not been disturbed by the psychic manifestations the house contained. The council purchased the property in 1982 and began restoring it as far as was possible to what it had been like centuries ago. It seemed as though the removal of the modern fittings and furniture had somehow released whatever was concealed behind them — or had stimulated strange forces from the past which the twentieth century furniture and fittings had been holding in check. According to Ed Williams it was after the old fabric came to the fore again that the strange voices and the sounds of children playing were released. He described how some visitors had felt as though their hair was being pulled and yet, just as with the phenomena at Bowden House in Totnes, the spirit presences in Llancaiach were friendly and mischievous. There was nothing sinister or evil in the old Tudor manor. When visitors were being taken on tours of Llancaiach they and the staff leading the tour frequently heard scratching noises that were normally attributed to the cat. The cat, however, was preying on the doves in the manor garden and a new home was found for it. It was only after the strange scratching noises persisted *although the cat had gone* that the paranormal nature of the persistent scratching sounds was realized. These mysterious scratching sounds are reminiscent of a strange and frightening mystery brought to the attention of the authors by a friend named Parker whom they met when he was attending one of their lectures. He had at one time worked at the Hedley Arms public house in the south of England.

One night, when he had worked late, the senior barman gave him permission to stay in the old hotel. The guest room he was allocated was very small: other than the door and window there was no means of access and both of these were firmly closed before Mr. Parker went to bed. During the night he was woken by a soft but terrifying scratching sound close to his head. Part of him longed for nothing more than to leap out of bed and switch on the light. Another part of him was terrified to move. There was no access via the small chimney, yet *something*, somehow, had ripped the wallpaper down and bitten deeply into the plaster during the night. Something had made enough noise to wake and terrify Mr. Parker. Could that *something* at the Hedley Arms have borne any kind of similarity to whatever made the scratching noises at Llancaiach?

Ed Williams reported that a friend of his who had stayed the night in the old manor house had seen a figure emerge from the fireplace and stand by the foot of his bed. One visitor was convinced that there was a strange figure — not of this world — in the back of her car as she drove away from the manor. Not only was it *visible*, but she could actually *feel* what seemed to be its knees pressing into the back of the driving seat.

One of the many other strange phenomena Ed Williams has witnessed is the distinct apparition of a Victorian gentleman outside the house. This particular spectre is one that has appeared on several occasions. He wears a top hat and is cloaked; other witnesses have observed him on the roadway near Llancaiach as well as outside the manor house itself. Some researchers have suggested that the reported footsteps from various locations in Llancaiach might in some curious way be connected with the flight path of

Concorde, which passes close to the old manor in excess of the speed of sound. The difficulty with that theory is that the footsteps were recorded long before any aircraft flew.

Fascinating old houses like Llancaiach Fawr Manor and Bowden House in Devon are undeniably mysterious, intriguing, and very well worth any researcher's time in paying them a visit.

Chapter 10
Did Atlantis Exist?

The historical evidence for the existence of Atlantis comes from two famous dialogues written by the great Greek philosopher Plato (427–347 BC), who was one of Socrates' students for almost ten years. Born into a wealthy, aristocratic Athenian family, Plato also studied with Euclid of Megara before going to Cyrene, Egypt, Italy, and Sicily. He was fascinated by the teachings of the Pythagoreans, but spent time as a slave after trouble overtook him on one of his many adventurous, academic journeys. He finally made his way back to Athens, where he founded his famous Academy in 387 BC.

The two dialogues that provide Plato's Atlantis information are *Timaeus* and *Critias*. Timaeus came from Locris in Italy. He was a dedicated Pythagorean as well as an active astrologer — and he was also an explorer. Critias, known as Critias the Younger, was the grandson of Critias the Elder who gave him the vital information about Atlantis, which he, himself, had obtained from the account written by Solon.

Critias the Younger was one of those ageless, energetic men — like fearless old Caleb in the Bible — who combined his political role as an Athenian statesman with his creative work as an orator, poet, and philosopher. He was also a soldier. Going fearlessly into battle at Aegospotami in 403 BC, he was killed in action. It was undoubtedly the way he would have chosen to go — he was over ninety years old at the time!

Who was the reputable and reliable Solon whose account of Atlantis came from ancient Egypt? Solon is perhaps best described as a merchant adventurer, an early Greek version of the later Arabian Sinbad type. He was also a successful soldier and captured Salamis for Athens. His greatest virtues, however, seem to have lain in the realm of statesmanship and constitutional law.

In 571 BC, Solon visited the priestly colleges at Sais and Heliopolis in ancient Egypt, where much old and mysterious knowledge was preserved by the learned priests. It was from these Egyptian priests that Solon heard the strange story of Atlantis and the disaster that overwhelmed it. Solon's own original notes on Atlantis have long since been lost, but Plutarch vouched for their existence.

In essence, an old priest from Sais told Solon that a great and glorious country had once flourished many centuries before on the site of Solon's contemporary Athens, but Phaeton, son of Helios — the sun god — had tried unsuccessfully to drive his father's blazing chariot across the skies and failed lamentably to hold it on track. To prevent a disaster of even greater proportions, Zeus had hurled a thunderbolt at the runaways. The old Egyptian priest went on to tell Solon how the greatest military glory of this proto-Athens had been their victory over the Atlanteans.

In this ancient Egyptian account, Atlantis — bigger than Asia Minor and Libya *combined* — had lain in the great Atlantic Ocean beyond the Pillars of Hercules (the Straits of Gibraltar). The arrogant and aggressive Atlanteans had posed a threat to all the nations of Europe and Asia Minor. After a battle of herculean proportions, the fearless proto-Athenians had destroyed the awesome Atlantean army and saved both Europe and Asia Minor from subjugation. Cataclysmic geological and meteorological disasters then submerged both Atlantis *and* proto-Athens.

Prior to its destruction, the kingdom of Atlantis was a great and prosperous island. It possessed vast wealth, augmented by the taxes and tributes sent in by the islands belonging to its extensive maritime empire. Among the produce of the Atlantean mines was *orichalc* and it was regarded by the citizens there as being second only to pure gold in value. Otto Heinrich Muck, the distinguished German engineer, physicist, and inventor who died in 1965, made a detailed scientific study of the Greco-Egyptian accounts of Atlantis and came to the conclusion that the material referred to as orichalc was a rich mixture of copper, arsenic, tin, and antimony of the kind frequently discovered in Cornwall in England. The Greco-Roman documentation also described the lush, abundant pastures, the wealth of timber, and the proliferation of domesticated Atlantean flocks and herds — as well as ample supplies of game for Atlantean huntsmen to pursue. Atlantis was said to be rich in herbs and spices and aromatic plants — together with gum and resin. The architectural skills of the Atlanteans were an appropriate match for the natural advantages of their huge island. The whole design of their kingdom, sometimes referred to as the Cross of Atlantis, shows how walls and canals surrounded their central city.

It is highly significant that this Cross of Atlantis design should figure so frequently and so prominently in many prehistoric henges and stone circles. Something very like it is carved on a stone in Rocky Valley near Tintagel, Cornwall, and Tintagel is one of the ancient sites connected with Arthur of the Britons.

The city of Atlantis, again according to this highly detailed Greco-Egyptian account, was richly supplied with temples, harbours, wharves, great houses, and palaces. Skilfully constructed bridges spanned the old Atlantean waterways. Their greatest temple was dedicated to Poseidon, the sea god, and was overlaid with gold, silver, and ivory. The description of its richness and beauty are reminiscent of the biblical account of the temple built by Solomon, king of Israel and Judah.

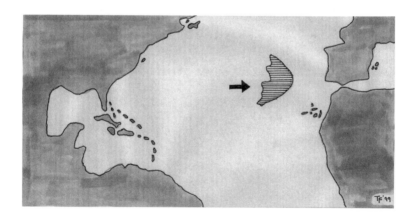

Was this the site of Atlantis? Drawing by Theo Fanthorpe.

Atlantis reputedly had vast armies and overwhelming naval power to match its rich flora and fauna, natural resources, and cultural, civil engineering, and architectural magnificence. There may even be some mileage in the theory that dim, confused memories of the old Atlantean glory indirectly gave rise to the strange medieval legends that circulated about the kingdom of Prester John.

During the Crusades, when things were going less than well for the European Christian armies, stories of a fabulous Christian king, Prester John, began to circulate. His army was invincible; his wealth was incalculable; and his arrival behind the Saracen forces was imminent and inevitable. For weary and disheartened Christian soldiers, the news of Prester John was a great comfort. He never came; but reports of his wealth and military prowess were remarkably similar to the Greco-Egyptian descriptions of Atlantis.

This same Greco-Egyptian evidence for Atlantis is remarkably firm in the matter of dates. According to what it seems that Solon may have heard in Sais, Atlantis was flourishing prior to 9600 BC The main reason for the unpopularity of the Greco-Egyptian Atlantis accounts in medieval Christendom was that current Jewish and biblical Christian dating took its beginning of the world back no further than 5508 BC at the very earliest. When the Bible was taken literally and the Jewish book *Bereshith* had equally high status, a definitive Greco-Egyptian reference to a civilization that was already flourishing five thousand years *before* the accepted Judaeo-Christian date of creation would be as dangerous as an attractive young harlot smuggled into a dormitory full of nervous, celibate monks.

When the unorthodox, pioneering archaeologist Heinrich Schliemann uncovered what he proclaimed to be the romantic ruins of ancient Troy, he set in motion a train of momentous events destined to reverberate controversially around the data at the back of the Atlantean evidence. On October 20, 1912, Dr. Paul Schliemann (Heinrich's grandson) wrote an account in the *New York American* of a bronze bowl he claimed Heinrich had bequeathed to him. This bowl — supposedly part of King Priam's treasure at the time when the Wooden Horse had finally penetrated the Trojan defences — allegedly carried an inscription in Phoenician: *From King Chronos of Atlantis*. Paul also referred to very ancient manuscripts that his grandfather had allegedly found in St.

Petersburg and that provided evidence that Egypt had originally been an Atlantean colony. Paul also referred to the famous Lion Gate at Mycenae, which was said to have borne an inscription concerning its history. The text of this highly controversial inscription was said to claim that the first temple in Sais had been built by Misor. The full text credited Misor with being an Atlantean priest who had, with a remarkable display of initiative and sound common sense, eloped with the beautiful daughter of King Chronos and sought refuge on the margin of the Nile.

Bearing in mind the legend of Paris escaping with the beautiful Helen and so starting the Trojan War, Misor's amorous adventure with Chronos's daughter stands in those indistinct and shadowy border lands between history and legend.

Did the ancients draw their circular maze diagrams as maps of Atlantis? Drawing by Theo Fanthorpe.

Braghine's interesting study *The Shadow of Atlantis* appeared in 1939 and is based on the earlier hypothesis of Carli and some other researchers that the Atlantean cataclysm was the work of a comet, asteroid, or meteor that was also responsible for the biblical deluge.

Charles Berlitz's work *The Bermuda Triangle* contains fascinating references to vast submarine structures not far from Bimini, and others on the seabed near Cuba, Haiti, and San Domingo. Berlitz reports that some resemble pyramids, while others could well be the truncated stumps of pyramids destroyed in some gargantuan cataclysm. If Berlitz's observations of just a few years ago are read in conjunction with the ancient Greco-Egyptian records preserved in Plato's works, it is perfectly possible to reconcile their seemingly variant accounts. The Platonic account credits Atlantis with being as large as Libya and Asia Minor *together*, and with having chains of small islands strung all around it. The Greco-Egyptian account refers to the accessibility of these small islands from the main Atlantean land mass, while from those at the western end of the Atlantean archipelago it was possible to reach a great continental land mass — presumable the substantial continents of north and south America. Is there any possible link between the mystery of Atlantis and the mystery of Oak Island and its inexplicable Money Pit in Mahone Bay, Nova Scotia?

Our erudite and reliable friend George Young, one of the leading experts on the Oak Island mystery, allocates considerable weight to the theories of Professor Barry Fell, who enjoyed a well-deserved world reputation in the field of ancient and arcane scripts and languages. Professor Fell's hypothesis was that the mysterious engraved stone found almost one hundred feet down the enigmatic Oak Island shaft during some nineteenth-century explorations was actually inscribed in a Phoenician dialect, or a script of similar age and style. Professor's Fell's translation of that stone suggested that perhaps a party of religious refugees had created the Oak Island workings many centuries ago.

As an ex-Royal Canadian Navy officer, George Young has expert professional knowledge of tides and currents, and his navigational calculations have proved beyond any reasonable doubt that Phoenician sailors *could* have made the hazardous voyage from the eastern Mediterranean, through the Pillars of Hercules (Gibraltar), and so out across the Atlantic Ocean to America and Canada.

If, like the proto-Athenians who allegedly defeated the Atlanteans in the great battle that kept the nations of the Mediterranean free, an advanced proto-Phoenician civilization also existed ten or twelve thousand years ago, could that civilization have crossed the Atlantic and been responsible for the Oak Island Money Pit, leaving their inscribed stone in the depths of that shaft?

When Charles Berlitz's comments about the submarine "ruins" off Bimini are linked with George Young's ideas and Professor Fell's translation of the stone, an interesting scenario begins to emerge. The strange old timbers found in Smith's Cove on the Atlantic side of Oak Island — where the creators of the Money Pit had gone to the trouble of creating an artificial beach to augment their ingenious flood tunnels — may have some tenuous links with other ancient submarine ruins along the Atlantic seaboard of Canada and the United States. *Whoever* dug the Oak Island Money Pit —*whenever* they dug it — had to create a sturdy coffer dam to hold back the Atlantic tides while their artificial beach was being prepared and the drains and flood tunnels were being created. Two or three later attempts to build a similar coffer dam during nineteenth-century explorations of Oak Island met with ignominious failure: the Atlantic surged in and destroyed it every time. The enormous old submerged timbers — some as much as a metre by a metre in cross-section — had had Roman numerals cut into them as though the structure had been carefully planned and prefabricated before being lowered into Smith's Cove to hold back the sea. These vast ancient timbers provide yet one more puzzling clue to the mystery of the Oak Island Money Pit, but their Roman numerals, of course, would suggest that they were manoeuvred into place thousands of years *after* the destruction of Atlantis, if it ever existed at all.

Evidence of a totally different kind is provided by oceanographers. A gigantic letter S traces the shape of the huge ridge running along the seabed from Iceland in the north to Tristan Da Cunha in the south. Historical geographers have from time to time put forward the theory that the most elevated portion of this vast submarine mountain range — around the Azores — might at one time have been well above current sea levels. If this mountain ridge, of which the Azores were once the highest peaks, had once been a large island — or chain of islands — then it might have been a starting point for theories of Atlantis and its submergence.

The difficulty with the theories in this group is that the geological evidence suggests that the Atlantic Ridge is very slowly *rising* and has been doing so for millennia. It is not the pathetic remnant of a great nation that was lost, but the possible territory of a great nation that is yet to be; at some remote period in the future.

The strangest, most daring, and esoteric theories of Atlantis could be allied to this possibility. Explorers of the paranormal who are prepared to consider the existence of parallel universes — so-called probability tracts or "worlds of if" — might suggest in their furthest flights of fancy that Atlantis exists, or existed — or perhaps *will exist* — in such an alternative universe. The Greco-Egyptian story may be one that came *back* to the old priest at Sais and to Solon of Athens not from a long lost period of history *but from a parallel universe or even from the remote future*. The visions of the cataclysm would then be prophecies rather than dim recollections.

The mighty mind of Francis Bacon turned to the Atlantis legend in *The New Atlantis*. John Swain put forward the theory that America and Canada had either been part of Atlantis or were actually Atlantis itself. The remains of a culturally advanced people living in and around the White's City area of New Mexico provide certain indications that a great deal more was going on in Canada and North America millennia ago than is always recognized by contemporary historians.

Other theories of Atlantis centre upon the idea of land bridges connecting Africa or Europe with the Americas. The route in prehistoric times might have been via Britain, Iceland, and Greenland, but the geological evidence suggests that such a bridge might have existed *millions* of years ago rather than mere thousands. The mysterious Sargasso Sea derives its name from the Portuguese word for "seaweed that floats," and that is about as effective a description of the Sargasso as can be arrived at. Early seafarers wondered whether the Sargasso covered shallows under which the ruins of Atlantis lay — but the weeds floating off the Florida coast cover over a half mile in depth of the Atlantic.

Other theories have tended to link Atlantis with the lost land of Lyonesse, which was supposed to have vanished off the Cornish coast many centuries ago. Romans, Greeks, and Phoenicians have left evidence of their visits to islands off the British coast that were rich in tin. Were they referring to the Scillies? The Scilly Isles, as they are today, are far from the description Plato left of

Atlantis, but the Lyonesse legends are interesting in their own right. Ample evidence exists for sunken land off the Cornish coast, which was undeniably farmed during the Iron Age. During the 1920s and 1940s — a period during which the great Charles Hoy Fort did much of his research — Edgar Cayce acquired his reputation as a psychic visionary and healer. Although unfamiliar with Plato's description of Atlantis, Cayce maintained that he had travelled back through time on the astral plane and visited the great, ancient civilization. His description of what he saw there was remarkably similar to the Greco-Egyptian accounts. According to Edgar, the Atlanteans had reached a level of technology which had placed nuclear power within their grasp and roundabout 10,000 BC one of their experimental nuclear explosions had led to the cataclysm. In Cayce's astral visit, he became convinced that North Bimini in the Bahamas had been part of ancient Atlantis. Bearing in mind that Cayce died in 1945 his forecast that further Atlantean artifacts would be discovered at the end of the 1960s seems particularly intriguing. Strangely enough, Dr. Manson Valentine, a noted zoologist and diver, discovered some very unusual structures off the north Bimini coast. In Valentine's opinion, he was investigating the remains of a gigantic harbour with massive quays and piers. Like all discoveries of lost cities, above or below ground, different expeditions have put forward different conclusions: some have supported Valentine, while others have maintained that the stones are purely natural and are merely the eroded remains of Pleistocene rocks.

In 1977, however, a Californian expedition led by Dr. David Zink retrieved a mysterious stone block that had quite clearly been cut with a tongue and grooved joint. In Zink's opinion, what lay below Bimini was an archaeological structure, not a natural geological one. Yet another group of researchers suggests that the Atlantis described in such colourful detail by the Greco-Egyptian accounts was somewhere in the Mediterranean rather than out in the Atlantic beyond the Pillars of Hercules. On the assumption that the Greco-Egyptian account not only made a mistake about the position, but was wrong in its dating by a factor of ten, a finger can be pointed in the direction of the Minoan culture of Crete and the Aegean. So then, if the sea in which Atlantis sat was the Mediterranean rather than the Atlantic and the date was not nine *thousand* years before Plato's time but only nine *hundred*, then we have information that links it very powerfully with the end of that great Minoan bronze age culture in roughly the period from 1450–1500 BC.

One of the greatest explosions the earth has ever seen was the blast that destroyed Krakatoa in 1883. The tidal wave it created was still six inches high when it reached the English Channel, and the material it flung into the atmosphere coloured the sunsets for three years. Round about 1500 BC something very similar happened to Kalliste — modern Santorini — halfway between the Greek mainland and the island of Crete. Deposits of volcanic ash thirty metres deep covered what might have been the Greco-Egyptian Atlantis. Unlike the ruins of Pompeii, the ruins of Kalliste contain very few preserved human corpses: it is likely, therefore, that a great many warning signs and sounds shook the earth before the colossal explosion destroyed the island. Perhaps it should be stated here that recent research into volcanic activity has led scientists to believe in what is called a pyraclistic cloud, which travels so fast it can go faster than people can run and this is what is now believed to have happened at Pompeii.

We can imagine the anxious refugees sailing and rowing towards Crete a hundred kilometres south of them as the smoke and tremors grew worse around Kalliste. Then the rock and white-hot ash blasted up into the air and rained down on the desperate refugees in their ships. There is evidence that over and above the horror of the choking air and burning ash all around them, the desperate refugees were swamped by a tidal wave almost a hundred metres high. Rushing outwards from the epicentre of the Kalliste explosion, it would have borne everything before it, destroying boats and sailors alike. At an estimated speed of some two hundred kilometres an hour, that vast volume of destructive water would have overwhelmed the Cretan civilization. Houses and harbours would have been swept away.

There are other interesting theories about what such a calamity might have done farther afield. Suppose that the wave had reached the Nile delta on the North African coast? One rather curious theory asks whether it might have been instrumental in the parting of the Red Sea at the time of the Exodus! The tonnes of ash from Kalliste covered several hundred thousand square kilometres. It would certainly have reached Egypt. Did it form one of the Egyptian plagues?

Did Atlantis Exist?

Some of the most convincing and scholarly work undertaken on Atlantis was undertaken by Rand and Rose Flem-Ath. Their intriguing book *When the Sky Fell: In Search of Atlantis* was published in Canada by Stoddart in 1995. Their research includes a description of how Albert Einstein in 1953 supported the fascinating theories of Charles Hapgood, professor of the history of science in New Hampshire. Hapgood's excellent work was published in the late 1950s under the title *Earth's Shifting Crust.* He set out to create a realistic and logical theory of why the ice ages had occurred and why certain major cataclysms had occurred alongside them. Those of us who have experienced problems that arise from driving a car when a newly changed wheel is unbalanced will sympathize with Hapgood's line of reasoning. He begins with the idea that the mass of the polar ice caps acts like those small lead weights which tire balancers fasten to the wheels of a car. As the solid crust of the earth rests on a layer of plastic or fluid magma, the eccentric weight of the ice at the poles would be more than capable of twisting the outer sphere over what lies below it.

Hapgood was also able to study an early sixteenth-century map showing far more detail of Antarctica than could possible have been known to sailors of the time. Because the rather sensational writings of Velikovsky and Von Daniken were not popular with the conventional scientists and historians, Hapgood's excellent work unjustly attracted the same type of sharp criticism the forces of orthodoxy aimed at Velikovsky and Von Daniken. In his scholarly and logical way, Hapgood quietly focused the readers' attention on the Piri Re'is map. That old Turkish admiral had had access to a portolans — a navigational aid that guided sailors from port to port — and which writers like Von Daniken and Louis Pauwels had put forward as "evidence" that "ancient astronauts" had visited our planet millennia ago. When Schwaller de Lubicz threw his twopenny's worth into the Atlantean cauldron, the orthodox archaeologists and Egyptologists began to get nervous get again. De Lubicz argued that Egyptian culture had blossomed in such a short period — from roughly 3000–2500 BC — that he did not feel it could have done so much on its own.

It was de Lubicz's opinion that the Egyptians had been helped and encouraged by survivors from Atlantis. Daring and romantic as Schwaller's theory is, it is logical and consistent and not easy to refute. An American researcher, John West, who specialized in

Egyptology looked deeply into de Lubicz's theories. Two facts rose stark and substantial as pyramids. The first was that what is now buried under the ice sheets of Antarctica seemed to have been accurately mapped and probably inhabited as much as seven or eight thousand years ago. At about the same time a culture with an advanced knowledge of the sea was not only flourishing, but appeared to have accurate information about South America, Russia, and China. West's own work focused on the theory that the ancient Egyptians had developed their knowledge of the stars by standing metaphorically upon the shoulders of giants who had been dead for thousands of years. Another of Schwaller's theories that particularly intrigued West was that the sphinx had possibly been built by Atlantean survivors and that it was thousands of years older than traditional Egyptology would allow it to be. Other conjectures of Schwaller's that interested West in particular were that the erosion showing around the sphinx was the work of *water*, not of wind-blown sand. How long can it have been since water flowed past the sphinx? Robert Schoch, a first-class geologist from Boston University, went with West to examine the weathering of the sphinx for himself; having studied it carefully, he concluded that it was a great deal older than was generally believed, perhaps as much as seven or eight thousand years old.

An ancient stone-age carving from Rocky Valley near Tintagel. Were they maps of Atlantis?

Another important contributor to the Atlantis mystery was Robert Bauval, who studied the rather odd arrangements of the major pyramids at Gizeh. The third one that had been built on the order of Menkaura did not seem to fit the alignment very well. It was in studying this apparent misalignment that Bauval saw a connection between the configuration of the Gizeh pyramids and the belt of Orion. Another of the mysteries of the Great Pyramid that intrigued Bauval was the curious small shafts that it contained. They pointed like torpedo tubes or bazookas: the idea being, perhaps, that they would direct the flying soul of the dead pharaoh to the paradise he was privileged to share with the gods of Egypt in the celestial afterlife in the Orion constellation. Supported by a great deal of complicated astronomical and mathematical evidence, Bauval hypothesized that the Great Pyramid might well have been intended as a sidereal chronometer of a very advanced type, a chronometer that had been started up round about 10,000 BC: one of the periods when the pyramids would have reflected the precise positions of the stars making up Orion's belt. Another of the outstanding contributions that the Flem-Aths make to the scientific study of Atlantis in their excellent book is focused on their studies of comparative mythology. If, as seems possible, many of the great myths and legends from all over the world came originally from the high culture that once inhabited Atlantis, then it is small wonder that those myths and legends have so much in common despite the distances separating them.

The mystery centred on Atlantis is by no means unique: a theory concerning a lost continent named Mu was put forward by James Churchwood, a colonel in the Bengal Lancers, in 1870 when the British Army was in India. Churchwood reported that he had been given the secrets of this lost continent by wise old Hindu priests. His mysterious informants showed him some strange tablets and taught him an almost unknown language called Naacal. Unfortunately, the tablets Churchwood was shown cannot now be traced. He did, however, claim that very similar ones had been found as far away as Mexico.

The Colonel reported that the tablets described how Mu had vanished below the ocean in a great cataclysm very similar to the one that had destroyed Atlantis. Mu's sixty-odd million inhabitants had been destroyed when their land was submerged.

Philip Sclater, a nineteenth-century professor of zoology in Britain, put forward the case for another lost continent he named Lemuria because of the lemur. The finding of lemur fossils as far apart as Malaysia and Africa gave Sclater the idea that a lost continent must once have existed somewhere in the India Ocean. He argued his case so logically and convincingly that he won the support of such leading scientists of their day as Haekel, the biologist, and Huxley — who was known affectionately as Darwin's bulldog. What conclusions can we reach about the supposed lost lands? Did Atlantis, Mu, and Lemuria ever exist? What happened to the lost land of Lyonesse that vanished off the Cornish coast? The evidence put forward by Colin Wilson, Graham Hancock, the Flem-Aths, De Lubicz, Hapgood, and John West is coherent, consistent, and challenging. An open-minded and imaginative approach to the whole question tends to lead the researcher towards the conclusion that the existence of Atlantis is probable rather than merely possible — but it is still a long way from being proven.

Chapter 11
The Zimbabwe Ruins

Three great riddles hover above the inexplicable ruins of four or five hundred ancient African stone buildings, among which Zimbabwe is the biggest and best known. Who built them? When? And for what purpose?

Theories about an ancient Atlantean civilization examined by Rand and Rose Flem-Ath and disseminated in their fascinating volume, *In Search of Atlantis*, are also put forward in much of Graham Hancock's exciting and stimulating work, including his highly readable *Fingerprints of the Gods*. Theories like these point to the *possibility* that the mysterious African stone ruins were inspired, and perhaps actually built, by Atlantean survivors on a site 160 miles south of Harare, the capital of the modern state of Zimbabwe.

According to these Atlantean-style theories, of which many variants exist, a global ellipsis over the magma beneath the earth's solid crust caused sudden cataclysmic temperature changes and dramatic polar relocations. The few survivors of the old Atlantean high culture found themselves more or less marooned, deprived of their advanced communications, and isolated from one another.

The cross-fertilization of cultural and technological ideas is the soil where discovery, invention, and progress grow most rapidly. With their communications severely damaged, our hypothetical Atlantean survivors would have been likely to try to share such residual knowledge and skill as they had salvaged with their less developed hosts, whose hospitable welcome and help had been essential to the survivors during those first vital weeks after the geological trauma that had left them scattered and vulnerable.

There is, therefore, a *possibility*, however remote, that the fascinating and mysterious Zimbabwe ruins owe their design, their origin, or both, to the arrival of a group of these supposed Atlantean survivors.

How *else* might the Zimbabwe ruins have originated?

Another cluster of theories, which do not necessarily contradict the Atlantean survivor hypotheses, but rather push the Atlantean factor further back into history, are those that look for links between the sturdy Zimbabwe ruins and the Sabaeo-Phoenicians. The term *Sabaeans* broadly includes the groups who lived in southwestern Arabia in classical times, and earlier. The Sabaeans originally occupied that territory which now includes the Yemen and its adjoining areas.

Fortunately for archaeologists, historians, and other researchers, the Sabaeans left numerous inscriptions behind them, and ancient Greek geographers also made references to them and their land. Babylonian and Ethiopian inscriptions mention the Sabaeans from time to time, and they also feature in the records describing the expedition of Aelius Gallus.

When spices and the ancient spice roads were of vast commercial significance, Sabaea was a source of both incense and spices and was an important stage on the route linking India, Africa, and the chain of Malayan islands.

It seems highly probable that some Arabian peoples emigrated to part of Africa in very early times, and there is no reason to doubt that Sabaeans *could* have reached Zimbabwe and created the puzzling stone ruins.

There is arguably just about sufficient evidence available now to compile at least a partial history of the ancient state once referred to as Ma'in, or Ma'an: the oldest nation in the Yemen area. The Greeks referred to its citizens as the *Minaeans* (not to be confused with the *Minoan* civilization of Crete) and there are records of the leading cities of Ma'in: Karnawu, Kaminahu, and Yathil.

The Minaeans also had well-established colonies and military garrisons guarding their important trade routes to Israel and Palestine.

It is a great historical truism that wars are triggered by religion, commerce (consider Homer's story of the Trojan War — due more to trading rivalry than to romantic fables about Helen), or a lethal cocktail of both.

The Zimbabwe Ruins

The almost equally ancient state of Kataban was a trade rival to Ma'in and Sabaea. Kataban and Sabaea fought first, then united against Ma'in, which was totally crushed round about 700 BC. But here again the basic principles of cross-culture fertilization as a consequence of disaster may be relevant. Overwhelmed by the combined military weight of Kataban and Sabaea (with whom the Minaeans shared much of their culture and technology), the refugees may have fled from Ma'in into Africa (consider the story told by Virgil that a surviving Trojan prince was ultimately responsible for the establishment of Rome).

Zimbabwe ruins. Drawing by Theo Fanthorpe.

Do these durable stone ruins of Zimbabwe date from a point where frightened, exhausted, dispirited Minaeans arrived following their long, arduous journey from Ma'in? Is it possible that the true nature and purpose of Zimbabwe is largely misunderstood by modern archaeologists, and that it was really created as a series of defensive fortifications?

The Minaeans were an effective people, and militarily well organized. Their first concern on arriving at a suitable new settlement would be to defend it. Romans threw up sturdy, durable fortresses wherever the empire expanded. During the conquest of England under William I, the Normans did exactly the same thing.

Another possible origin for Zimbabwe can be traced back to the Phoenicians, founders of Rome's formidable trading rival and bitter enemy during the three notorious Punic Wars. Carthage — such a sharp and poisonous thorn in Rome's side — was originally a Phoenician colony, while Phoenicia itself was a semi-determinate strip of seaboard along the coasts of Syria and Lebanon, running from Mount Carmel in the south to Eleutherus in the north.

At the height of their power, the Phoenicians extended south as far as Dor and Joppa and went way beyond Eleutherus to Aradus and Marathus in the north. Natural forces of coastal deposition, however, were not on the side of Phoenicians. As centuries passed, the harbours that had played such a vital part in their maritime trading history silted up.

It is particularly interesting to note, however, that although Sidon, Tyre, and Aradus are now connected to the mainland, the ancient cities stood originally upon islands. This seems to have been a strong preference among Phoenician town planners and designers. Island cities were evidently convenient for the Phoenician navies and were far easier to defend from attack than cities on the mainland. When the existence of these original island cities is considered in conjunction with the legends and mythology of Atlantis, an arguable case can be made for the hypothesis that seven Phoenician island cities, ringed by earth and water alternately, bear a close resemblance to the traditional descriptions of Atlantis itself.

Is it remotely possible that an ancient Phoenicia, on the site of the one known to classical history but thousands of years older, once stood where the relatively modern biblical Phoenicia stood during the time of King Solomon? Was it the destruction of this proto-Phoenicia by something akin to a flood of biblical proportions that gave birth to the legends of Atlantis as recorded by Plato in the *Timaeus*?

According to Old Testament records (together with the Amarna Tablets, which date from approximately 1500 BC, and various Egyptian and Assyrian evidence), Acre and Beirut, along with dozens of other cities, can trace their history back to its Phoenician roots.

Much of our contemporary knowledge of ancient Zimbabwe came from the work of Adam Renders, a hunter and prospector from America. He reached the fascinating Zimbabwe ruins in 1868 and was so intrigued by them that he went back in 1871, accompanied by a German geologist, Karl Mauch.

They measured and described what they found there then. This consisted of the great enclosure with its circumference of almost a thousand feet, the sturdy circular double walls with their large stone tops, and the impressive conical towers constructed of solid granite. For them then, as for us today, the great question of *who* built Zimbabwe was paramount.

It is the nature of the ancient stonework that is so impressive. The whole of the large complex includes a maze of courts, monoliths, and wide staircases. The amazing *accuracy* with which the great stones were shaped and fitted together is an achievement. What is particularly significant is that this method of building was employed with equal success by the Incan architects of Peru.

The question then becomes unavoidable: how did a sophisticated and durable dry-stone building technique appear both in South America and in South East Africa? And did they appear in those distant continents more or less *simultaneously*?

Unfortunately, because their knowledge of African history and African skill and ingenuity was incomplete, Mauch and Renders convinced themselves that the builders of Zimbabwe had come from outside Africa. The two nineteenth-century explorers wondered whether King Solomon's men had had some hand in this structure. Had it been the Queen of Sheba's architects? Mauch even went so far as to suggest that the great temple of Zimbabwe *might* have been based on Solomon's designs in Jerusalem. The German historian's mind was full of biblical history and in particular of references to the Solomon and Sheba era.

He also knew of Ophir — the gold-bearing land from which Solomon's wealth had come — at least in part. Mauch thought of Ophir as a biblical equivalent of the South American El Dorado, and the account of Ophir in the ancient records in the Book of Genesis situated it somewhere in Arabia or further south.

Renders and Mauch compared the magnificent Zimbabwe ruins they were studying with the basic lifestyle of the Mackalanga people who were living in the area when Renders and Mauch visited it. Neither of the two nineteenth-century researchers seemed able to accept that civilizations tend to rise and decline. Romano-Britain, for example, did not take very long to descend into the Dark Ages, rocked by Saxon and Viking invasions.

There was no logical reason why the nineteenth-century simplicity of the Mackalangan lifestyle precluded the Mackalangan people from being the descendants of a technologically and culturally advanced society that would have been more than

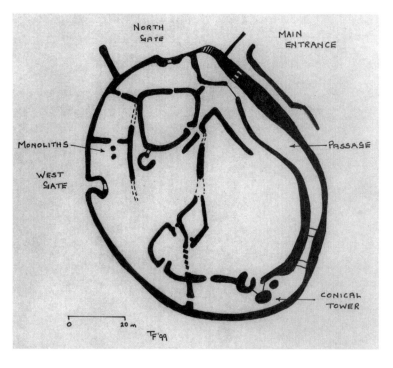

Conical tower at Zimbabwe. Drawing by Theo Fanthorpe.

capable of building the great structures at Zimbabwe a thousand years and more before Renders and Mauch came on the scene.

Further research in the Zimbabwe area has produced evidence that the great ruin and the civilization capable of building it was only a small component of a much broader cultural group — the Azanians. These highly intelligent and industrious people constructed wells and canals and worked hard and efficiently in their gold mines. From such evidence as can be studied today, it seems as though the Azanian empire flourished for three or four centuries and enjoyed a dominant cultural position in the Zimbabwe area until some five or six hundred years ago.

Certainly, while the English poet Chaucer was writing *The Canterbury Tales*, citizens of Great Zimbabwe were using their fine granite complex as a centre for ceremonial worship and a final resting place for their royalty. Although Zimbabwe's date remains highly controversial, there is broad agreement among many orthodox scholars that it goes back at least to the seventh or eighth century and possibly rather further. Such was the sturdiness and durability of Great Zimbabwe that it lasted three or four centuries longer than the Azanian culture of which it had been a part. It may well have been the rise of the Zulu nation that brought the Azanian culture and its centre, Zimbabwe, to ruin.

Scarcely two generations had passed since Zimbabwe's overthrow and abandonment when Renders and Mauch came on the scene. Yet relatively recent as the demise of the city and its people had been, Mauch and Renders had great difficulty in finding anyone in the locality who could tell them about the history of the intriguing ruins.

Mighty as it is, the ruined city of Zimbabwe is by no means alone among African mysteries. Scattered throughout the great continent, isolated examples of standing stones are there to be studied. A stone circle at Msoura in Morocco is well over fifty metres in diameter and is every bit as impressive as many of the famous stone circles discovered in Britain and Europe. Another rich area as far as African stone circles are concerned is the Senegambian region, which occupies the territory between the Saloum and Gambia waterways. Senegambia has many fascinating stone structures of considerable antiquity waiting for further research. In the forty thousand square kilometres the territory occupies, there are over eight hundred ancient stone circles:

approximately the same number as were erected in Britain over the centuries.

As though these circles were not impressive enough, the Senegambia territory also includes some two thousand menhirs. Some of these are octagonal in cross-section, although the majority are either circular or have D-shaped profiles. Other standing stones exist on the far side of Africa, in Kenya for example. Almost all of them are arranged as circles or at the very least as significant alignments and groupings. Near Lake Turkana there are numerous stones bearing geometrical patterns and representations of animals; these are remarkably similar to the Pictish stones at Meigle in Scotland.

One of the sites close to Lake Turkana is covered by two rows of stone pillars — a dozen in each. One of the rows runs north-south: the other runs from west to east. African researchers are convinced that many more ancient menhirs and stone circles wait to be discovered.

There are experts on the period and the mysterious structures who have put forward the hypothesis that the ancient and skilful people who built the European megaliths came from Africa *originally*, and moved northwards through the Spanish peninsula until at last they reached the United Kingdom. Other theories give India, the Russian Steppes, the Middle East, or the lost continent of Atlantis as the likely origin of those who raised the circles of stone.

North America has its megalithic mysteries as well. The New England states on the Atlantic coast reaching up towards southeastern Canada contain scores of strange mounds covering ancient stone chambers. There is one in particular, close to South Woodstock in Vermont, that researchers believe to be orientated astronomically. Historians who prefer to explain these curious structures by giving them a more recent date argue that they are storage cellars erected by seventeenth- and eighteenth-century colonists and that the great protecting stones were positioned defensively to keep animals away from the contents of these storage areas.

Considering the size of some of the megaliths — there is one, for example, at a site known as Calendar II, which is over four metres long — some early colonial farmer must have gone to a great deal of trouble to keep the beavers away from his onions!

One of the most intriguing locations in North America and Canada is to be found in New Hampshire. Mystery Hill, as it is called, covers a full thirteen acres. It contains monoliths, dolmens, what appear to be megalithic chambers, and a sinister slab deeply cut with grooves that look as though they were meant to drain the blood of sacrificial victims. Researchers who have studied the alignments that radiate from the structures on Mystery Hill maintain that they are linked to various stellar constellations. Radio carbon tests have suggested a date as early as 2000 BC.

If the mysterious structure below Nova Scotia's Oak Island and the standing stones in Vermont and New Hampshire might conceivably have been connected with a lost continent in mid-Atlantic, or to have shared some common ancestry with the amazing ruins in Zimbabwe, it is much more difficult to account for the great stone circle in Arizona that goes by the name of Zodiac Ridge. Researchers who have worked on this secret location in Arizona have claimed that the stone ring was capable of indicating important solar events as well as those connected with the moon.

A long-established group of indigenous Americans living in the Zodiac Ridge region have compounded the mystery by their ancient folklore tradition of "star priests" who performed their esoteric ceremonies at Zodiac Ridge.

Even taken in isolation, the mysterious ruins at Great Zimbabwe present an archaeological and historical mystery to the open-minded researcher; but when examined in conjunction with the theories put forward by Hapgood, Cayce, the Flem-Aths, De Lubicz, Hancock, and the penetrating mind of Colin Wilson, the mystery deepens into something challenging and profound, which demands a careful reappraisal of the traditional, orthodox explanations for these strange phenomena.

Chapter 12
Grimes Graves

If the religious and astronomical purposes of the great megaliths and stone circles are not yet fully understood by contemporary researchers, there is one very old and mysterious site hidden among the forests of Breckland in East Anglia whose purpose is clear. To crawl through the mysterious chalk miners' tunnels as the flint diggers did four thousand years ago is a gripping experience. Back in the 1950s, when we first visited the site, it was possible for visitors who felt so inclined to move through those narrow tunnels from which the ancient flints needed for Stone Age tools and weapons had been dug millennia ago. We were conscious, even as modern researchers who had no need to dig flint as we crawled, of the claustrophobic weight of the chalk above our heads. Although the site is still as fascinating as ever, today's health and safety regulations preclude visitors from crawling through those old workings as the two of us did nearly half a century ago. A first glance at the Grimes Graves site gives the impression that it could have been a tank training area or a heavily bombed battled site from the first or second world wars, but these hollows with their covering of grass, shrubs, and small trees were there long before Romans, Saxons, and Vikings fought for the possession of Britain.

The area was known to the locals as Grimes Graves long before the Normans arrived in AD 1066. To the Anglo-Saxon mind this heavily cratered landscape must have been the work of a god or a demon. Some etymological traditions associate Grime or Grim with the Devil, but Grim was also associated with Woden, who ranked high in the Anglo-Saxon pantheon. Neither did the word *graves* mean burial places. In the old tongue it stood simply for holes or hollow places. To medieval man Grimes Graves seemed like a battle ground between the forces of good and evil.

Early historians wondered whether it might have been a settlement of the ancient Britons long before the Roman invasions. Further theories considered that it was a Viking camp or that the Danes had been there. In 1870 an industrious and scholarly clergyman named Greenwell, who had the time and resources that were the privileges of many nineteenth-century clerics, began to excavate the site. He started by digging down with his team into one of the mysterious hollows with which the whole Grimes Graves area is covered. Canon Greenwell and his helpers soon discovered that what they were digging into was a shaft about forty feet deep that had been refilled by whoever had dug it thousand of years before. In a way this back-filled shaft had something in common with the Oak Island Money Pit off the Nova Scotian coast when Smith, Vaughan, and McGinnis first discovered it in 1795. As the boys dug into the Oak Island working they could see the original pick marks in the sides of the shaft while they excavated the soft back-fill had been thrown into it when the work was completed. Similar clear evidence that back-fill had been returned to the shaft showed Greenwell and his team that they were examining something human miners had made. This was no random act of capricious natural forces. The Grimes Graves shaft, some forty feet deep, cut down through sand, boulder clay, and finally the chalk layer so characteristic of the geology of that part of Breckland. Once Greenwell's team reached the bottom of the shaft, they discovered the radiating galleries that were then blocked with chalk rubble — the same galleries the two of us explored almost a century after Greenwell's time.

He and his helpers began clearing and exploring these mysterious little tunnels: what they found there made it abundantly clear to them that they were excavating an ancient Stone Age flint mine. Five thousand years ago good quality knapping flint had been as important to neolithic culture as the silicone chip is to us today. It was their plastic, their steel, the essential raw material for the tools and weapons that meant survival. If the high-quality flint that was essential lay forty or fifty feet below the surface, then our neolithic ancestors would focus mind and muscle into extracting it.

Geologically, veins and bands of high-quality flint tend to occur in chalk. It comes in all shapes and sizes. Some nodules of flint are large and irregular; others are rectangular; quite frequently, the flint turns up as small pebbles. Scientifically, flint is best described as a form of hydrated silica. Pure flint is translucent but various impurities create varieties that are coloured and opaque and frequently brown or black. From the point of view of those who used flint for tools and instruments, the best-quality flint was black and very hard; the less useful type was grey and brittle. Why flint nodules turn up in horizontal veins through chalk strata is not fully understood, but is probably the result of the activities of ancient marine organisms — sponges and the like — which used silica for their own vital, biological purposes and left it behind when they died. Because flint is a hydrated silica, there are conditions during which the water content evaporates so that a thin coating of white silica known as a patina is left behind on the exposed surface of the flint. This patina plays strange tricks on the appearance of the stone. If it is thin, the black flint below it takes on a bluish tinge; where the patina is thicker the whole stone looks white. Flint proper is totally impervious to water, although the external patina is relatively porous. It is this waterproof quality of the flint that led to so many Norfolk houses being given a flint covering to protect them from the weather and this was a highly successful and durable building technique for centuries. When flints with characteristic porous patina are found in gravel beds where iron is also present, the patina takes on a yellow pigment. Chemicals present in peat also stain the patina of the flints.

Our early forebears, with their belief in magic, talismans, and charms would pay close attention to the colours, shapes, and sizes of the flints they discovered in mines such as Grimes Graves. Tribal wizards and wise-men who read such omens would see symbols in the flint much as Roman soothsayers did in the entrails of animal. Evidence of this can be found where flints with patched patinas — particularly common in East Anglian gravel pits in England — were known as toad-belly flints; and the toad was frequently associated with witchcraft and the old vestigial traces of nature religion that persisted throughout the Middle Ages. It is interesting to speculate whether the neolithic religious leaders of those who dug for flint in Grimes Graves passed on their superstitions in an unbroken tradition to the East Anglian witches and "cunning men," some of whom were still practising in Norfolk villages as recently as the early nineteenth century. As far as working flint was concerned, neolithic craftsmen soon discovered that flints could be fractured by striking them, by pressure, or by sudden changes of temperature. The flint knappers of the Grimes Graves area were as skilful as those who mined their raw materials were fearless — as they scrambled like moles through the small chalk tunnels at the foot of the pits.

Striking a lump of flint in such a way that the force of the blow was concentrated at one point would cause the flint to break so that a cap-shaped piece could be taken off. This exposed a shape best described as a double cone. It was more or less in the form of a broad-angled cone adjoining the apex of another with steeper sides and a truncated end. This type of percussion flaking, or knapping, invariably left a shoulder of flint where the two cones joined. The small cap-shaped piece knocked off as a result of this percussion has a hollow that is the mirror image of the twin cones. Characteristic marks are left on both the flakes that come away and the instrument, or weapon, that is being made. One of these — a partially formed cone — is referred to as the bulb of percussion. Lines frequently appearing on the flake also provide evidence that *deliberate* knapping by the percussion method has taken place, and the artifact so formed is no mere natural occurrence. So distinct are the lines left by percussion flaking that in some ways they resemble the magnetic lines of force formed by iron filings on the paper covering magnets when experiments are done by students in school laboratories. Small flake scars known as *éraillure* can be detected on the surfaces.

Pressure flaking was another technique neolithic people used and it is one still practised by indigenous Australians.

Because flint is a good insulator — another reason why it is popular as a surfacing material for Norfolk houses — it is vulnerable to sudden changes of temperature. If heat is applied to the outside of the flint, the interior is unable to keep up with the external expansion and a series of fractures occurs. The characteristic bulb seen on percussion flints is missing on those that have been broken by such temperature changes.

Although flints of the kind retrieved from Grimes Graves were very popular tools for Stone Age people, they were not the only raw material available to them. Where flint was not readily accessible, Stone Age craftsmen would turn to chalcedony or chert. Almost any type of fine-grained rock was used when flint was not available. Seven main types of Stone Age tools and instruments have been categorized by researchers. First there are the *coups de poing*, which are also known as hand-axes or *bouchers*. These are characteristically boldly flaked with irregular edges and are roughly pear-shaped. Later and more sophisticated examples were rather finer and flatter than the earlier avocado design. These hand-axes were used widely by the lower paleolithic peoples.

The second category, scrapers, were notable for their very sharp, convex edges. Much used by the Mousterians, scrapers would have been vital for preparing animal skins.

The awl was used for making holes. It would have been one of the most difficult flint tools for the knapper to prepare.

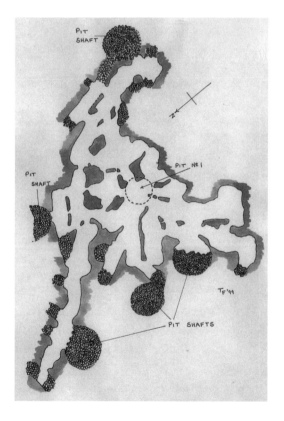

Layout of Grimes Graves, Norfolk, England. Drawing by Theo Fanthorpe.

The very sharp knapped flints known as *points* were clearly used as lance tips, others known as *audi points* and *gravette points* seemed to have been used as knife blades. They were frequently single-sided with a sharp edge opposite to a blunted one on which the user could press without damaging his hand. The fifth group of flint tools were sometimes designated as pygmy instruments and were undoubtedly fitted into handles and shafts. They normally had one blunt edge, which was the one that was hafted to prevent it from cutting or splitting its handle. Later more perfectly finished, ground, and polished tools were known as *celts* — like the ethnic group of the same name. These are clearly neolithic instruments and were not known in paleolithic or mesolithic cultures. The northern European type differs from the western type in that northern celts tended to be squared and flattened, the western variety developed into a more chisel-shaped instrument.

The seventh major group consists of the different types of arrowheads. Some were winged and tanged, others were shaped like leaves or lozenges. The skilled neolithic knappers who dug and worked at Grimes Grave four thousand years ago were experts in all these types of sophisticated flint work. The finest of the Norfolk flints, referred to as floor stones, were located in a relatively small area close to the Suffolk border and there can be little doubt that the industrious Grimes Graves miners dug their perilous pits in order to extract the precious floor stone. It is interesting to note that there are as many separate shafts as days in the year. Did this have some strange significance for neolithic people? It may well be, of course, that more than three hundred and sixty-five shafts exist and that a number were so perfectly refilled that they have remained invisible to later archaeological expeditions. The actual workshops with the knapping floors are sometimes located at the tops of the shafts and sometimes on the barren heathland close to them. Axe heads seem to have been one of the most popular products.

What kind of tools did the Neolithic miners use? The antlers of the red deer served as very effective picks, flint hammer-stones were popular — as were other picks made of bone — and deer shoulder blades made effective shovels.

During the Stone Age, and certainly well up until the middle of the fourth millennium BC, the early Britons had lived by hunting, fishing, and gathering wild fruits and berries when they were available. Permanent settlements were not compatible with following the movements of game, and the Stone Age hunter-gatherers were not able to create permanent settlements in one spot.

A few thousand miles to the east of Britain, however, a quiet revolution was taking place in human culture and economy. It was beginning to dawn on people that *keeping* flocks of animals, which you could kill and eat as needed — or from which milk and cheese could be produced on a regular basis — was a more secure means of living than hunting. These eastern cultures also worked out that if you went to the trouble to plant food crops near to where you lived, that would make life much easier than if scouring the countryside to find scarce food crops in their natural habitat. The earliest Norfolk farmers began to create clearings in the vast forests that up until 3500 BC had covered most of Britain. Flint axes were needed to fell trees. Simple flint blades set in wooden handles could be used to cultivate the ground. Ash from burning the felled trees was dug into the soil to improve it. Hunting, fishing, and gathering were still vitally important to survival, but small-scale farming had begun — no matter how inefficient it was in its primal beginnings. No metal was yet available to these neolithic farmers. Wood, bone, and flint were turned into tools and weapons: although they were no match for the iron and bronze axes that were to come later, and far behind modern steel, the stone axes used by these neolithic East Anglian farmers were remarkably efficient, considering their date. As a recent experiment showed, a small pine tree — some seven inches in diameter — was felled in five minutes using a neolithic flint axe.

Something strange seems to have happened round about two millennia BC. Previous to that date there seems to have been quite a brisk trade in polished stone axes, which were brought down to East Anglia from workshops in the west and north of Britain, and from Cornwall, Wales, and the Lake District. From 2000 BC onwards this trading in polished stone axes died out, while simultaneously the mining for top quality flint in the chalk at Grimes Graves slid into a high gear. The excellent flint axes produced at Grimes Graves had a serious impact on the local agricultural economy. With these excellent tools to assist them, the early farmers began cutting their way deeper and deeper into the forests as they cleared ever greater areas of trees and undergrowth. Once the shafts had been dug and the miners had been able to reach the lower levels, where the excellent floor stone flint was to be found, it was almost certain to have been hoisted to the top of the shaft in a sling made of skins and hides. A sturdy tree trunk would probably have been laid across the top of the pit. Such primitive techniques made from inadequate hide ropes and dangerously primitive ladders must have led to many fatalities.

Despite all the advantages of nineteenth- and twentieth-century tools and equipment, the Canadian Oak Island Money Pit has claimed its fair share of lives and more as one party of adventurous treasure hunters after another have risked everything as they battled with the island's flooded labyrinth.

Do the ghosts of the neolithic miners who died extracting their flint from Grimes Graves linger on in East Anglia's bleak and sinister Breckland? Flint represented wealth, and wealth was always an invitation to a local war leader to come and help himself.

Because the Grimes Graves shafts were some thirty or forty feet in diameter, enough light would have reached their bases during normal daylight hours to enable the miners to hack away with their deer antler picks; but in the small chalk tunnels into which they crawled to extract their precious floor stone flint, artificial light would have been needed. Pine wood torches there would have been in plenty, but among the many strange artifacts discovered at the foot of Grimes Graves there have been numerous chalk cups filled with animal fat and a wick. These would have produced an uncertain, intermittent, smoky light by which the miners would have worked. In the pit numbered 15 on modern archaeological plans of the Grimes Graves site, a very interesting find was made: a female figure carved from chalk — the ancient goddess of fertility — was found there with other Stone Age religious emblems nearby.

On a heap of flints near the statue of the goddess, seven antler picks had been laid as though they were meant to be a religious offering. The flint in pit 15 is not very plentiful and its quality is low. Researchers have suggested that seven miners working in that disappointing shaft had given their picks as offerings to the goddess in an effort to gain her favour so that the next mine they dug would provide them with better flint in greater quantities.

In addition to the carved chalk statue of the strange old fertility goddess, many sketches on stone have been found showing deer and other animals.

Grimes Graves is a very atmospheric site. Crawling through those narrow chalk tunnels where neolithic miners crawled four thousand years ago is like crawling back into the past. The weight of time, as well as the ponderous weight of the chalk, seems to separate the explorer from the modern world. Whatever they lacked in technology, the neolithic miners certainly did not lack courage, tenacity, or determination. Standing at the foot of the shaft, the researcher cannot help but feel that the courage and willpower of our remote ancestors who dug these pits and worked in them in such dangerous conditions has somehow been absorbed by the flint and chalk of the mines themselves. Over the centuries, inevitably, strange legends and tales have arisen concerning forgotten sights and sounds associated with these mysterious ancient flint mines.

Chapter 13
The Mysteries of Niagara Falls

Aside from the well-known grandeur and spectacular beauty of Niagara Falls itself, there are three very human mysteries attached to this place.

The first of these concerns the legend of the Maid of the Mist. According to local indigenous American legends, a beautiful teenaged princess, daughter of a chieftain whose people hunted on and around the American-Canadian border in early times, was greatly distressed on behalf of her beloved people because the game on which their lives depended had moved away from their regular hunting grounds.

The princess was a devout believer in the Great Spirit. She believed he manifested himself and his powers in a sacramental way through the dramatic power of the Falls themselves. She was also convinced that alongside the power of the great god of the Falls there was mercy and compassion — if only she could take the necessary message to him. Such were the tribal beliefs in which the princess had been reared that she had convinced herself that some great sacrifice was necessary in order for the message to be conveyed effectively to the benign god of Niagara Falls. Without saying a word to her father and brothers, who she knew would have prevented her, she packed a small canoe with her most treasured possessions, the toys she had loved and played with during her all too recent childhood, and pushed her frail craft out from the bank into the mighty stream of the great river flowing north from Lake Erie to Lake Ontario.

As the current took her and her boat ever closer to the crest of the Falls she stopped paddling and prayed to the Great Spirit to bring back the game upon which the lives of her people depended. With her eyes closed and her arms upraised in supplication on behalf of her beloved tribe, the altruistic little princess plunged over the Falls. According to the legend, the benign and merciful entity dwelling in Niagara was deeply moved by her heroic sacrifice. As her frail craft hung poised amidst the spray between the sky above her and the terrifying plunge pool below, the great Niagaran spirit transformed her into an immortal deity like himself and she became his eternal and radiantly happy bride.

Sensitive observers claim to have seen her exquisite and euphoric face bejewelled with rainbows — gifts from her divine, adoring husband.

Early natural religions and pagan interpretations of the universe have peopled waterfalls, caves, lakes and pools, wells, springs, and rivers with their own guardian spirits. The great, creative mind of C.S. Lewis populated the mythical kingdom of Narnia with the spirits of trees, centaurs, and fauns. Is it possible that these animistic concepts are more than the simple blundering towards spiritual truth of early races whose culture did not include scientific explanations of natural phenomena? If, as many researchers — including the authors — believe, human personality has a spiritual core that transcends and survives the death of the physical body, is it possible for that eternal, personal *essence* to be transformed or transmuted into something else? Greek and Roman myths are full of instances of favourites of the gods who were transformed into one natural phenomenon or another at the end of their mortal lives.

If, as many researchers have theorized, those phenomena often referred to as ghosts, phantoms, or spectres are in fact *impressions* that have been absorbed by the fabric, stone, soil, or bricks and mortar that were *close* to those beings during their normal mortal life span, might not the dynamic fabric of Niagara Falls have been particularly receptive to the extremely powerful emotions radiating from the princess who intended to die for her people?

Amherst, Nova Scotia, was the scene of one of the most amazing and well-documented poltergeist cases in the history of psychical research. Esther Cox was the centre of a number of dramatic disturbances that have remained stubbornly inexplicable to the present day. When those disturbances began, Esther was a very young woman. The disturbances troubled her for many years and only faded away some time after her marriage.

Traditionally, poltergeist phenomena seemed to focus on, or be generated by, a young boy or girl going through puberty. Does what Freud would have referred to as the *libido* generate surplus mental and psychic energy simultaneously with these pronounced physical changes in the human body? Is it possible that the "Maid of the Mist" phenomenon, reported by sensitive observers while viewing the coruscating rainbow light in the myriad water droplets around the face of the princess whom they claim to see over the Falls when conditions are right, is some form of residual poltergeist phenomenon?

Niagara Falls on the Canadian border.

It is only one theory among many possible explanations and the authors (who always enjoy a happy ending!) would like to think that the original indigenous American explanation — that the altruistic goodness of the young princess was rewarded by eternal euphoric happiness — has a basis in fact, after all.

This mystery prompted co-author Lionel to write the following poem several years ago, following a visit to the Falls:

NIAGARA: MAID OF THE MIST
A gentle, firm, determined step —
Avoiding flowers —
She walks head high and unafraid:
Her braided hair like ravens' wings
Entwined with stars;
Brown eyes that matched the depths below the fall,
And, like the sun, outranged the earth's horizon.
With gentle, firm determined hands
She packs all that she loves
Into the frail canoe —
Crafted in secret in the sacred grove
Among the slender birches.
She kneels in prayer among the restless reeds
Hearing their soft and solemn whispering:
Faint echoes of the One Great Voice —
Her Summoner who shall not be denied.
She glides, the shadow of a dream,
Princess of Destiny,
Maid of the Mist, she passes through the spray
And Lives again,
Serene and smiling
Bride of the One Great Voice,
Triumphant, sacrificial ...
Immortal Priestess of a thousand rainbows.

There may well, of course, be nothing to the reported phenomena whatsoever, except what dwells within the imaginative minds of the observers. But this explanation itself raises yet another possibility. A group of psychical researchers working in Toronto produced inexplicable phenomena said to be "the ghost of a sixteenth-century Englishman named Philip" — actually a totally hypothetical character whose entire life story had been written for him by the psychical experimenters concerned, and who had had no physical existence whatsoever. Yet when the right people were present and concentrating upon him, Philip was able to respond with all the traditional paraphernalia of a Victorian seance room. The conclusion the Toronto researchers drew was that there are amazing powers in the human mind that make telekinesis more than an empty theory.

Whether what the Toronto group had created had, in any sense, developed *consciousness* and genuine personality of its own in some weird disembodied limbo is a matter of speculation. What was proved beyond a shadow of doubt by the experiments the group conducted was that when a sufficient number of intelligent and sensitive people concentrate their mental powers on the creation of something not physical, they succeed to an almost frightening degree.

Do the observers of the Maid of the Mist phenomenon at Niagara Falls *produce* the face of the beautiful indigenous American girl with her decorative rainbow jewels in the same way that the Toronto experimenters "created" Philip? Such are the curious, often paradoxical, mysteries of modern physics that a number of serious scientists have lent credence to the idea that the observer — and what he or she *expects* to observe — are vital parts of the interaction between the human mind and the external universe. If a sufficiently powerful, sensitive, and creative mind was convinced of the truth of the indigenous American legend centred on the Maid of the Mist appearing in the spray at Niagara, *could the creative psychic power of such a mind bring that maid into existence?*

And, if it could, would the phenomenon so created have any degree of consciousness?

Madam Blavatsky, the mystic who cofounded theosophy, gave a vivid account of something similar that occurred during one of her trips to Tibet. She was intrigued by what she had learned there of the power to create a thought form or tulpa. Always an intrepid experimenter, Helena Blavatsky tried to create such a being herself.

As she and her companions trekked on through the snow-covered heights, she *imagined* the figure of a smiling Tibetan monk astride an ambling mountain pony who had just joined their procession. To her amazement and — at first — to her delight, a small, bald-headed, smiling monk joined the party and ambled along with them. As far as Helena was concerned the theory of tulpa creation was proved. She had done it herself. And the amiable monk that she had made was all the evidence that she needed.

Such psychic experiments seem in the experience of most researchers to have a dangerous propensity *to go wrong.* This was certainly the case with Blavatsky's monk. She reported that the benign smile and innocuous ambling slowly changed to something sinister and purposeful. The smile became a grin of demonic mockery and the figure of the monk became the epitome of dangerous evil casting a sinister threat over Blavatsky and her companions.

Her next move was an attempt to imagine it out of existence. But Blavatsky found that, like the mill that ground salt in the folk tale, such strange phenomena were a great deal easier to initiate than to remove. It was almost as though she had opened a door into an invisible realm through which *something* had forced its way and was now obdurately refusing to return. Blavatsky wisely called in the aid of some very senior Tibetan monks. They, themselves, only succeeded in removing the unwelcome and dangerous tulpa she had created by combining their own very considerable white psychic powers.

If Madam Blavatsky was able to create the little monk whom she *believed* she had created, is it possible that observers believing enthusiastically in the Maid of the Mist at Niagara may have functioned in a parallel *and actually brought what they believed in into being?* There is a wonderfully erudite ancient Chinese proverbs that runs: "Be careful about what you want — because there is a strong possibility that you will achieve it."

The second great mystery of the Falls involves Jean François Gravelet, better known by his stage name of Charles Blondin. Gravelet was born at St. Omer in France on February 28, 1824, and died in London on February 19, 1897, just a few days short of his seventy-third birthday. When his incredibly adventurous life — filled with almost compulsive risk-taking — is taken into account, the fact that Blondin actually reached his three-score and ten — and then some — is in itself a miracle.

He was only five years old when his parents sent him to the École de Gymnase at Lyons, where he was trained as an acrobat for a few months and then made his first public appearance billed as "The Little Wonder." As a tightrope walker and acrobat Blondin had few if any equals. It was the mysterious charisma that seemed to radiate from Niagara Falls that brought him international fame and fortune.

In 1859 Blondin slung a tightrope over a thousand feet long, a hundred and sixty feet above those turbulent waters. Not content with crossing it successfully in 1859 at the age of 35, he did it again blindfolded, and once more in a sack. On another occasion he trundled a wheelbarrow across. Once he did it on stilts. He carried a man on his back. He sat down halfway across to cook and eat an omelette. However massive Charles Blondin's acrobatic and tightrope-walking skills were, it was as though some unseen power protected him. Having won worldwide acclaim for his feats over the great Falls, he appeared at London's unique Crystal Palace, where, on a rope high across the central transept a hundred and seventy feet above the ground, he performed somersaults on stilts. His skill and courage never left him throughout his long life and he was still performing well when he gave his farewell performance in Belfast in 1896 when he was seventy-two years old. If there is any genuine mileage in the concept of some great benign force in or around Niagara, it would seem that it sought to reward the altruistic courage of the indigenous American princess and the fearless skills and abilities of the great Charles Blondin.

The third mystery, however, ended in tragedy. Captain Matthew Webb, the stalwart English Channel swimmer, was born at Dawley in Shropshire on January 18, 1848. He became famous on July 3, 1875, when at the age of 27 he did a marathon swim from Blackwall Pier in East London down to Gravesend in Kent: a distance of twenty miles. It took him less than five hours and his record stood for almost a quarter of a century. In the same year he swam the Channel from Dover to Calais. That took him twenty-one hours and forty-five minutes. Just as Niagara had brought international fame and fortune to Blondin in 1859, so the great Falls brought death to Matthew Webb on the July 24, 1883.

It may be significant that Webb was *not at the Falls themselves* but was attempting to swim the whirlpool rapids below them when he met his death. The psychic mystery surrounding Webb's tragic death at the age of 35 is centred on his native Dawley in Shropshire. According to local accounts, at the time of Matthew's death he was seen swimming along the old canal at Dawley and was also observed passing through the wall of the Congregational Hall there.

The brilliant poet John Betjeman described the event in one of his superb pieces called "The Shropshire Lad." According to Betjeman's account, Webb's ghost was discussed from Iron Bridge to Coalbrook Dale, as well as from the old Dawley canal to the Congregational Hall where it was alleged to have been seen. People in nearby Oakenbridge could speak of nothing else for days.

It has to be asked whether some great psychic force manifesting itself at Niagara was somehow responsible for projecting, or transmitting, the symbols and images of Matthew Webb's tragic death to the area he had known and loved as a boy.

But what of the historical background and geological features of these unique falls, with their three intriguing personal mysteries? The great Niagara River flows north from Lake Erie to Lake Ontario covering almost thirty miles as it does so. That same Niagara River forms part of the boundary between Canada and the United States, where it separates New York State from the Canadian province of Ontario. It serves effectively as a massive drainage outlet for the four upper Great Lakes, which have together a vast basin area in excess of two hundred and fifty thousand square miles. The awesome river has a discharge of almost two hundred and fifty thousand cubic feet of water per second at its maximum. For the first five miles there is only a single channel. This is then split by Strawberry and Grand islands. The United States channel to the east is fifteen or sixteen miles long, the Canadian channel to the west is two or three miles shorter. At Grand Island the two channels merge for the next three miles on their way to Niagara Falls.

Once the grandeur of the Falls has been passed, there are seven miles of gorge, after which the river flows across a broad lake plain for seven or eight miles as it links with Lake Ontario. The Falls themselves are in two main parts and Goat Island acts as the separator. The Horseshoe Fall is on the Canadian bank almost a hundred and sixty feet high with a crest not far short of a thousand metres. On the right bank the American fall is roughly ten feet higher but only three hundred metres wide.

The Falls came into being because of unusual geological formations. In the Niagara gorge the rocks are in horizontal strata and descend only six or seven metres every mile. The top layers over these rocks consist of very hard Niagaran dolomite; underneath there are soft layers that are quickly and easily eroded by the power of the water. It is this hard dolomite layer above the softer supporting strata that ensures the water cascades vertically from its overhanging ledge.

The Niagara River dates back at least to the Pleistocene era when a gigantic continental ice sheet retreated and exposed the Niagaran dolomite. Water from the Lake Erie basin then began flooding over it. If the speed of recession is carefully calculated, the Falls would seem to have been in existence for at least seven thousand years and possibly for as much as twenty-five thousand years. Is it merely coincidence that the consensual estimate of about ten thousand years for the age of the Niagara phenomenon coincides with the generally accepted date for the submergence of Atlantis?

The authors have made research visits to Niagara on several occasions and have never failed to be impressed by its awe-inspiring power and grandeur. If there is any truth at all in the ancient idea that certain charismatic natural phenomena harbour psychic forces, then Niagara has a major claim to be one of the earth's most mysterious sites.

Chapter 14
Magnetic Hills

Some of the most mysterious places on earth owe their reputation to their apparent ability to contradict such basic natural laws as gravitation. The coffins in the Chase-Elliot vault at Oistins, Christchurch, Barbados seemed to have been able to defy gravity. Weighing close to a tonne apiece, these lead containers seemed to have floated about inside their sealed vault. Over the years, gravity appears to have been challenged in other curious ways. Many of the legends associated with the vast bluestones of Stonehenge have hinted that Merlin the magician, or another wonder-worker from the long forgotten past, had been able to transport them by some form of gravity-defying levitation.

Researchers into the great pyramids of Egypt and South America have wondered whether the builders and designers of those vast structures had possessed some kind of anti-gravitational device unknown as of yet to contemporary science. Saint Joseph of Copertino (who lived from 1603 until 1663) was reported to have flown through the air whenever he became spiritually excited. Originally from Apulia in Italy, Joseph was from a peasant family and became a Franciscan at the age of 22. Often in front of witnesses, Joseph would suddenly rise into the air. On one occasion he flew over the altar during Mass and was severely burnt by the altar candles. On another occasion, walking through the gardens of the monastery with a Benedictine colleague, Joseph suddenly flew into a tall olive tree and had to be rescued with a ladder. His flights were not only witnessed by a surgeon and two or three cardinals, but were also seen by Pope Urban VIII himself.

Saint Teresa of Avila, who lived a century before Joseph, also experienced what were described as mysterious periods of weightlessness. She described feelings of buoyancy when levitation overtook her. Feats of levitation are frequently connected with other systems of religion. Joseph and Teresa were Christians, but Hindu mystics and worshippers of the gods of ancient Egypt have also reported instances of levitation. Daniel Dunglas Home was a Victorian spiritualist who apparently performed a spectacular feat of levitation on the December 16, 1868, in front of Viscount Adare and Captain Wynne.

Although he had been born in Scotland, Home made his name in the United States. In August of 1852 nineteen-year-old Home was conducting a seance in the home of Ward Cheney in Connecticut. F.L. Burr, who was editor of the *Hartford Times*, was one of the witnesses and Burr's account is all the more remarkable because he was noted for his pragmatic scepticism. In Burr's own words, "without any expectation on the part of the company, Home was taken up into the air. I had hold of his hand at the time and I felt his feet — they were lifted a foot from the floor. He palpitated from head to foot."

A French explorer, Alexandra David-Neel, spent fourteen years exploring the mysteries of Tibet. She described her encounter with a group of mystics keeping watch over a companion who was held down with heavy chains. They explained to Alexandra that the spiritual exercises that he had undertaken had made him so physically light that without his iron chains he would simply have floated away. On the June 6, 1936 the *Illustrated London News* published some unusual photographs of Subbayah Pullavar, an Indian yogi, going through a levitation process step by step. P.Y. Plunkett who was a witness, said that the performance had taken place close to midday with the sun directly overhead so that the witnesses were not confused by shadows. Subbayah apparently levitated inside a small tent, which was then removed by his helpers to reveal him floating unsupported in the air.

Nijinsky danced so brilliantly in the Russian ballet that there were moments when he appeared to be almost weightless. There were reports from Shepton Mallet that a twelve-year-old lad named Henry Jones had levitated there in 1657, a singularly dangerous time to demonstrate anything that could be construed as witchcraft or magic.

If there is some power in the human mind that can in certain abnormal circumstances temporarily overcome gravity, it would go some way towards explaining two cases of abnormal lifting that took place during the Second World War. In the first an unexploded German bomb weighing some nine hundred pounds lay on the deck of a British warship. A young naval rating weighing scarcely 140 pounds, and incapable of lifting even a quarter of the weight of the bomb swept it up into his arms and dropped it over the side. Neither he nor his shipmates were ever able to explain how the feat had been accomplished.

The other account concerns a blitzed house in the East End of London. A toddler was trapped under a beam in the debris and his mother simply crawled under the beam and pulled him clear. Did the minds of the sailor and the young mother provide their bodies with a great surge of unusual physical strength, or were they able in some way to *levitate* the bomb and the beam? Is it possible that the mystery of Magnetic Hill at Moncton, New Brunswick, Canada, is connected more with some abnormal terrestrial anti-gravity phenomenon than with the levitational powers that appear to be latent in the human mind? Earth's gravity is very rarely measured at sea level so that scientific corrections for height must be applied mathematically as gravity varies with elevation.

A brilliant mathematician named Pierre Bouguer worked out a method for comparing the gravity at different points on a land surface with those at sea level. He noted that there was an additional effect because of the neighbouring mass and by making calculations with a theoretical formula involving a horizontal slab of thickness h and uniform density p the gravitational pull of such a slab could be calculated in centimetre-gram-second units. His work is known as the *Bouguer Anomaly*. By including this complicated Bouguer calculation it can be predicted that gravity decreases with the increasing height of land surface at roughly 0.2 milligal per metre. This short extract from Bouguer's work is quoted as one small sample indication of the complexity of earth's gravity: "A basic law of engineering and mechanics is that the simpler a machine is the less likely it is to behave in an unexpected, anomalous, or faulty way. The greater the complication, the greater the likelihood of malfunction or aberration."

Are there any abnormal geographical or geological features in and around Moncton that might in some way relate to the magnetic hill phenomenon? Situated in Westmorland County in the southeastern part of New Brunswick, Canada, Moncton is approximately forty kilometres from the mouth of the Petitcodiac River. It's the largest city in the province after St. John, which is just over a hundred miles to the southwest.

The history of Moncton goes back a long way. The site was occupied by indigenous Canadian Micmac villagers long before explorers and settlers arrived from Europe. The French Acadians took over in 1698. Pennsylvanian Germans arrived in 1763, and a group of Empire Loyalists appeared twenty years later. Moncton was then known simply as The Bend. In 1855 the city was renamed to commemorate Lieutenant-Colonel Robert Monckton, who was the leader of a British military expedition that attacked the French fortress at Beauséjour.

The university there was founded in 1864 as St. Joseph's College and Moncton became an important cultural centre for New Brunswick's Acadians. Because of its location on the deep water inlet, Moncton prospered during the nineteenth century as a ship-building city; but its great days were the days of sail, and as steam began to take over at the end of the century, the ship-building industry became less important.

Modern Moncton is an important rail junction, port, main highway city, and airport. Its most unusual natural feature apart from the mystery of Magnetic Hill is the tidal bore — like the famous bore on the River Severn in England. The Petitcodiac River bore can be as much as two metres high and surges along its course twice a day.

Can there be any possible connection between Moncton's origins as a Micmac settlement centuries ago and the riddle of Magnetic Hill? As an example of the length of time the Micmac people have lived in Canada, the Shubenacadie waterway system is an interesting starting point. The entire waterway consists of over a hundred lakes and rivers and was a vital link for the Micmac people as they travelled between the Bay of Fundy and Halifax Harbour. There is evidence that some early indigenous Canadians have occupied the area for at least ten thousand years and the earliest of their settlement sites on the Shubenacadie route goes back at least four thousand years.

Magnetic Hills

Is it possible that the religious leaders and medicine men in ancient times developed some powers similar to those of the levitationist reported from Tibet, saints like Joseph and Teresa, or later levitating mediums like Home? If there is any minute shred of mysterious truth in the legends of the English Stonehenge bluestones being moved by paranormal means, is it remotely possible that that same paranormal knowledge of anti-gravity was known to the early Canadians? Was this ability to move great weights against gravity one of the secrets that went down with Atlantis, if Atlantis ever really existed? Suppose that it had, and that its survivors took those secrets with them north, south, east, and west as they fled from the destruction of their homeland. Is some ancient, gravity-defying wonder buried beneath Moncton's so-called Magnetic Hill?

Although extremely unusual the Moncton phenomenon is not unique; there is another so-called anti-gravity hill not far from Crickhowell in Wales. The Welsh magnetic hill is far harder to locate than the Canadian one at Moncton, but by travelling towards Crickhowell along the A40 and looking out for a gas station, the researcher will find a road opposite to it: a left turning close to the old castle walls. Follow that road past the high school over the traffic lights and bridge. An immediate right is signposted to Llangattock. The explorer follows that road and then turns right over a humped-back canal bridge. The road then leads on over a cattle grid and on to a rugged Welsh mountain, where it comes out on yet another road with a turn to the right, where the landmarks are dry-stone walls and a lonely, corrugated-iron shed in a field. Drive to the junction. Turn your car around so that it is facing the road along which you have just come. Drive slowly to the dip in the road, which the marks the start of the hill. Stop the car; slip it into neutral *and it will roll slowly up the hill — unless this apparent gradient is only an optical illusion.*

If it's not, could it be something to do with ley lines, or some strange old power dating back for millennia? Are the mysteries of the magnetic hills at Moncton, in Canada, and Llangattock, in Wales, indicators that something from millennia ago now lies buried there waiting to be rediscovered?

Almost since the very first settlers arrived in the Moncton area in New Brunswick, there were strange stories of wagons running up against the back legs of horses while they seemed to be pulling them uphill.

155

On that curious little road below the Lutes Mountain there were tales of barrels that rolled uphill and bales of goods that tumbled upwards instead of down.

It was Alex Ellison who was the press superintendent of the *Saint John Telegraph Journal* who brought the story to the attention of John Bruce, the news editor. Like all good journalists, Bruce was always keen on a good story with an unusual angle. He took with him reporters Jack Brayley and Stuart Trueman and the three of them set out for Moncton in the early hours of August 10, 1933. Bruce was driving a 1931 Ford Roadster at the time.

For hours they were unable to find the mysterious magnetic hill that Alex Ellison had told them of. By eleven o'clock in the morning they were about to give up and tell Ellison what they thought of his legend when they stopped at one final hill immediately before the intersection of the main highway. Life is full of ironies and those who explore the paranormal seem to find more than their fair share of them. So it was for John Bruce, Trueman, and Brayley on that memorable August morning. They left the Ford Roadster in neutral while they got out to stretch their legs before the long drive back to Saint John. As the three journalists watched in amazement, the roadster slowly began rolling backwards up Magnetic Hill. With mounting excitement the pressmen spent hours taking photographs and doing everything they could to test out the mystery.

Before finishing their work and heading back to Saint John, the three journalists stopped to buy ice cream from a local kiosk run by young Muriel Lutes. Being a local lady, she was, of course, familiar with the story of the hill and had already recognized its commercial possibilities.

Whatever the secret of its apparent ability to defy gravity, she saw that the hill could become a great tourist attraction for Moncton — and so it has proved. Close on a million visitors a year now test out the mysterious slope where cars and water *appear* to run uphill.

There is always the possibility that the so-called magnetic hills in Wales and New Brunswick are simply very curious optical illusions; but they could also prove to be two of the most intriguing and mysterious places on the face of the earth.

Chapter 15
Chinese Mysteries

The Canadian Sasquatch or Bigfoot, with its counterpart the Yeti of Tibet and Nepal, seems to have another cousin in the vast and mysterious land of China. On May 14, 1976, a group of workers from Shennongjia, part of the Hubei province in central China, came across a strange anthropoid lying in the road ahead of their vehicle. It was perfectly motionless and covered with reddish-brown fur. The driver focused the headlights on it while his companions went to investigate. One of them tossed a small stone towards it to see if it was still alive, whereupon it stood up and shambled away into the darkness. The Chinese observers took careful note of the creature. They were certain it was not a bear nor anything else they had ever seen. They reported their findings to the institute of Paleo-anthropology and Vertebrate Paleontology at the Chinese Academy of Sciences. Theirs was by no means the only sighting of the creature in that area. Known as *Yeren*, these Chinese variants of the Sasquatch and Yeti seem to have left frequent traces, including hair and excreta.

In 1957 a teenaged Chinese girl, Wang Longmei, was guarding some cattle near Zhuatang village, part of the coastal province of Zhejiang, when she was attacked by what seemed to answer to the description of a Yeren. When she called for help her attacker retreated and became stuck in a deep marsh. Courageous women from Zhuatang ran to help the girl and killed the creature with sticks. Convinced that the monster had been a Yeren they cut off its feet and hands and sent them to the local authorities. Preserved by a science teacher specializing in biology, these hands and feet were examined several years later, but according to scientific analysis they belonged to some large, unknown species of monkey, not to a Yeren.

This tied in with another report from a lady named Gong Yulan who saw a strange creature scratching itself against a tree trunk while she was gathering grass. Running back to inform her friends in the Qiaoshang commune in Fangxian County, Gong led a search party back to the place where she had seen the strange creature. On the tree which she pointed out and on the ground near by, a considerably quantity of hair was found. When sent for examination this was found to be of a type appropriate for higher primates and was very different from the fur of a bear.

Very many footprints have been found by Chinese scientists and researchers over the years and, by studying these, experts have suggested that a Yeren could be up to two and a half metres high and weigh in the vicinity of two hundred and fifty kilograms. It would have had a stride of approximately two metres. Many of the footprints that the Chinese experts examined were basically human in form with the major difference involving the big toe, which turned outwards. If the Chinese Yeren is related to Sasquatch and the Yeti, then perhaps the monster of Menbu Lake in China is similarly connected with the Canadian Champ and Ogopogo — as well as with Morgawr of Falmouth and the monster of Loch Ness. Menbu Lake has a surface area of almost a thousand square kilometres and many local witnesses have reported seeing an aquatic creature in it. The body is reported as being the size of a house. The neck is very long and the head is surprisingly large, considering the length and slenderness of the neck. At least one local farmer was reportedly dragged down and destroyed by the Menbu monster while out on the lake in his boat. Cattle straying too close to the side of the lake have also reportedly been dragged into the water by *something*.

Many miles from Menbu in the Jilin province stands Lake Tian Chi. What makes this particular Chinese mystery so intriguing is that Lake Tian Chi is relatively recent. It is in fact the crater of Baitoushan, which exploded in 1702. Popular theories that set out to explain the Loch Ness monster, Ogopogo, and Champ as vestigial traces of prehistoric dinosaur families cannot be applied to something sighted in a lake that is barely three centuries old. Whatever is living in the volcanic depths of Tian Chi would seem to be a family rather than one individual monster. As many as half a dozen have been reported at one sighting. Far smaller than the Menbu monster, the Canadian beasts, or whatever is in Loch Ness, the Tian Chi creature is described as having a beak similar to that of the Australian platypus. The head is bovine rather than serpentine and the body is rather larger than that of a horse or bullock.

Piao Longzhi, a sensible and reliable witness and professional meteorologist, fired several shots at the Tian Chi creature when he saw it and believed that at least one of his bullets had grazed its head. Another particularly interesting Chinese mystery concerns the so-called speaking rocks of Dong Ting Lake in the Hunan province. It has been reliably reported on numerous occasions that calls for help have apparently been heard coming from one particular rock standing out prominently from the waters of the Dong Ting Lake.

Many experienced researchers into the paranormal have concluded that just as an audio tape or video is capable of recording sights and sounds, so under certain conditions stones and other materials may well be capable of absorbing such impressions on their own. When conditions are favourable and when the witnesses and observers are in the right locality, the sights and sounds absorbed by the rocks can be played back. As so many of these reported hauntings appearing to be replays or re-enactments of past events are frequently associated with past events possessing strong emotional overtones, it seems likely that the cries of victims drowning in the lake would have reached the Dong Ting rock with a psychic impact fuelled by the emotion of those who were drowning there.

A Chinese mystery of a totally different type was reported from Yunnan province, where a mysterious tree seemed to respond to particular forms of music. Observers had noted that when quiet, gentle, pleasant sounds were played in the vicinity of the tree, *it seemed to move*. When the experimenters used louder, harsher, military-style music, the tree remained motionless. Further reports suggested that the tree was responsive not only to music but to other sounds, and that the key factors were that the sounds should be soft, gentle, and mellifluous. Witnesses observed that if they stood near it and spoke quietly, the tree seemed to be aware of them and its leaves moved gently. If, however, voices were raised to angry shouts, the tree was apparently impervious to the stimulus.

Of all the stirring events and significant achievements in China's long history, the construction and subsequent preservation of the Great Wall must rank with the best. Extending fifteen hundred miles from central Asia to the Gulf of Chihli on the Yellow Sea, it is unquestionably the greatest single building work ever undertaken by the human race.

Small, walled Chinese cities had built their own local defensive walls for many centuries, but almost two and a half thousand years ago Ch'in Shih Huang Te united the whole of the great Chinese nation and linked up some of the walls that were already there — together with new sections — thus creating the Great Wall, which was intended to defend his people from the Hsiung-Nu or Huns to the north. Constructed of stone and earth, the Great Wall's eastern sections were brick-faced. Later portions were as much as thirty feet high and wide enough for troops to march along them. At approximately two hundred metre intervals great towers were raised thirteen or fourteen metres high. It was part of the brilliant Chinese culture and architecture of the Ch'in and Han periods to express kingship and strong, stable government through architecture and roads as well as through military might. During the reign of Han Wu Ti from 140 to 87 BC, enormous pleasure palaces were built and these were even more sumptuous than the magnificent buildings of his predecessors.

What is particularly significant is that a number of Han Wu Ti's great structures were intended to establish contact with the supernatural world. They were regarded as *gateways* through which mortals and immortals could pass and meet. They were doors between the visible and invisible worlds. What mysterious ancient wisdom had reached Han Wu Ti and his ingenious architects?

It seems almost impossible to believe that the vast empires of China and Rome could have coexisted on the same planet without any communication taking place between them. Is it remotely possible that intrepid Chinese merchant adventurers with rare silks and costly spices, beautiful carvings in jade and ivory, met up with Roman merchants? If there was any intercultural connection between these extensive ancient empires, could it have been stories of the Great Wall of China that inspired the later Roman military architects to build Hadrian's Wall across north Britain? The earliest known Roman fort at Corbridge, near Newcastle-upon-Tyne, was probably built round about AD 80 when Agricola, having penetrated into Scotland, created a series of fortifications to try to maintain his hold on the recently conquered territory. Standing as it does at the junction of Dere Street and Stane Gate, which runs across to Carlisle, the original Corbridge fortress must have been of immense strategic importance. The great wall runs from Bowness in the west, through Carlisle, Gilsland, Chollerford, Heddon-on-the-Wall, and Throckley before passing through Newcastle-upon-Tyne and finishing at Wall End close to the Tyne estuary. Just as the Great Wall of China had its fortresses at two-hundred-metre intervals, so Hadrian's Wall had its mile castles. Some of the forts that have served the wall ranged from two acre sites — like the one at Drumburgh with its infantry battalion of five hundred men — to the ten-acre site at Stanwix, which held a full cavalry regiment of a thousand Roman horsemen.

The tough and aggressive Scots and their northern allies proved to be more of a problem than the wall could contain. Much of Scotland was abandoned before the end of the first century AD and half a century later the Antonine Wall that had run between the Forth and the Clyde was abandoned, and Hadrian's Wall was powerfully defended.

At the end of the second century AD large-scale damage had been done to the wall, which had to be rebuilt by the Emperor Severus. At the end of the third century, another successful attack on the wall led to its having to be rebuilt by Constantius Chlorus. Just over half a century later it was attacked again. The last rebuilding was undertaken by Count Theodosius and at this point the wall fortresses became fortified villages. Before the end of the fourth century, however, the wall ceased to be occupied: the Western Roman Empire was sinking into its twilight. So many similarities exist between the Great Wall of China and Hadrian's Wall. Both are among the most mysterious places on earth. It would be fascinating to speculate whether some future archaeological evidence will establish a link between the two. Did some intrepid Roman traveller see the Great Wall of China and bring his report back to Rome? Or was it a daring Chinese explorer who brought the news to the land of the Caesars?

Chapter 16
Giants, Horses, and Mysterious Designs

Some of the most famous of these strange figures carved into the earth, sketched on desert sands, or preserved in chalk on the hillsides are the mysterious lines in the Nasca Desert in Peru. The first serious study of them was made by Paul Cosok, an American, who came across them in 1940 in the course of his research into old irrigation systems. Cosok was understandably surprised by what he found: the inexplicable lines fanned out across the desert in all directions. Some came to abrupt endings on the tops of cliffs, others apparently carried on regardless of obstacles like hills and mountains that got in their way.

Their refusal to be diverted was reminiscent of the mysterious Devonshire footprints in the snow, which managed to travel over walls, haystacks, and the roofs of houses.

The great lines at Nasca were frequently geometric shapes — but they included outlines of fish, monkeys, birds, and other creatures. The designs had been made visible by the simple expedient of removing an upper layer of dark-coloured stone from the desert, which then revealed the lighter-coloured earth beneath. This technique was very similar to that which was used in Britain to make the outlines of the white horses and giants.

Cosok flew over the Nasca Desert in order to study the lines more extensively. His theory that the lines had some kind of astronomical significance attracted the attention of Maria Reiche, an astronomer and mathematician from Germany. The first glimmerings of the idea of possible astronomical alignments had occurred to Cosok as he and his wife had watched the sun set one early June evening. It was, in fact, the southern hemisphere's winter solstice — and as the Cosoks looked they saw that the sun was setting *precisely* along one of the Nasca lines. In all fairness to them and without any undue scepticism, there was such a proliferation of lines along the Nasca plain that it would have been very difficult for the sun to have avoided them all! It is equally easy to understand why Cosok was sufficiently impressed to describe the Nasca lines as a very large book on astronomy.

When he and Reiche worked on the lines together they came up with a theory that the whole structure was intended to be some sort of agricultural calendar to guide farmers in the vicinity to the ideal dates on which crops ought to be planted. Reiche and Cosok believed that the gigantic drawings were intended to represent constellations. Shepherds and sailors observing the ancient star patterns of the west in the northern hemisphere certainly reached a number of highly imaginative concepts about the constellations the stars formed. The Plough, or the Big Dipper, is understandable enough, but many of the other colourfully named constellations are very much in the eye of the beholder. It is possible that the great drawings of Nasca did represent southern hemisphere constellations, as they appeared to the creative imaginations of early Peruvian observers.

Sadly, Cosok died at the end of the 1950s, but Maria Reiche continued to study the mysterious lines with great enthusiasm for many more years. Hawkins, a gifted American astronomer, had checked the alignments at Stonehenge with a computer. With that experience to support him he visited Nasca to try out his theories there along astronomical lines. His work at Stonehenge had been based on the hypothesis that if there was any genuine statistical significance in the so-called stellar alignments, then the lines would need to point unerringly and consistently to some particular observable astronomical event. Hawkins also hypothesized that all of the lines — or a very significant majority of them — would need to fulfil these astronomical alignments if there was any mileage in the basic idea.

He began by programming the computer to identify those lines that would point to obvious observable locations of the moon or the sun. Only about 20 percent of the sample tested managed to achieve that. The result was so close to pure random chance that for a scientist like Hawkins it was practically meaningless. Not a man to give up easily, however, Hawkins turned his computer's attention to the stars, and provided it with a data base going back twelve thousand years. Hawkins' results seemed to indicate that whatever else they might be, the lines at Nasca had never been used as any kind of stellar, lunar, or solar calendar. The stubborn questions persist: if the lines at Nasca have no astronomical alignments that are detectable, then what purpose did their makers have in mind? Allied to this is the great question as to whether those patterns could have been made unless they were observed from the air in the way that Cosok observed them. But what ancient Peruvian people would have had the power of flight?

To try to understand the Nasca lines more thoroughly, it may well be necessary to try to understand the Peruvian people and the South American attitude to life. To study the lines with the people would seem the ideal approach for any serious researcher, explorer, and filmmaker. Tony Morrison is extremely knowledgeable about the Nasca lines — perhaps, along with Maria Reiche, he's the ultimate working authority on them. Morrison's hypothesis regards the lines as basically *religious* in origin. His studies of the Andean peoples has enabled him to create a data base of their fondness for small wayside places of worship connected by pathways. The shrines themselves are known as *wak'as* and the paths that link them are called *siqis*. Wak'as are sometimes mere heaps of small boulders and stones, and the siqis may be so faint that goat tracks are like motorways when contrasted with them. As a result of his research both on site and into the history and traditions of the area, Morrison feels that the Nasca lines can best be explained as holy tracks that connect desert shrines. Certainly small heaps of rocks and stones are present among the Nasca drawings. If Morrison is correct and the Nasca drawings have a religious significance — rather than some theory based upon their having been placed there for the benefit of visiting extraterrestrials at some remote period in the past — then their visibility from above may, perhaps, be explained very simply by a naïve belief on the part of their designers and makers that if they were intended for the benefit of the gods rather than men, the gods would presumably be able to look *down* on them from above. As Occam would have said when applying his metaphorical razor to a problem in philosophy, "Let us cut away everything that is unnecessary."

165

Morrison's sharp, practical mind soon realized that just as Roman soldiers were able to construct long straight roads by using a simple series of signal fires or surveyor's poles, so the long straight lines of Nasca could also have been created at ground level with no problem at all. Morrison was also successful in explaining the way that some of the animals, birds, and other designs might have been produced. It was clear to him that if a small drawing had been made first, it would not have been beyond the wit of the Nasca line constructors to scale it up with their ranging poles or signal fires as they moved over the surface of the desert. Comparing what the lines look like at ground level with what they look like from the sky still leaves the question at least partially unresolved.

There was so much room for doubt in the mind of fearless adventurer Jim Woodman that he decided to put it to the test. Flying over Nasca, he traced one absolutely straight line for a distance of ten kilometres: it deviated not at all even when passing over mountains. His own straight flight for such a distance convinced Woodman that whoever had constructed those lines, or at least whoever had been responsible for supervising their construction, had been able to observe them from above. Woodman, a practical man as well as an Indiana Jones-style adventurer, discovered from his researches that the indigenous people of the Nasca area had been more than capable of producing strong reliable ropes and textiles that were so tightly woven that they were capable of acting as *envelopes for hot air*. Excited by these technological discoveries, Woodman, with the assistance of Julian Nott — an expert balloonist — constructed the hot-air balloon *Condor I* using only materials he knew from archaeological samples to have been available to the indigenous Peruvians who might have constructed the Nasca lines centuries before. The basket for *Condor I* was constructed from reeds that came from Lake Titicaca on the border of Bolivia. On a memorable November morning in 1975 Woodman and Nott took off. With her capacity of over two thousand cubic metres, their primitive hot-air balloon found a ceiling just under a hundred metres above the desert, but that was high enough to give them an amazing aerial view of the Nasca lines. Satisfied that the line builders might have been able to fly in a very similar balloon, Woodman and Nott began to bring their frail craft down. Six or seven metres above the ground, when the last stage of the descent looked particularly perilous, the two intrepid balloonists whipped off their safety belts and leapt clear of the reed gondola as it landed heavily in the Nasca desert sand. Woodman felt vindicated. His point had been proved.

Among the latest thoughts on the figures at Nasca is the hypothesis that the people who made the lines had experienced a dramatic drop in rainfall and were experiencing a loss of vegetation and the animal life it supported. The lines are supposed to represent the animals that had formerly grazed on the vanishing vegetation, and stylized representations of valleys the indigenous people would walk in during religious ceremonies to try to persuade their gods to restore the life-giving rain.

The amazing figures drawn in the Nasca desert are not by any means the only mysterious designs in the South American theatre of mysteries.

When the Spanish conquistadors sailed towards the coast of Peru they were awe-stricken by what contemporary chroniclers described as an enormous "candelabrum." It stood high above the Bay of Pisco. The Andes themselves are rich in other drawings of enormous size. Far to the south of Nasca is the Chilean desert of Attacama. A high-ranking Chilean air force officer had once photographed the figure of a giant he had seen on one of the Attacama mountains.

Woodman saw a copy of the photograph and was fascinated by it. He came down and studied the area in great detail, being particularly intrigued by the Sierra Pintada, or painted mountain, covered with huge geoglyphs that could, perhaps, have been intended as landmarks to assist traders in Incan times. Woodman also examined the Sierra Unica, or solitary mountain. It, too, is situated in the Attacama Desert. Here to Woodman's amazement was the largest carving of a human figure existing anywhere in the world. Beside the giant of Attacama, the Colossus of Rhodes is a pygmy and the Cerne Abbas giant in Britain is a mere doll. Even the Statue of Liberty, in New York, pales into insignificance beside the huge figure on Sierra Unica.

The giant of Attacama is a hundred and twenty metres long. He has boots on his feet and something that looks like a crown on his head. Patterns of lines run from him in all directions. Did the line builders of Nasca also cut the Attacama giant? Certainly he is almost a thousand miles from Nasca, but Nasca and Attacama *occupy parts of the same vast desert.* Is it conceivable that the same ancient peoples made both the giant *and* the strange figures on the Nasca plain? Archaeologists believe that a technologically capable culture flourished in the Attacama/Nasca region about two thousand years ago.

Could there possibly be any cultural connection between the people of Nasca and Attacama in South America and those in Britain who created the White Horses, the Long Man of Wilmington, and the Cerne Abbas Giant? If those ancient designers did have anything in common, *who gave them their knowledge?* Who might have been the source of the technology that enabled both groups to leave their signature for millennia on the surface of our mysterious planet? There is a great deal of sense in Jim Woodman's answer to the question so often raised about these great drawings. Why should those early artists have worked so long and so hard to create vast designs visible *only from the air?* Jim Woodman, who ranks among the world authorities on these strange figures, is the first to grin and say frankly: "I don't know".

Arthur C. Clarke, who has an irrepressible sense of humour as well as a great deal of knowledge of the paranormal, is on record as suggesting that there is a deep-seated urge in human beings to leave their mark behind for posterity — part of the human quest for immortality. He says with a chuckle that the vast outlines sketched on the earth's surface are merely multi-mile pieces of graffiti saying the equivalent of: "Kilroy was here." That particular piece of graffiti that appeared all over the world at one time — as though Kilroy was magically ubiquitous — may be traceable to a quality control inspector named Kilroy who, having looked at goods that were to be sent worldwide, chalked on the lid of the inspected and approved cases: "Kilroy was here." This meant simply that the quality control inspector had seen them and passed them as fit to leave the factory. When these cases and crates began turning up all over the globe, it amused those who were puzzled by Kilroy's apparent ability to go everywhere at once to take on his identity and leave his famous message wherever *they* went too.

Another theory put forward by Arthur C. Clarke was that if the huge designs on Sierra Unica in the Attacama Desert, along with those on Sierra Pintada and further north at Nasca, were meant to be viewed by the gods from above, perhaps those who had constructed them were hoping for a little divine favour in return. Just as Jim Woodman had been impressed by what he learned on his flight along the Nasca lines and his later adventure in *Condor I*, so way back in 1932 another aviator named George Palmer was flying from Las Vegas, in Nevada, to Blythe, in California. Scanning the desert below him as he flew, Palmer saw an amazing figure not far from the Colorado River.

He was so surprised by the glimpse he got of it that he turned his plane and made a second flight by the river's edge. His first impression had not been wrong. There below him, with a body thirty metres long outlined in stone, was the enormous figure of a man. Not far from it was another, this one a quadruped: a cow, a dog, a horse perhaps? Palmer reported his find to the Los Angeles Museum, which sent Arthur Woodward out to have a look at the figures Palmer had reported.

The astonished museum man found three distinct groups. The first of these was the outline of a human being inside an enormous circle. He was accompanied by a four-legged beast with a tail and *something* coiled up that could have been a snake. Woodward measured the largest figure, that of the man, and found it to be almost a hundred feet from head to toe. The ring was a hundred and forty feet across and the quadruped wasn't far short of forty feet from the tip of its nose to the tip of its tail. The little snake, however, wasn't much more than ten feet across its coil.

One of the famous white horses cut into the chalk hillside.

The second discovery Woodward made was that of a solitary human figure almost a hundred feet long and twenty feet wide. His third and final discovery was of another group of three figures: human, quadruped, and serpent, somewhat bigger than in the first group. The human outline was over a hundred and fifty feet long and the artist had gone into rather more detail over the hands and feet. The correct number of fingers and toes was present.

Similar figures in Britain had been known long before the American excitement in the 1930s. Areas like Wiltshire, in England, were ideal for the production of white horses and human giants. Chalk shows up very well and can easily be exposed by lifting a layer of turf. Many parts of the West Country have steep hillsides from which these chalk figures can be seen for long distances. Although it is highly probable that many of these mysterious figures were cut into the chalk centuries, if not millennia, ago, several are far more recent and easily explained. Regimental badges were cut by the troops stationed in the area during World War I and as soon as one regiment had proudly left their mark on the chalk other soldiers would follow suit for pure regimental pride.

One of the Wiltshire horses, of the New Pewsey specimen, was put there by George Marples for the 1937 coronation ceremony. A school proprietor named Gresely allowed a party of his pupils to cut the Marlborough White Horse in 1804. A grocer named Taylor was responsible for the Kilburn Horse in 1857. The Cherhill Horse was cut in 1780 by Dr. Christopher Allsop, who used the simple expedient of marking out his design with white flags and directing the work through a megaphone. For the researcher of ancient mysteries, the numerous recent white horses are something of a disappointment — but the great White Horse of Uffington in Berkshire is both ancient and mysterious.

The recent white horses frequently bear a clear resemblance to the work of George Stubbs, the artist so famous for horse pictures during the eighteenth century. The old White Horse of Uffington is nothing like the recent horses based on Stubbs' design. Some researchers and historians believe that the beaked, almost bony, head of the ancient Uffington Horse makes it more *dragon-like* than equine. In fact, Dragon Hill is not far from it. This is the site where Saint George is said to have killed the dragon. Twelfth-century records, however, mention the Uffington Horse and record that it is accompanied by a foal. Somehow or other the foal has vanished. During the reign of Henry II reference is made to one Godrick of Abbingdon who owned land near "the Hill of the White Horse." Records from the fourteenth century compare it to Stonehenge. One theory put forward by Thomas Baskerville in the seventeenth century, and supported by the famous John Aubrey, was that the horse was placed there in honour of Hengist, whose name actually appears to have meant "the horse" or "the stallion." It would not have been uncharacteristic of the belligerent Jute leader to have had himself immortalized in this way. He is also supposed to haunt parts of Kent in the form of a white horse.

Others wonder whether the horse was cut on the orders of Alfred the Great. Uffington was certainly once included in his kingdom of Wessex. Did it commemorate Alfred's victory over the Danes in AD 871? If it did, the dragon theory would be more likely to apply, as the banner of Wessex was a golden dragon.

Other theories include the idea that it was the totem animal of a horse-worshipping tribe. Similarities have been noted between the Uffington Horse and the horses depicted on Iron Age coins. Does that help to date the carving? Some of these Iron Age coins seemed to be copies of currency that had been minted by Philip of Macedon, father of Alexander the Great.

Professor Stuart Piggott, who lived in the area and made a close study of the Uffington Horse for many years, was of the opinion that it had been cut by the Celts at least a century before the birth of Christ. Horses were very important to the Celtic Icenii tribe of East Anglia and there are some historians who believe that a branch of this tribe eventually became the Epidii of Scotland.

The village of Cerne Abbas in Dorset, England, is overlooked by the stark figure of the Cerne Giant on a hillside above. He stands a full fifty metres high, and carries the sinister club that every giant and ogre in folk tales invariably carried. Even the benign Fenland giant, Thomas Hickathrift, fought with the axle of a cart as his club and one of its wheels braced as a shield across his brawny left arm.

The Cerne Abbas Giant is not solid white like the hillside horses. Only his outline has been sketched in with chalk trenches up to sixty centimetres in width. Sometimes referred to coyly as the "*rude* man of Cerne," the giant's sexual organs are very clearly drawn and are positioned almost exactly in the centre of the pentagon that could be constructed around him.

The great club that he carries in his right hand combined with this central point of the pentagon provides a curious link with Nicholas Poussin's mysterious painting, *The Arcadian Shepherds*. Some researchers consider this canvas to be a vital clue to the mystery of the treasure of Rennes-le-Château in southwestern France. The Poussin painting was made in the seventeenth century and although there are at least two versions in existence, the pentagon and shepherd's staff as depicted in the later work may have connections with the esoteric tomb that stood for years at Arques very close to Rennes-le-Château.

Before it was destroyed a few years ago, the Tomb of Arques was an almost perfect replica of the tomb in the Poussin painting. Although this replica seems to have dated only from the early years of the twentieth century, it is generally accepted that it stood over a far older tomb on the same site — above the labyrinths of limestone caves in the Rennes area. Did an aperture at the bottom of the tomb connect with a secret passage leading to the Rennes treasure store? A number of researchers believe that they have uncovered a link between Nicholas Poussin, who painted the canvas of the shepherds in Arcadia, and Fouquet, the extremely powerful and influential minister of finance during the reign of Louis XIV — the so-called Sun King of France.

The staff in the hand of the shepherd is a vital part of the geometry of the Poussin painting. That staff — if measured correctly and applied appropriately to the composition — shows that Poussin was working on a pentagonal plan that went outside the frame and was centred on the head of the shepherdess. The tomb, which is central to the theme of the painting, bears the inscription: "*Et in Arcadia Ego.*" Implying to most translators of the Latin that "even in Arcadia the idyllic land of youth, love, and beauty, death, symbolized by the tomb, is present."

The club of the Cerne Abbas Giant happens to be just same length as the side of the pentagon that can be drawn around him. His stylized — but unmistakable — genitalia form the centre of this Cerne Abbas design: just as the head of the shepherdess in the Poussin canvas forms the centre of that painting's pentagon. The Cerne Abbas figure is not art in the way that Gainsborough and Constable understood it, but it *is* art of a kind that the unbridled imaginations of Pablo Picasso or Salvador Dali would have appreciated.

Further research into the mystery of Rennes-le-Château has suggested that Nicholas Poussin was a party to some great secret — possibly a secret that was known to other members of the elite inner core of the artists' guild of his day. It has also been suggested that Poussin hid this information in his carefully coded canvases.

The brilliant and thorough Canadian Ogham expert George Young, of Nova Scotia, has detected Ogham letters in many of Poussin's canvases. The human figures in some of Poussin's compositions are holding their hands in positions that clearly indicate Ogham script. At least two Ogham letters are discernible on the body of the Cerne Abbas Giant. The clearly marked ribs that are also very close to the centre of the pentagon can be construed as part of an Ogham alphabet. If George Young is right in his hypothesis about Ogham codes in the Poussin canvases, and if there is some strange hidden symbolic connection between Poussin's message in the pentagon and the message inside the Cerne Abbas pentagon, then the dating of the Cerne Abbas figure become critical. Who exactly is the Cerne Abbas Giant, or whom does he represent?

An obvious theory is that he is some kind of blatant fertility symbol and dates back to an ancient British fertility cult — which was a Celtic or Anglo-Saxon echo of Baal-worship in the Middle East. When the sun rises on the first of May over Dorset it is directly in line with the centre of the pentagon and the giant's genitalia. Whether this is significant is arguable, but a great many local legends and much fertility folklore have gathered around him; and certainly the May Day celebrations at Cerne Abbas regularly included May Pole dancing. Local girls in search of husbands or lovers once believed that walking around the giant would help to achieve their objective. Others used to think that making a courtesy call on the giant a few days before their weddings would have a beneficial effect on their future lives as wives and mothers. The idea that making love on the giant's genitalia will ensure the couple's fertility is an old magical belief that still survives.

It is, of course, perfectly possible that the Cerne Abbas Giant is the work of a genuinely ancient pagan fertility cult that flourished thousands of years ago in that part of Dorset. The area around Cerne Abbas has its fair share of early settlement sites, battlefields, fortresses, and henges. If the giant is contemporary with any of these, then his age can be counted in millennia. The most difficult argument against a claim to his having any great age, however, is the almost total absence of early references to him in the relevant literature.

In 1751 a clergyman named Hutchins who had written a Dorset guidebook communicated with Dr. Lyttleton, who was then dean of Exeter Cathedral. Hutchins referred to "a giant delineated on the side of the hill ...of vast dimensions." Surveys carried out in the fourteenth and early seventeenth centuries made no mention of the giant.

Another tradition suggests that the giant was cut — possibly on the orders of Henry VIII — when the local monastery was dissolved. According to this theory the giant represents Abbot Thomas Corton who was allegedly lascivious, decadent, and a tyrant as far as local people were concerned. Close inspection of the giant's feet seems to suggest that he is walking down the hill and away from Cerne Abbas: was this Corton's departure? A different theory, which gave the giant a recent date rather than an ancient one, suggested that the figure was meant to represent an unpopular local landlord named Holles, whose chronic ill treatment of his servants and tenants had led to a rebellion against him. But what if the connection between the Poussin school of art and the Cerne Abbas Giant can be established? If the figure was cut within a century either side of Poussin's dates (mid-seventeenth century), then it may well be that the secret — if it exists — of the Tomb of Arques in France is in some tenuous way connected with the giant in his pentagon on that Dorset hillside.

But if the Cerne Abbas Giant is not relatively modern, but a genuinely ancient work, whom does the figure represent?

A ploughman working in the 1940s on Hod Hill near Blandford Forum turned up some very interesting Celtic objects, including a bronze handle showing the figure of the god Nodens. The feet on this bronze handle point the same way as the feet of the Cerne Abbas Giant on his hillside. And the man on the handle also carries a club or cudgel. Other theories have suggested that the Cerne Abbas figure represents Hercules, and apparently at one time the figure had a cloak on his left arm that may have been a depiction of the Nemean Lion's skin that Hercules carried along with his club.

The Roman emperor Commodus led a cult in which his followers venerated him as the personification of Hercules in their

174

day. It was a group that certainly flourished in Britain and there is some evidence of it at Whitley Castle in Northumberland.

Wilmington in east Sussex is not far from Eastborne. It is close to the place where the self-styled black magician Alastair Crowley died, and where the allegedly haunted car with its sinister number plate of ARK 666Y was exorcised at the request of its owner, number plate dealer Keith Ferrataglio.

Like the Cerne Abbas Giant, the Long Man of Wilmington is cut as an outline in the chalk. He is over seventy metres high and his body looks anatomically accurate and well muscled. He is a far more herculean figure in that respect than the outline at Cerne Abbas. It is difficult to establish the age of the Wilmington man, but no records relating to him have been found going back any further than 1799. When he was originally cut — if that date is approximately correct for him — he seems to have had agricultural instruments in his hand: a rake in the right and a scythe in the left. If he did, the heads of those implements have disappeared with the passage of time.

One of the most interesting theories about him suggests that he was intended as a representation of an *idealized* agricultural labourer — rather on the lines of the handsome and muscular worker-heroes who were depicted in Soviet communist art after the Revolution.

A few years ago there a mysterious red horse was visible at Tysoe in Warwickshire, England. It was so well known a few decades back that the area was described as the Vale of the Red Horse and the picture scoured on it was also referred to as the Nag of Renown. The red colour resulted from the figure's having been cut from turf that covered red soil instead of chalk. Old records have suggested that the horse was destroyed by a local innkeeper roundabout the time of the Napoleonic Wars. Two tireless researchers, Ken Carrdus and Graham Miller, finally succeeded in locating the site where the Red Horse of Tysoe had once stood out so clearly. The Red Horse was very large indeed and may well have had Anglo-Saxon origins, or perhaps dated from an even earlier period. The name Tysoe itself provides a few interesting historical clues. It can be roughly interpreted as "the spur of land sacred to the god Tiw." This Tiw was a Saxon war god — their version of Mars. A red horse was particularly appropriate for him.

The great white horse of Mormond Hill in Aberdeenshire, Scotland, has a gallant, romantic history. Captain Fraser's war horse was shot from under him during the Battle of Gilzen in the Netherlands in 1794. Sgt. James Henderson, who was devoted to Captain Fraser, immediately leapt from his own horse and offered it to his commander; in the moment of doing so, Henderson was killed by the enemy. When the war was over, Captain Fraser had the Mormond Hill Horse created as a memorial to his faithful sergeant. A brass memorial to Henderson in the Old Free Church at Strichen adds authenticity to the story.

Although they are not visible any longer, the Gogmagog Giants give their names to the Gogmagog Hills in Cambridgeshire, England. They're about five miles southeast of Cambridge just off the A1307 road. The site is accessible to visitors and is administered by the Cambridge Preservation Trust. The site was thoroughly investigated in the 1950s by T.C. Lethbridge, who reported that he had traced the outlines of Magog — alias Epona the Horse Goddess — plus a warrior and the sun god. Lethbridge based his report on findings he made with a sound-rod. He dated the figures from around 200 BC and associated them with the Iceni.

Giants and horses, fertility symbols, ancient gods, more recent cartoons of unpopular landlords or abbots — many researchers are understandably intrigued by these strange, giant figures adorning the landscapes of the world.

Chapter 17
The Riddle of Tunguska

On June 30, 1908, four years before the *Titanic* went down and six before World War I started, a remote area of Siberia leapt suddenly into the ranks of the world's most mysterious places. In the remote Tunguskan region there was an explosion, an impact of such magnitude that trees were blown flat in a great circle radiating out from the central point of the devastation. As far away as London the night sky became so bright that newspapers could be read out of doors at midnight. In Sweden it was bright enough for the early cameras of 1908 to record sharp clear pictures of the scenery around the photographer.

Many investigations have been made, dozens of theories have been put forward, but the Tunguska explosion still remains as big a mystery as it was in June 1908. Some astrophysicists suggested that it could have been a black hole that somehow encountered the earth. Others suggested that it was anti-matter: something based on the theories Paul Dirac, the Nobel Prize winner. Dirac's hypotheses suggested that matter and anti-matter would be cataclysmically annihilated if they ever met. Some other writers took up their position in the challenging but shadowy borderlands that occupy the metaphysical territory between science fiction and science fact. These theorists were of the opinion that a nuclear-powered spaceship, crippled and crashing as the one at Roswell was alleged to have been in 1947, had exploded over Tunguska when its nuclear pile went critical. Versions of this theory credited the hypothetical pilots of this theoretical spaceship with a high level of altruism, suggesting that knowing that their own end would be swift and inevitable, they had piloted their dying ship as far as they were able *away* from any large concentrations of human habitation. Other scientists theorized that it was a comet of enormous size travelling at vast speed that had made the terrific Tunguskan impact. Time passed: the First World War began and ended — leaving four million dead, many more crippled, and untold numbers of families grieving. The Bolshevik Revolution sent its troops to Siberia to rid that vast empty wilderness of Admiral Kolchak and the White Russians.

It was not until 1921 that Lenin endeavoured to enhance Russia's standing in the international scientific community by promoting the work of the newly established Soviet Academy of Sciences. It was as their representative that Leonid Kulik was given the task of gathering data about meteorites on Russian soil. Kulik came across a description of the Tunguskan event of 1908 and was totally fascinated by it. The first information that reached him described what was believed to be an enormous meteorite that had impacted along the Trans-Siberian Railway Line close to Filimonovo Junction.

According to the information in the press cutting that reached Kulik thirteen years after the disaster, the *sounds* of the cataclysm were as terrifying as the sight and the physical impact that was felt for many miles. The train driver and his passengers were said to have alighted in fear to see what was causing the awesome disturbances.

Like the good scientist that he was, Leonid Kulik spoke to as many eyewitnesses as he could and began putting their reports together with information gathered by meteorologists at the time. Newspapers serving Krasnoyarsk, Irkutsk, and Tomsk all carried their individual reports of what had taken place on that fateful day, June 30, 1908. One of these journals, *Sibir*, reported that in the village of Nizhne-Karelinsk eyewitnesses had seen something shining in the sky so brightly that, like the sun, it was impossible to look at it with the unprotected human eye. Instead of being a golden yellow, this light was a strange whitish blue. Witnesses described how it had been seen moving downwards like a celestial climber descending on an abseil rope from a starry cliff. When the shining object, which looked roughly cylindrical to the eyewitnesses, touched the ground, there was a flash, a crash, and a massive cloud of thick black smoke. According to *Sibir* the witnesses described the sound as being *unlike* thunder. Some said it was like the noise of large stones falling down a mountain, or gunfire. Observers in the area reported that buildings were shaking violently and huge tongues of flame were seen leaping through the cloud around the impact site. Many observers were terrified and distressed, believing that the end of the world had come.

Report after report reached Kulik, each one more puzzling than its predecessors. Vasiley Okhchen reported to Kulik that he and his family had been sleeping peacefully in their tent, when all of them were hurled into the air by the force of the Tunguska blast. Vasiley and his family were members of the Tungus nation who depended at that time on their reindeer for their livelihood. As a result of the horrendous explosion many of their terrified beasts never returned.

Leonid Kulik who spent his life researching the Tunguska mystery. Drawing by Theo Fanthorpe.

Koso Lapova brought another strange account to Kulik. On her way to fetch water from the spring, she described seeing the sky apparently open, and fire seemed to pour out of it and land on the ground. She got the impression that rocks were dropping from the heavens. She rushed home as fast as she could and found her father had fallen unconscious beside the family barn. Koso, like other witnesses, said that the light she could see was brighter than the sun.

When all the evidence had been gathered, sorted, and analyzed, Kulik was still convinced that a huge meteorite had caused the problem. After some ten years of searching he had still not been able to find the site where he thought its great mass must lie.

With the help of Il'ya Potapovich, whose brother had been injured when he was an eyewitness to the Tunguska devastation, Leonid Kulik began fighting his way towards the spot where he believed the great Siberian meteorite had most probably fallen. At last the two men found themselves at the Mikerta River. From this vantage point Kulik noticed that a number of small hills looked very different from the rest of the landscape. Their summits seemed to have taken the brunt of some enormous force. There was forest and undergrowth in plenty *below* them; but these small hills were completely clear of trees and foliage. As Potapovich and Kulik examined these outcrops of devastated higher ground more closely, they could see that where some immense force had struck them the fallen tree trunks all lay in one direction.

The explorers climbed to the top of the Khladni Ridge and looked around as far as the eye could see. There below them stretched mile after mile of bleak destruction. From what he had heard and read, and from the information he had received from eyewitnesses, Kulik had expected to find some evidence of a serious major explosion — but this vast arena of flattened trees was a sight beyond his wildest dreams.

A few months later Kulik returned with a fresh expedition party and more equipment. He pressed on with grim determination until he arrived at what he was to call in his later reports "The Cauldron." This was a depression more than a kilometre across, which seemed to be the centre of the devastation.

Kulik was undoubtedly a great man and a great scientist, but he made one disastrous error. All research must be open-minded. Explorers and investigators are entitled to their favourite theories and their pet hypotheses, but they must also be prepared to switch

without demur or regret to a new and more probable explanation
of a phenomenon when fresh data appears. To begin with a
preconceived certainty and then to search assiduously for the data
and arguments that will support it, is more likely to lead to a
frustrating dead end than to an exciting new discovery about the
universe. That is as true of theology and philosophy as it is of the
scientific examination of an amazing area like the strange site of
the devastation in Tunguska. Scientific progress is an intricate
and complex formation dance in which data has to lead theory. In
the great courtroom of science, verdicts are passed before the
evidence has been heard are very likely to be overturned at the
appeal court of posterity.

A while before Kulik began his explorations of the great
Tunguskan crater, Daniel Barringer had done pioneering work on
the huge Arizona crater in the United States. Barringer was so
certain that the Arizona evidence pointed to an impact with
something massive from out of space that he actually went to the
lengths of buying the land that contained the crater in order to
carry out his assessment. His obsession almost ruined him
financially, but Barringer was lucky. His prejudice was the correct
one. Devil's Canyon, Arizona, was made by a meteorite, not blown
out by a volcano. Because a coin gives the gambler heads on one
spin, there is no guarantee of what it is going to do next time. Kulik
convinced himself that the Siberian devastation in Tunguska was a
carbon copy of Devil's Canyon, Arizona. It was not.

It was another part of Kulik's tragedy that he had no
knowledgeable and experienced Siberian companions with him to
explain the real source of what he thought were holes where
fragments of the meteorite that he believed in had gone deep into
the soil. Any regular Siberian traveller could have demonstrated to
the enthusiastic Kulik that the holes were by no means confined to
the Tunguska impact cauldron, but were caused quite naturally by
ice penetrating upwards through the peaty surface soil and then
turning to water during the summer. This melting ice left behind it
the characteristic "flat holes" that misled Kulik.

Kulik's report was received with great acclaim and excitement
by the Academy of Sciences, and he had no difficulty in raising
funds for a second expedition in 1928. He was accompanied now by
a tough and phlegmatic cameraman named Strukov who came from
Sovkeno and had the dour determination that kept him filming

even when Kulik came close to drowning in white water when his boat overturned. Malnutrition and mosquitoes played hell with the expedition, but Strukov captured it all on film — a film that duly impressed the Academy of Sciences when the party finally returned.

A third expedition that persevered through 1929 and 1930 was struck by frostbite and other painful medical problems. Despite the most rigorous search, Kulik and his indomitable companions failed to find any trace of the meteorite he so firmly believed in. The second in command, Krinov, found a tree stump in one of the "flat holes." He photographed it but hid the picture from Kulik. Krinov calculated that if there was a tree stump at the bottom of the hole it could not possibly been caused by a fragment of a meteorite. But Kulik's single-mindedness had now become so totally focused on his meteorite theory that Krinov saw little or no point in trying to turn the unswerving stampede of Kulik's thoughts. A fourth expedition in 1937 to 1938 that was greatly assisted by aerial photography came up with interesting evidence about the flight path of whatever had come down and caused the havoc in Tunguska. An area of two thousand square kilometres had been blasted by *something from above*. Yet in the centre a number of trees still stood — branchless but *vertical*.

The most curious fact of all that now seemed to be emerging from the investigations was that there was no indication of what might be termed impact damage.

It was typical of Kulik's phenomenal courage, dedication, and determination that with Hitler's Nazi army penetrating his beloved Russia, the great scientist-explorer volunteered to join the Red Army and fight. He was well over 50 at the time. Wounded and taken prisoner, the heroic Kulik died in captivity, never knowing the real cause of the Tunguskan phenomenon he had studied so hard and so long.

Eyewitnesses seemed to agree that the light in the sky had first appeared over Lake Baykal and had apparently been moving from a southeastern direction towards a northwestern one as it hurtled downwards. Those who believed that the object was some kind of spaceship whose nuclear pile had exploded felt that this evidence of its change of course was relevant and significant. A totally inanimate object such as a comet or meteorite would be unlikely to do an aerial equivalent of a handbrake turn over Tunguska and Lake Baykal.

The Riddle of Tunguska

After nuclear bombs had fallen on Hiroshima and Nagasaki it was noted that the centre of the blast area was relatively far less damaged than the wider area of destruction all around it. Whatever hit Tunguska had been hundreds of times more powerful than the bombs that destroyed Hiroshima and Nagasaki. But there were disconcerting similarities between all three scenes of horrendous destruction. Reindeer in the Tungus region had developed blisters after the 1908 explosion. Cattle in New Mexico had shown radiation burns after the Alamagordo tests. Were any other signs of radiation present at or near the Tunguska site?

A scientist from Tomsk University reported that dramatic genetic changes seemed to have affected plants and insects in Tunguska after 1908. He was not able, however, to detect any evidence of high radiation levels.

Another curious and interesting point is that when hydrogen bombs were being tested in the 1950s, very bright lights similar to the aurora borealis were seen at the antipodes. Ernest Shackleton was busily exploring the Antarctic in 1908 when whatever-it-was hit Tunguska. Shackleton and his companions reported an abnormally bright and persistent display of the aurora.

Yet another intriguing piece of evidence came to light when further comparisons were made between the Tunguska phenomenon and the results of H-bomb tests: the damage pattern in Siberia in 1908 made it clear that whatever had exploded there had exploded *several miles high* — roughly as far as the peak of Mount Everest stands above sea level. When further research in Tunguska produced globules of silicate and magnetite that were quite clearly of extraterrestrial origin, Zolotov, among others, assumed that they were almost certainly the vestigial traces of an exploded, nuclear-powered spaceship that had come to grief over Siberia. Researchers who support the spaceship theory suggest that it was heading for Lake Baykal, which would have provided the alien astronauts with the largest source of freshwater on earth.

Jackson and Ryan, relativity specialists at the University of Texas, worked on a miniature black hole theory and concluded it would have burst through on the other side of the globe somewhere between Newfoundland and Iceland. No reports of anything strange in that area in 1908 have yet been found in the archives. The anti-matter theory was thoroughly investigated by Cowan and Crannell in Washington together with Atluri and Libby in California. Anti-matter theory demanded that a significantly raised radiation level would have been the inevitable consequence of any kind of interface between matter and anti-matter. No such discoveries were made in the Tunguska region.

All that can really be deduced is that something with a mass of thousands of tonnes and a diameter of at least five hundred metres exploded with the force of many nuclear bombs at a height of around ten kilometres above Siberia. It caused some of the most extensive damage the earth has ever seen. It apparently produced genetic changes in plants and insects. It burned and blistered reindeer and it left behind curious traces of silicate, nickel, cobalt, and iron — which looked as if they had an extraterrestrial origin.

If it wasn't a meteorite, or an exploding nuclear spaceship, what might it have been? Whipple believed that it might have been a comet. From time immemorial comets have been regarded as astrological harbingers of great events — normally cataclysms and disasters. As contemporary astrophysics seems to suggest that comets can be described in their most simplistic form as "dirty snowballs," then perhaps it was such a mass of frozen gas and cosmic dust that blew hell out of the Tunguskan forest in 1908 — while still some five miles above the area of devastation.

Two almost insurmountable objections seem to militate against the comet theory. Comets can normally be observed for several days. If it was a comet that blew up over Tunguska, why did nobody see it until its final moments? The second objection lies in the consideration of how an exploding comet could have produced the sort of devastation that would normally be associated with an atomic explosion? Counterarguments suggest that a comet would not be easy to see if its trajectory took it close to the sun as it skimmed out of the early morning sky on its way to Tunguska. A perfect example of this was the comet "Mrkos," which had looped around the Sun, passed by the Earth, and was not observed until it was on its way back. There was, it must also be noted, a comet named "Encke" with an ephemerally short life span that seems to have been on its rounds at about the same time as the Tunguska disaster. Was it "Encke" that disintegrated so traumatically five miles above Siberia on June 30, 1908?

As recently as 1965, a mystery that might have been a miniature version of the Tunguskan episode was reported from Revelstoke in Canada. Citizens in the area heard what they described as a loud explosion above their heads and cosmic dust was later found in the district. Another significant piece of evidence comes from a discovery that Lovell and his team made as far back as 1947. There are unsuspected meteor showers that pass the Earth only in daylight and so are almost impossible to observe.

A group known as the Beta-Taurids contact the Earth on the thirtieth of June of each year. It may be no more than coincidence, of course, but it was on the June 30, 1908, that the Tunguskan phenomena took place.

It is not possible to conclude the theories of the Siberian meteorite without reference to Nikola Tesla. He was born on July 9, 1856 and was in his early 50s when the Siberian explosion took place. Tesla was acknowledged as one of the great pioneering electrical scientists of his time. Marconi, the radio pioneer, was one of Tesla's contemporaries, but whereas Marconi was primarily interested in the transmission of radio waves, Tesla was interested in the transmission of electrical *power* — vast amounts of it. In 1899 he used an enormous coil that generated millions of volts and so succeeded in pumping millions of watts into the air before the generator itself gave out. Tesla was working in Colorado Springs with a huge copper ball a metre in diameter at the top of a two-hundred-foot tower. He had built primary and secondary coils in a building below it. The basis of his revolutionary theory was that a resonating radio and electrical system would come into being, would go on reinforcing itself, and would draw current from the earth. The core of Tesla's ingenious theory was that high-frequency radio waves would be capable of travelling across the world and then returning. He reckoned that if he had tuned them successfully to coincide with the natural frequency of the oscillation of the earth's own electrical currents, the voltage pushes in his two-hundred-foot mast would be reinforced and the current being drawn from the earth itself would be increased.

Tesla's gadget was a spectacular success to begin with. Lightning bolts fifty metres long crackled and spat their way from the copper ball at the top of his tower. How far had Tesla's global experiments developed by the June 30, 1908? Almost thirty years after the Tunguskan cataclysm Tesla went on record as saying that he had created a secret electrical weapon that he claimed: "will destroy anything, men or machines, approaching within a radius of two hundred miles." There are those, impressed by Tesla's unique engineering genius, who seriously believe that a machine of the type he described could have been responsible for the Tunguska devastation in 1908. As far back as 1900 Tesla had described the basic principles of a prototype laser. Those same basic principles would have been applicable to a particle gun. The Colorado Springs demonstration was a very attenuated miniature of the force that blasted Siberia, but Tesla did succeed in creating bolts of energy fifty metres long from his huge copper globe at the summit of its two-hundred-foot tower. It is only a very remote possibility that links the electrical engineering genius and the devastation in Siberia, but it is a link that ought not to be totally ignored when explanations for the Siberian explosion are being considered.

Chapter 18
The Mysteries of Malta

The Maltese Islands consist of Malta itself, Gozo, Comino, Cominotto, and Filfla. The five islands together contain only just over a hundred and twenty square miles of land — scarcely the size of the Isle of Wight off the coast of Britain. Despite their small size, the Maltese Islands have been occupied for seven or eight thousand years. It is possible that the earliest neolithic farmers came across from the direction of Italy or Sicily.

The life of the neolithic Maltese farmers seven millennia ago was made richer and more interesting by their trade with Pantelleria and Lipari from where they obtained obsidian, a tough volcanic rock that made for excellent tools. Archaeological explorations at the Skorba site have provided evidence that the religion of these neolithic farmers seemed to have centred around various fertility cults.

One of the great mysteries of Malta centres on the arcane temples that intrigue modern historians. Characteristically, the chambers are in the form of semicircular apses. Many are trefoil-shaped or lobed so that their ground plans resemble biological organs rather than designs for buildings. It is almost as though the temples had grown out of the living rock rather than having been constructed by human builders. When the interior designs of the Xemxija grave chambers are compared with the designs of the temples themselves, there is clearly close similarity between them. Articles found with the remains in the tombs would seem to suggest that there was a cult of the dead, probably some form of ancestor worship, in addition to the neolithic farmers' devotion to their well-built fertility goddess. The temples might well have been designed symbolically to mimic the graves, but the temples did not seem to have been used themselves as burial places. The presence of sharp flint knives in the temples would seem to suggest that sacrifice was a central part of the ceremonies involved in the worship of the fertility goddess.

She is further connected with the temple designs, particularly those which have a five-apse formation, in that the ground plan actually *resembles* the statues of the goddess that have been found in so many places.

Here, too, there are interesting parallels with the ground zodiacs of Glastonbury and Rennes-le-Château. At least one Rennes researcher has suggested that the entire village of Rennes is laid out in the form of a ship of the dead carrying some giant warrior to the afterlife. The five-apse temple plans may well, therefore, represent the complete goddess figure, while the three-apse plans are her head and shoulders. In some of the later temples, such as Hagar Qim, a number of chambers have been added at a later date to an original design which may have been intended to follow the five-apse shape of the goddess plan.

The great stone balls which were used to move the vast stones of the Maltese temples.

In Rugeley in Staffordshire, England, there is a fascinating underground structure hidden below the site of the now-demolished Hagley Hall. Although it is not currently open to the public, the authors were able to examine the sealed entrance and talk to local residents who recalled exploring these strange subterranean chambers years ago. Like the Tarxien Temples, and the village layout of Rennes-le-Château, the plan of this mysterious structure at Hagley *is in the form of a human figure holding aloft what might be a rectangular banner in its left hand.* There are many possible mysteries attached to it; enough to merit months of further research. It could, of course, turn out to be merely be an unusual eighteenth-century folly. It is far more likely to be a Rosicrucian temple-tomb, or a sinister cult-centre for black magicians or Satanists who flourished during the era of Francis Dashwood and the notorious Hell-fire Club. It could even be something far older and stranger — a temple to Mithras, perhaps, dating back to Roman times. It is cut into the solid sandstone. Its origins might go deeper even than Roman times....

Close to the Tarxien temples in Paola is a mysterious building known as the *hypogeum*. It is a multistorey structure extending to some thirty-five by twenty-five metres and its stairs, corridors, halls, and chambers seem to have been cut successively by one generation of builders after another ever further into a limestone hill. The hypogeum is extremely ancient. It is certainly contemporary with the Egyptian pyramids and possibly goes back to a much earlier period.

The ancient temples are fascinating, but the mysterious hypogeum (the name is based on the Greek word *ipogaion)* is even more so. Its full title is the "Hal-saflieni Hypogeum." This amazing underground structure — thousands of years old — was not rediscovered until the year 1902. A shaft was being dug for a water tank when the workmen discovered a cavern some four metres below the road. They went in to explore the complex labyrinth of which it was a part.

During the first decade of the twentieth century vast numbers of human bones belonging to many different individuals were found in the hypogeum. They gave every appearance of having been deposited there haphazardly, in some disorder, and it seemed as though it had been the practice to remove decayed remains from their original burial place and tip them into the hypogeum. As excavations proceeded, however, it became clear that the structure had served for purposes other than secondary burial.

Once the soil and rubble had been carefully removed, a large hall was revealed, which gave every appearance of having been used for religious ceremonies. The hypogeum was also a veritable treasure house of tools and instruments. Mortars, sling stones, and querns, along with hard stone mallets and polished axes, scrapers and other ancient tools and implements, were found there. It looked very much as if it had been customary for the dead who were placed here randomly, almost casually, to be left in possession of their jewellery and ornaments. Pendants and necklaces were frequently found among the heaps of ancient bones — although no metal of any kind was uncovered during the explorations. Were the living, perhaps, afraid of dark, psychic reprisals if they robbed the dead?

Foretelling the future by means of dreams, technically known as oneiromancy, seems to have gone on most frequently in one particular hypogeum chamber. Its ceiling was decorated with circles and spirals, below which the dreamer would have slept, possibly under the influence of hallucinogenic herbs or smoke.

Co-author Patricia Fanthorpe researching the ancient Maltese and Gozitan temples.

The discovery of an ancient statue of a sleeping woman suggested to some researchers that oneiromancy was also practised in the hypogeum's small side chambers under the direction of the priests who maintained it.

It has also been hypothesized that pregnant women in particular, who were devotees of the fertility goddess, would have come and rested in one of these cubicles while the priest lit some of the sacred herbs that, it was hoped, would induce visions of the future. If this hypothesis has any foundation in fact, it would seem probable that the expectant mothers participating in these prophetic rites would be hoping to foretell the good things that the future held for the child they were about to bear.

Unlike the mysteries surrounding Stonehenge and Avebury in Britain, the very ancient Maltese temples contain clues as to how their great megaliths were moved. Close to the external walls of the Tarxien temples many of the beautifully rounded stone spheres the builders used can still be seen. In some cases these huge ball-bearings have been found jammed under the great stones they once helped to move. The Ggantija Temple in Gozo still rises to a height of over seven metres, and when it was in pristine condition five millennia ago, it would undoubtedly have been considerably higher. How did the early Maltese raise those slabs weighing several tonnes to a height of ten metres, perhaps more?

Part of their success would have depended upon the use of the inclined plane up which the great slabs could have been dragged — but there is also evidence that they lifted heavy weights with an ingenious device best described as a sea-saw lever. A sturdy timber frame would be constructed up to the height to which they desired to raised the block. A long double lever would extend on both sides of this vertical structure. The block would then be placed on a small platform in the centre of the structure at ground level. A team of sturdy builders would then raise one end of the sea-saw device, which would in turn lift the block. Wedges would be placed under the opposite side of the central structure; the sea-saw would be lifted in the other direction; the block would be lifted again; further wedges would be placed in to maintain the new height, and the process would continue until the block had reached the top of the central structure. A fascinating theory concerning the mystery of these very ancient Maltese temples — dedicated as they were in all probability to a religion combining the worship of a fertility goddess with communion with the dead — would very probably have had a major place for attempts to foretell the future by various other forms of divination, as well as oneiromancy.

The discovery of sharp sacrificial flint knives opens up the possibility that — just as was the practice among the soothsayers of ancient Rome — the entrails of the sacrificed animals would have been viewed as symbols of what was likely to happen; and as characteristically good or bad omens.

Another mysterious feature of the Tarxien temple is the ancient spiral design on its main altar. This resembles the mysterious spiral-maze design carved on the stone at Rocky Valley near Tintagel in Cornwall, England. Such spirals and mazes — like the great labyrinth of Knossus on Crete — undoubtedly had major significance in the thought of our neolithic ancestors. Is it possible that they bear testimony to the concentric circles that were allegedly the basic design of the great city state of Atlantis? If the Greco-Egyptian tradition is correct and Atlantis existed well before the ancient temples to be found on Gozo and Malta, it is possible that Atlantean refugees took their culture to these beautiful Mediterranean islands. Further evidence exists in the temples in the form of decorations consisting of another type of spiral or maze

Co-author Lionel Fanthorpe researching the ancient Maltese and Gozitan temples.

in the shape of the letter S. In and around these maze-decorated locations are numerous niches originally packed tight with half-burnt bones, skulls, and the horns of many goats, oxen, and sheep that had been sacrificed there.

Ceremonial basins have been found in which holy water used in the rituals was almost certainly stored. From the earliest times alchemists and other magicians have regarded sacrificial fire and holy water as two of the essential ingredients of magic and religion. Some of the great stones in the temples have been found drilled through by holes that may well have been used originally for ropes — perhaps to secure sacrificial victims.

Like many other ancient sites, the temples of Malta and Gozo contain carvings of animals. The Tarxien temples contain the mysterious low relief carvings of three such beasts. One is quite clearly a bull with short curved horns, a pronounced hump just behind the head, and quite a lengthy tail — very like the Brahmin bulls of modern India. A sow is shown clearly carved rather lower than the bull and facing in the opposite direction. A second bull is facing in the same direction as the sow, and it is probable that these carvings represent strength, virility, and fertility.

But these ancient, pagan temples and burial places with their mysterious magic were only the beginning of Malta's fascinating archaeological history.

Not far from the Church of St. Paul at Rabat are the famous St. Paul's catacombs. Many of these are of the type known as loculi. These are horizontal recesses that look very similar to berths in the cabins of ships. It is likely that they were cut to size, and the body would be wrapped in white linen, covered with sweet-smelling spices and myrrh, then laid in its narrow cell. The front would be covered by a stone slab that would be cemented into place. Inscriptions were often cut into the slab or inscribed on the mortar before it dried. During the Byzantine Christian period, chapels were often erected over the graves of martyrs or notable Christians.

In the Maltese catacombs circular stone tables were often cut out of the rock, and it is probable that these were used for washing and anointing the bodies of those who were to be buried there. Another theory is that the funeral party would use the stone table for a farewell feast in honour of the departed before they left the catacombs. Taken altogether then, the ancient pagan temples and the centuries-old catacombs have provided the islands in the

Maltese group with a long and mysterious history. It is small wonder that many folk tales and legends have arisen around these intriguing islands whose roots go so far into the past.

The Stone Age farmers from seven thousand years ago, followed by the builders of the Ggantija temples, Phoenician traders two thousand years before the birth of Christ, Greeks a thousand years afterwards, then Carthaginians and Romans: all left their timeless signatures on Malta and on Gozo and its legends in particular.

Saint Paul was shipwrecked on Malta roundabout the year AD 60. During their heyday both Vandals and Goths left their influence on the Maltese Islands. In the sixth century they were back under the control of the Eastern Roman Empire. Arabian forces held the islands from 870 until Roger of Normandy defeated them in 1090. The famous and heroic Knights of St. John ruled the islands in 1530. A Turkish raiding party took most of the Gozitans into slavery in 1551. The French arrived in Malta in 1798 during the turbulent times of the Revolution and the reign of the Emperor Napoleon I. By 1800 the Maltese Islands were part of the British Empire. Independence came in 1964 and the Maltese Republic was founded ten years later.

One of the great Maltese heroes who is particularly revered on Gozo is the famous San Demetri who gives his name to a cape on the rugged western side of Gozo, where the sea batters the rocky coastline relentlessly. According to legend a small isolated chapel dedicated to San Demetri stood close to the shore which bears his name today. Not far from San Demetri's chapel lived an elderly woman named Zgugina. She was a widow with an only son who was the centre of her life. A devout woman Zgugina went to San Demetri's Chapel every day to pray for her son's health, happiness, and safety.

Zgugina and the boy lived during the turbulent period when Turkish pirates made incessant raids on the Maltese Islands. On one of these raids, boatloads of savage marauders raided the area around San Demetri's Chapel and Zgugina's impoverished home. They took what few belongings she had, including her small store of simple food, and carried off her beloved son as a slave. Zgugina watched in despair as the pirates rowed away with all that made her life worth living. Then she did what she had always done and struggled to San Demetri's Chapel where she prayed yet again for the warrior-saint to help her.

According to the legend her miracle then took place. The sacred mural that included San Demetri on his great horse began to move and vibrate, and the figures became lifelike. The saint and his horse grew to full size and leapt from the painting in dazzling splendour and vitality as though lit by some internal heavenly radiance. San Demetri rode swiftly from the chapel and galloped away towards the coast in the direction which the pirate ship had taken. The holy horseman bounded through the shimmering sea surrounded by foam and spray as he headed purposefully towards the Turkish galleon. It was already too far out to sea for Zgugina to observe what was taking place, but within a few moments the saintly horseman was back at his chapel carrying her son safely in his great arms. Overwhelmed with joy and scarcely able to believe the miracle, Zgugina embraced her beloved son. By the time she turned to pour out her undying gratitude to the warrior-saint, he and his magnificent horse had faded back into the mural above the altar.

She showed her gratitude for the rest of her life by keeping a small oil lamp alight by night and day in front of the painting of the saint. There is an epilogue to the legend of Zgugina and San Demetri that is almost as strange as the original story. Although the ruins of Zgugina's house are still pointed out by local Gozitans, of the chapel itself there is now no trace. The legend tells how a prodigious earthquake shook the area some years after Zgugina's time and the chapel was submerged in the aftermath. It remained miraculously whole and continued to stand tranquil and strong on the bed of the sea.

Many years after the earthquake a peaceful merchant ship was anchored off the Cape San Demetri coast. When it tried to leave, the anchor refused to come up from the seabed. A diver went down to investigate but did not swim back. Two rescuers went down to see what had happened to him; they also failed to return. When all hope had been given up for the three men they suddenly returned to the surface in a state of great excitement. They told of a beautiful chapel they had found on the ocean bed. The door had stood open and they had gone inside. The interior was filled with fresh pure air as though the chapel still stood as it had done before the earthquake submerged it. A small oil lamp was still burning in front of the altar and by its light they could see the painting of San Demetri on his great steed.

There is, perhaps, in the legend a faint echo of the prophet Elijah who fed the widow's son throughout the long famine when the cruse of oil was never exhausted and there was always a little meal left to sustain the three of them day by day. The San Demetri legend may also encapsulate a very ancient thread of neolithic sympathetic magic. Cave paintings and carvings left by our Stone Age ancestors were believed to have been used to invoke the reality portrayed in the image.

The mysterious Ghar Dalam caves in Malta.

The neolithic hunters painting aurochs on their cave walls may well have done so in the belief that the image could in some way influence its real counterpart. There is also, perhaps, a connection with Pygmalion the sculptor from Amathus in Cyprus. Having carved the statue of a girl of surpassing beauty, Pygmalion fell in love with it. In the legend, the goddess Aphrodite, to whom Pygmalion was devoted, miraculously brought it to life for him. The full creative power of the human mind is only partially understood. The visual and audible hallucinations accompanying what are diagnosed as some forms of mental illness are another dimension of this apparent ability of the mind to produce what appear to be external stimuli. The psychical researchers in the Toronto group who produced the very realistic "Philip" phenomenon may also shed useful light on the Gozitan legend of San Demetri. Examined from this angle, there may be something in the theory that psychic mediums are not so much contacting another world as actually *creating it subconsciously.*

Nikola Tesla seems to have had this power to a very high degree. On numerous occasions Tesla demonstrated his ability to set up complex electrical experiments in a sort of alternative reality that did not seem to have any existence except in his own mind. He demonstrated his ability to visit this mental workshop and monitor the behaviour of the non-physical "machinery" he appeared to have set running there. One of the most striking examples of Tesla's abnormal mental prowess occurred in Budapest in 1882. Tesla was walking through the city with his friend Szigeti when he switched into that special alternative reality mode so characteristic of his creative mind. For want of a better term, Tesla saw a "vision." It showed him clearly how the alternating current electric motor could be built and made to run. Tesla was so preoccupied inside his mental workshop with its alternating current electric motor that Szigeti had to lead him out of the way of the city traffic. Wherever Tesla's consciousness was at that moment it was certainly not strolling through the busy streets of Budapest. The brilliantly imaginative C.S. Lewis used a similar device in *The Voyage of the Dawn Treader,* where the painting of the ship came to life and transported the central characters of the story from our world to the alternative reality of Narnia.

The strange legend of Ulysses and Calypso's cave is also attached to the island of Gozo. The beautiful beach of Ramla Bay, with the remains of ancient Roman baths nearby, stands between two attractive, well-wooded hills forming the sides of the fertile valley separating the villages of Xaghra and Nadur. A steep cliff on the western side of the bay contains the mysterious cave of Calypso.

Expert scholars who search for the realistic geographical locations cloaked in Homer's *Odyssey* are in general agreement that Gozo is the mysterious island of Ogygia — one of Ulysses' ports of call as he returned from the siege of Troy. According to Homer, following storms and thunderbolts, Ulysses finally struggled ashore in Ramla Bay. The whole of the island was a natural, earthly paradise; full of flowers, delicious fruit, pure streams of water, and beautiful women. Attracted by the sound of enchanting, mysterious music and the sight of beautiful girls dancing around the fire by the mouth of a cave, Ulysses drew closer. When we ourselves paid a research visit to Calypso's cave we met a friendly Gozitan orange seller and his young grandson eager to offer assistance. They not only sold us candles and matches, but the young grandson offered his services as a guide to the cave. His small, agile figure disappeared ahead of us into a narrow opening leading down into the depths of the cavern. We could not help but conclude that either the cave opening had contracted since Ulysses ventured into it or that the great Greek hero had been considerable slimmer than co-author Lionel. In the legend, despite Ulysses' endeavours to return to his homeland of Ithaca and his faithful wife, Penelope, he was detained by Calypso for a full seven years before being able to resume his journey. Are there overtones in this part of the Odyssey of some kind of alternative reality? Did the two time systems run at a different rate? So many stories and legends from all over the world concern human adventurers straying into caves or magical realms where they believed they had spent only a few hours — or at most days — when, by the normal terrestrial time system, they had been away for years or even centuries.

Is this ancient Maltese cauldron five thousand years old — or more?

198

Are there echoes of the Neolithic fertility cult of Malta in the story of Ulysses, and Calypso, the magical queen-goddess of Ogygia? To what degree do history, mythology, and the ancient Gozitan cultures blend into an integrated and understandable framework?

Another strange Gozitan legend that ties in with ancient history and tradition is associated with the hill named Ta'gelmus not far from Victoria. Ta'gelmus is famous for the golden-coloured dust coating its rocks. Alchemical legends claimed that for those who knew the secret of the transformation, this dust could be turned into real gold.

Going right back to the days of the neolithic farmers with their fertility cults — some of which might have been brought to the island by Phoenicians — and linking the story with the bulls carved on the ancient temples, the tradition of the golden calf of Ta'gelmus becomes a very plausible one. In the legend, an impoverished Gozitan farmer once lived and worked on the Ta'gelmus slopes. A mysterious stranger one day visited the hill and shared an astonishing secret with the poor farmer. According to the stranger, a golden calf of enormous value lay hidden in the hill waiting to be uncovered. The mysterious messenger urged Sidor, the farmer, to begin searching for this vast treasure. After several weeks of digging and searching while his other work was being neglected, Sidor struck some bright metal object. He had found the horn of the golden calf. He wrapped the precious object in sacking and made his way home with it as quickly as he could. His wife was as delighted as he was when she saw what he had found, but the two of them were very concerned about how best to turn their golden statue into the money they so desperately needed. They did not want the authorities to know what they had found in case it was simply confiscated and they received nothing. At last they decided that they could trust a man named Pupull whom they knew slightly and who was a wealthy merchant trading mainly in cotton. Sidor knew that Pupull was supposed to be a close friend of the hakem or governor.

When night fell Sidor wrapped his golden calf carefully in sacking again and made his way to Pupull's house. The merchant convinced the simple farmer that the golden calf was an ancient pagan idol and was by law the property of the governor. Pupull deliberately frightened Sidor into believing that he would receive some terrible punishment if the governor learned that he had found the calf and not reported it immediately. The terrified farmer begged the wily Pupull to help and advise him. The treacherous merchant gave Sidor a few coins and told him to leave the calf there, promising to use his influence with the hakem if there should be any trouble in future.

When Sidor got home and told his wife how little he had obtained for their treasure, she became furiously and uncontrollably angry with Pupull the merchant. She told everyone she knew of the discovery and of how Sidor had been treated by the greedy and deceitful Pupull. Within days the story reached the ears of the grand master. Meanwhile, Pupull and the hakem had decided to hide the statue until it could be profitably disposed of to a suitable goldsmith or perhaps a collector of valuable antiques. The grand master's officers returned to Malta convinced that the story of the golden calf had no real basis in fact and was merely a piece of gossip that had got out of hand.

The grand master went to Gozo to find out what was happening for himself. His suspicions were aroused when he spoke to the hakem. He was able to trace Sidor, the farmer, and got the whole story from him. The hakem was immediately dismissed and was lucky to escape with his life, but the wily Pupull tried to wriggle out of the situation and did his best to persuade the grand master that he knew nothing about it. Pupull was arrested shortly afterwards and interrogated more thoroughly by the grand master. He finally confessed that Sidor was telling the truth but would not tell the grand master where he had hidden the golden calf. Pupull was imprisoned in the dungeons of Fort St. Angelo to await the grand master's pleasure. This consisted of having Pupull flogged three times a day on the understanding that the punishment would go on until he disclosed the whereabouts of the golden calf. The merchant proved stubborn and died in the dungeons *without* disclosing where the golden calf of Ta'gelmus was hidden.

This is the kind of legend that has threads of fact running through it and it seems possible that some ancient pagan treasure dating from thousands of years in the past *is* hidden somewhere on Gozo. If the golden calf of Gozo has tenuous links with the Golden Calf of the Israelites, which Aaron constructed while Moses was on the mountain, then the sinister cavern of Il Belliegha has equally strange links with the legend of Tannhäuser and the Hörselloch in Thurginia. This mysterious cavern deep in the side of the Hörselberg Mountain is notorious for the strange sounds emanating from the subterranean waters that flow through its dark depths. Once believed to have been the entrance to the palace of the goddess Venus-Aphrodite, the Hörselloch acquired a sinister reputation as a place into which travellers vanished, never to return.

In the Gozitan version of the story, the Maltese name *Il Belliegha* carries strong implications of danger and unknown mystery. According to legend a widow named Selika was the mother of seven beautiful daughters. The family lived at a time when Gozitan peasants went in constant fear of "the evil eye." It was genuinely believed that certain witches, wizards, and sorcerers had the power to bring evil on their victims simply by exerting the malicious power of their eyes. The Gozitan villagers took careful precautions against such workers of evil and put their trust in a variety of charms, talismans, and amulets, which they believed would turn away the evil eye should it be aimed in their direction.

Selika had a particular phobia about the evil eye being cast on her beautiful daughters by some jealous witch, so she had made a variety of defensive charms from seashells and carved stone. During the period when Selika and her girls lived in Il Belliegha, many of the Gozitans were terrified of a wild and unkempt hag who came down from the hills periodically, always accompanied by a goat. As this strange old woman walked she supported herself on a stick, one end of which was carved in the form of a skull.

None of the villagers in Il Belliegha had any idea where this frightening apparition lived or what her purposes were. Such was the terror in which she was held by the locals that whenever she appeared they went indoors and barred their houses against her. While Selika's daughters were at work in the field one day at harvest time, the hag rose up from behind a boundary wall cackling insanely and waving her stick in the air in the direction of the girls.

The crone and her goat shuffled away across the field out of Selika's range of vision. That night, when the eldest daughter went to fetch water from a spring in a nearby cave, she failed to return. One after another, her sisters went to look for her. None of them returned. Finally Selika herself went in search of her missing daughters. She reached the cave from which the fresh clear stream emerged. There was no sign of the girls. Their water pitchers were also missing. As she was leaving the cave Selika saw to her horror that the charms her girls had worn to ward off the evil eye were lying pathetically on the steps.

Suddenly Selika found herself confronted by the hideous hag with her skull-topped stick. "Where are my daughters?" demanded Selika. Her only answer was a gesture with the stick and a cackling laugh of insane evil. Selika's daughters never returned. The cave became a place of fear and loathing and the name Il Belliegha ("the place that Swallows") became attached to it. The local villagers finally blocked it with rubble but just as at the Hörselloch the strange sound of the gurgling waters can still be heard within and those who are familiar with the tragedy of Selika's daughters aver that their sad lost voices can be heard blending with the sound of the waters.

When it is remembered, however, that Turkish pirates and slave traders frequently raided Gozo at this time, there may be a perfectly rational and simple explanation for the disappearance of seven attractive Gozitan girls. If the crazed old hag was working in conjunction with the slavers, her terrifying presence would have had the desired effect of keeping people off the streets while the abductions were being carried out.

Just as eighteenth-century British smugglers spread stories of ghosts and hauntings to keep superstitious country people away from their stores of contraband, so a grotesque figure believed to possess the power of the evil eye might well have had a similar effect and assisted the slave raiders carrying out their work on the Gozitan coast.

A Maltese writer named Guze Diacono conducted some fascinating research into ghosts connected with the Maltese Islands. According to Diacono's records a pious Maltese Capuchin monk was on a mission to a Maltese community in Tunisia, where he was preaching and conducting spiritual exercises for them. In search of accommodation, he was finally taken to an empty house owned by a local shopkeeper. "I have not been able to let it," replied the shopkeeper, "for no one is willing to stay in it." When the Capuchin questioned him the owner became rather evasive but hinted that the young holy man might be able to put right whatever was causing the strange psychic atmosphere of that house.

That night the Capuchin monk felt disturbed and depressed. There was a strange atmosphere in the place. In the small hours of the morning he was disturbed by a demanding knock on the door. He felt strangely chilled and frightened as he asked who was there. A gruff voice demanded that the door should be opened.

Interiors of the mysterious Gozitan and Maltese Temples.

There was a strange, supernatural quality to the sound and the young Capuchin hesitated. He wondered if perhaps it was an urgent demand on behalf of someone who was dying and wanted the last rites. With his sacred duties in mind he overcame his fear and reluctance and went to the door.

"We can come past a closed portal," came the strange voice from outside and the monk felt another shiver of fear according to Diacono's account. Summoning all his courage, the Capuchin opened the door. Two men entered and pushed past him. One appeared to be in his early 70s, the second was a little younger.

"Write what I tell you," said the older visitor in a commanding tone the young monk felt unable to disobey. The trembling he had experienced on first hearing the strange voice did not subside and he had to do his best to write in spite of it.

"Tell the man who owns this house that when he inherited it from me he knew that I had come by it by trickery," said the older man. He paused and pointed to his companion. "My son here was also aware of my evil doing. Tell him that he must restore this house to its rightful owners or one day he will suffer as we are suffering."

This note of warning seemed to be a very close echo of Marley's ghost in Dickens' *A Christmas Carol*. Whatever his selfishness and greed had been during his earthly life, Jacob Marley at least had the redeeming virtue of wanting to help his old partner Ebenezer.

The young monk, according to Diacono's account, was now perfectly well aware that he was in the presence of two spirits of the dead who had come to try to restore some wrong that they had done in life. He finished writing what had been dictated to him and turned unsteadily to the older spirit — as he believed it to be.

"Will you sign it?" he asked. The ghost with the long white beard took the pencil and signed what the young monk had written. The Capuchin allegedly said that where the pencil in the spirit's hand touched the paper, the paper was burned. Next morning the monk took the evidence to the shopkeeper who had allowed him to stay in the house. As a result it was returned to its rightful owner and no further spiritual manifestations occurred.

Such is the account as Guze Diacono recorded it. It is a very strange story, but the data was presented with honesty and in good faith. It fits in with an account of a haunting recorded by the late Canon Noel Boston, who was at one time the vicar of East Dereham in Norfolk. Noel tells of a similar purposeful ghost, the spirit of a departed monk, who haunted the muniment room of an old cathedral. Those who had seen it and testified to its existence said that it always looked as if it was searching for something and was in some distress at being unable to find it. When repairs and renovations were being carried out in that room by members of the cathedral staff and a team of volunteers, a silver groat (a fourpenny piece) was found between two old floorboards in the room where the monk had appeared. As far as Noel could ascertain, the ghostly visitor was a past treasurer or assistant treasurer who had been deeply distressed when he failed to balance his accounts by this fateful four pence. After the coin was solemnly placed in the cathedral offertory box, Noel records that the ghostly impression of the ancient monastic treasurer was not seen again.

Victorian spiritualists and psychic investigators frequently spoke of a substance they called ectoplasm, which looked a little bit like mist, candy floss, or cotton wool. Many fascinating accounts of hauntings in Malta have involved descriptions of something witnesses have referred to as "a ball of mist." Joseph Attard is one of

Malta's most accomplished writers and a painstaking and impressive researcher into the paranormal. His bestselling *The Ghosts of Malta* contains an intriguing chronicle about three friends who were on their way home to Vittoriosa after attending the festival at Zabbar.

Albert Ferrugia and his two friends were enjoying the warm September moonlight when they heard the unmistakable sounds of a donkey's hooves on the road and the squeak of the wheels of the cart it was drawing. Albert recognized the cart and its driver immediately. "That's Ausonio coming home from the festival," he said to his two friends. One of them was American. She asked, "Who is Ausonio?" Albert explained that his nickname was "Sonu" and he was a nougat maker who sold his products at festivals. The driver of the cart wore his cap at a rakish angle that was characteristic of Ausonio. The three friends looked away for scarcely a moment as Albert added some friendly comment about Sonu the nougat maker. When they glanced back there was nothing to be seen and there was no place to which Sonu, the donkey, and the cart could have vanished. They looked at each other in stunned silence and then from the spot where the man and his cart had vanished, a ball of mist began moving towards them. They moved back in alarm as though they felt instinctively that they must not let it touch them. The indistinct globe passed among them. Attard recalls that they described it as having a thick, uneven texture more like white candy floss than mist. They also reported feeling a blast of sinister chilled air as it came close to them. They watched in silent terror as it moved away from them faster and faster in the direction of Vittoriosa. Finally it disappeared into the invisible distance.

The strange manifestation of these apparently supernatural balls of mist or ectoplasm is not unusual in the records of Maltese ghosts. The history and mystery of the fascinating Maltese Islands undoubtedly qualifies them for inclusion among the world's most mysterious places.

Chapter 19
The Tower of London

Co-author Lionel worked for the Phoenix Timber Group of Companies of Raynham, Essex, from 1969 until 1972 as their chief training executive and metrication and decimalization officer — the timber trade was in the process of changing over to SI metric measure and the decimalization of British currency was imminent. During that period the Phoenix Timber Group were interested in acquiring the U.K. franchise for an extruded plastic manufactured by Royal Dutch Shell and known as "Wavin-x." It was thought that this might be a serious challenge to timber as a cladding material and the Phoenix Group thought, wisely, that it would be commercially sensible to be in on the ground floor if that turned out to be the case.

The new product needed some promotional photography that could be shown to potential customers: architects, surveyors, and builders. A top professional photographer was called in to undertake this work. His name was Sid. He had recently retired from Fleet Street. He was a friendly character with a vast stock of interesting anecdotes based on his Fleet Street career. Like most journalists, he enjoyed a drink and he was chatting with Lionel in the Phoenix pub in Raynham, Essex, where many of the Phoenix Timber staff tended to congregate because of the name.

As Lionel was also a former journalist, he and Sid got on very well together and Sid also knew of Lionel's keen interest in the paranormal and the extensive research he had undertaken in that field.

"I'll tell you one of the strangest things that ever happened to me," confided Sid, downing another pint. "It was just after the Second World War, and we had not long since finished celebrating V-E Day. The Ministry of Information were planning a big publicity project with the aim of showing how well Britain had survived the war and especially showing how well London had come through the blitz. Churchill was still prime minister and was so popular following V-E Day that his name was pure gold and his word was law. To my surprise and delight," Sid continued, "I was summoned to Downing Street in connection with this Ministry of Information project for which I'd been commissioned to do the photography. I was given a pass signed by Churchill himself, which authorized me to go *anywhere* without let or hindrance to take pictures in connection with the Ministry of Information project. Among the other photogenic sites that I wanted to include was, naturally, the Tower of London. I was looking for some artistic old stonework with a saucily defiant raven or two perched on it. I reached the tower, showed my seriously impressive prime ministerial pass, complete with Churchill's signature, to the senior man on duty, and got a rather strange response. He asked me in an awesome whisper whether that pass included "*the lower levels,*" and he asked it in a way that whetted my pressman's appetite for a unique story. 'Oh yes, of course,' I replied; but until that moment I hadn't the faintest idea of what he what talking about or that any "lower levels" even existed at the Tower."

Lionel liked Sid and always regarded him as a good professional and an honest sensible colleague; but it has to be accepted as part of life's rich tapestry that the most honest and reliable reporters *do* exaggerate on occasion and that sometimes a story can be hammered around a little for the sake of sensationalism and a neat, crisp, tabloid ending.

We think there is a solid core of truth in what Sid said. When the opportunity arises, we are definitely going to pursue it — with or without a pass issued from 10 Downing Street!

Sid went on to describe how he was taken through a series of locked doors and escorted down into a series of deeper and ever deeper dungeons that appeared to be of greater and greater age the farther they descended below the ancient White Tower. Sid told of storeroom after storeroom stacked with armour and ancient weapons and even of sinister dungeons in which skeletons of long-forgotten prisoners still mouldered.

The Tower of London

The Roman emperor Claudius had put a fortress on the site a thousand years before William the Conqueror built his great Norman stronghold there — and it is certainly possible that Britons or Celts had occupied it before the Romans came.

The site was very well selected: the great military structure could command the river route to the city and it provided a place of refuge for the Norman king and his courtiers should the citizens of London ever decide to take action against them. The temporary building would almost certainly have been timber, with a defensive ring of stakes around it, but by 1078 King William had commissioned a military architect named Gundulf, who was also a monk, to erect a permanent stone tower. The work took some twenty years to complete and the stone for its construction was imported from Caen in Normandy. The tower's design was based on Rollo's Tower in Rouen. Rollo was the first Norman duke and Rouen was his capital. Caen stone is very easy to cut, but "sets" very hard when used for building.

Kings came and went and the great fortress was enlarged and modified, refurbished, redesigned, and improved. A network of walls and towers encircled the original keep Gundulf had built for William I. Before the year 1300 Richard the Lionheart had the idea of surrounding the tower with a moat supplied from the River Thames itself.

The Tower of London.

Today the tower is roughly rectangular and two lines of defensive walls protect Gundulf's original structure, the White Tower. The inner wall has thirteen small towers set around it. The outer wall is protected by six towers facing the river, and two great bastions at the northwest and northeast. The tower has seen many changes during its long history. It has served as a royal observatory, a zoo, a mint, and a record office — those functions moved to other locations long ago. The tower guards the Crown jewels, an armoury, and is still officially a garrisoned fortress and royal palace — although the last king who actually lived in it was James I. The tower's most sinister purpose over the centuries was to be a prison — particularly for those who offended against the state. It was to London what the Bastille was to Paris.

Co-author Lionel Fanthorpe at London's Roman Wall near the Tower of London.

Traditionally, the Tower of London is under the direct control of whichever king or queen is on the throne of Britain and is commanded by a constable appointed by that sovereign. The first man to hold this office was a Norman knight named Geoffrey de Mandeville. The constable has direct access to the king or queen. At one time he was required to live in the tower itself, but this no longer applies. The resident governor who acts for him lives in the queen's house on the tower site. The tower is normally approached via Tower Hill, where a permanent execution scaffold used to stand in Trinity Square. The scaffold dated only from 1465 but records show that Simon of Sudbury — a rather unfortunate Archbishop of Canterbury — lost his head on that spot in 1381 at the hands of Watt Tyler's men. The most recent execution was that of Simon Frasier, Lord Lovat. Frasier was involved in the Second Jacobite Rebellion and was executed in 1747.

The Lion Tower is wide and semicircular in shape. Henry I kept lions here and Frederick II gave Henry II a gift of three leopards in 1235. (Three leopards had been the English standard before the adoption of a lion.) A white bear arrived as a gift from the King of Norway, followed by an elephant given by Louis of France. The animals from the tower were all transferred to Regent's Park in 1834. The redundant Lion Tower was then taken down.

The middle tower dating from the thirteenth century is reached via a causeway, and the archway is defended by a portcullis. The Byward Tower, which is situated by the ward — hence its name — is still protected by a ceremonial password that the sentry demands during the hours of darkness. Beyond the Byward Tower and the outer ward is Water Lane, and Mint Street is nearby. The Royal Mint was here until 1810 and gave its name to the street. The Bell Tower on the southwest corner of the inner ward dates from the thirteenth century and at one time the bell from the belfry at the top was rung as an alarm. At this signal, portcullises were lowered, drawbridges were raised, and gates were secured. When the bell rings today it is to advise visitors that it is time to leave.

Queen Elizabeth I was imprisoned for a few weeks in this same Bell Tower while her half sister Mary I was queen, the first woman in English history to be queen in her own right. Elizabeth took her meals in the lieutenant's quarters and exercised by walking along the battlements that have been known ever after as Elizabeth's Walk. Other famous parts of the tower complex include the Saint Thomas Tower and the Traitor's Gate below it. This was created in the year 1230 when Henry III arranged for a channel to be cut through the wharf and the outer wall so that the royal barge could go directly into the tower and allow passengers to embark and alight. The Saint Thomas Tower is named after the martyred archbishop of Canterbury, Saint Thomas Becket.

The Wakefield Tower stands opposite Traitor's Gate. For

almost a hundred years the Crown jewels were kept safely here before being moved to the Waterloo Block. Another sinister landmark in the ancient Tower of London campus is the Bloody Tower. Its original name was the Garden Tower and it acquired its present dark title because of the numerous gruesome and gory happenings in the sixteenth century. According to a tradition for which there is reasonable evidence, the young Princes Edward (V) and Richard of the House of York were killed there in 1483. The finger of suspicion points to Richard, Duke of Gloucester, who came to the throne as Richard III — but his defenders suspect Henry Tudor, who came to the throne as Henry VII (Lancastrian) of being responsible for the death of the Princes. Henry VII later married Elizabeth of York, the elder sister of the two murdered princes. According to tradition Sir Robert Brackenbury who was constable of the tower in 1483 was asked to participate in the murder of the young princes and resolutely refused despite the danger to himself, but a ruthless opportunist named James Tyrell later turned up at the tower and ordered Brackenbury to surrender the keys for one night. Tradition states that Tyrell's hired killers found the young princes asleep, suffocated one, and knifed the other. The bodies were then carried down a narrow stairway and buried in the basement under a crude heap of rubble.

When the horrified Brackenbury discovered what had happened, he ordered a priest to give the boys a proper Christian burial. Again, according to this tradition, they were reburied next to the White Tower, but the priest who conducted the funeral disappeared and Sir Robert Brackenbury died fighting at the Battle of Bosworth. Almost two centuries later, when Charles II was king, two young male skeletons were discovered near the White Tower. Charles, assuming that these were the murdered princes, arranged for their bodies to be transferred to Westminster Abbey. In 1933 the bones were exhumed and examined by experts, in whose opinion they were indeed those of the two tragic young princes.

The White Tower that forms the great central keep of the Tower of London is a ponderous structure even by modern standards. The walls are fifteen feet thick and there were no doors at ground level. The White Tower would have been a very difficult place to storm in medieval times. This impressive old building was the centre of royal family life and government in the Middle Ages.

The legend of the Tower Ravens is a particularly interesting one. It is said that they have been there since the tower was built and even today they, are normally seen strutting around on Tower Green as though they and not the yeoman warders were the senior people in charge. It is also rumoured that if the ravens ever leave the tower, England will fall. (Just in case there is any truth in the prophecy their wings are clipped to prevent them escaping!) Six of the birds are officially on the strength of the British army and are under the command of the yeoman quartermaster of the tower. Although they are traditionally raw meat eaters and scavengers, the tower ravens actually prefer raw eggs.

The Salt Tower, which was built by Henry III in 1235, contains much interesting historical graffiti. Hew Draper was imprisoned there for witchcraft in 1561, and below a complicated diagram intended to assist with the casting of horoscopes there are the words: "Hew Draper of Brystow made this spheer the thirty daye of Maye Anno 1561."

Another fascinating mystery connected with the Tower of London concerns the remarkably adventurous, swashbuckling Colonel Thomas Blood who attempted to steal the Crown jewels. After the restoration of Charles II the jewels were kept safe in the Martin Tower. Blood disguised himself as a priest and cultivated the friendship of Talbot Edwards, who was responsible for the safety of the Crown jewels. One May morning in 1671 Blood turned up with a friend he claimed was his nephew and asked to see the royal regalia. The unsuspecting Edwards opened the door and was immediately struck down and seriously injured. Blood and his henchmen were escaping with the jewels when Talbot's son disturbed them and all three thieves were captured in the scuffle that followed. Many a man in those days would have expected to be hanged or beheaded for a far smaller offence (poor old Talbot Edwards died of his injuries not long after). Blood, however, was granted an audience with Charles II, who admired his daring, pardoned him, granted him a pension, and gave back his Irish estates. There are many shrewd historical researchers who strongly suspect that Charles II and Blood were in on the deal together and that the original intention was that the jewels would be sold overseas and the king and the colonel would share the proceeds in due course; thus providing the prodigal Charles with the extra money he always wanted. (This, however, is debatable because

Charles II was able to secure income from three different sources, one of which was Louis XIV of France, which kept Charles more or less financially independent from Parliament.) It is also hypothesized by historians who support this collusion between Charles and Blood argument that a second part of the deal was: if anything went wrong, Charles would see to it that Blood came to no harm. The king's remarkable leniency after Blood was captured may have been the result of loyalty to their pact — if such a pact existed — or, more cynically, to Charles' fear that if Blood was not looked after well, word of the plot would reach dangerous and powerful ears. Charles II of all people knew all too well since his father's execution that even a king was vulnerable and Parliament ought not to be crossed. (On the other hand, however, despite what the country had suffered during the puritanical Commonwealth and the lamentable failure of Oliver Cromwell's son — Tumbledown Dick — it must be remembered that Charles was actually *sent for*: hence the restoration of the monarchy by warm and popular invitation in 1660.)

Part of St. James' Palace Complex, London — said to be haunted by Henry VIII's unhappy wives.

With such a long and checkered history, it is small wonder that the Tower of London is the central focus for many reports of hauntings.

One such account tells that it is not the ghost of an executed victim or even the headsman who swung the fatal steel, but the shadow of the axe itself that glides across the site where so much blood was shed on Tower Green and then leaves its black outline silhouetted against the ancient Norman keep.

Sir Walter Raleigh's ghost has been reported from the tower moving noiselessly down the long passages and from cell to cell where Raleigh once walked during his years of captivity. A woman in white appears on Tower Green and vanishes again with equal speed. She is thought to be one of Henry VIII's unfortunate queens. Sentries listening by night claim to have heard the tortured screams of Guy Fawkes stretched on the rack to confess.

In 1864 the officer of the watch was doing his rounds when he found a rifleman of the Sixtieth Rifle Regiment flat on the ground and out cold. The sentry was court-martialled on a charge of sleeping at his post. He said in his defence that a figure in white had approached his position, that he had challenged it, but that it had come on regardless. He struck at it with his fixed bayonet, met no physical resistance of any kind, and fainted in terror as a result. It was as he lay unconscious following that collapse that he had been found by the officer of the watch.

It was fortunate for the young rifleman that two witnesses came forward to testify at this court-martial that they had looked out of one of the tower windows prior to going to bed and had seen a white figure approaching the sentry. They were also able to testify they had heard him issue his challenge and had seen him strike at the figure with his bayonet before collapsing. He was duly acquitted.

Over the years that followed other sentries reported seeing the same strange spectre. Edmund Lenthal Swifte was so impressed by an incident that had occurred while he was keeper of the Crown jewels that he wrote an account of it for posterity. Edmund Swifte was a distinguished, deservedly respected and reliable public servant who had the responsibility of guarding the Crown jewels from 1814 until 1842. He was also a man of great individual courage, which he demonstrated by taking a leading role in preserving the jewels during a disastrous fire in 1841. In October of 1817, when he had been in charge for some three years, he was having supper with his wife and son and his wife's sister. The family party was sitting in the Jewel Room. The doors were shut and the heavy dark curtains were drawn over the windows. Two large candles were the only illumination in the room.

Edmund was sitting at the foot of the table with his son on his right; his wife was sitting in front of the fireplace and her sister was opposite. Swifte had just passed a glass of wine to his wife who was raising it to her lips when she stopped suddenly and cried out that she could see something strange. Swifte turned to follow her gaze and saw what he described as a cylinder like a glass tube about the thickness of a human arm. It was hovering with no visible means of support between their dining table and the ceiling. It looked to him as though it was filled with some dense white milky fluid with a pale blue tinge. He described it as being very similar to a cloud in a summer sky, and whatever the misty substance was, it was rolling incessantly inside the cylinder.

Edmund and his family watched it for a full two minutes, after which it began to move slowly in front of his wife's sister, tracing its path along the oblong shape of the table in front of Swifte and his young son. Swifte got up so he could observe its movements more closely and was standing quite close to his wife, who suddenly cried out that it had got hold of her.

Years later, when Swifte wrote his account for posterity, he said he could still feel the horror of that moment almost half a century after the event. He snatched up a chair and struck at the mysterious misty cylinder, and his blow went clean through it and struck the wainscot behind. The cylinder then moved to the upper end of the table and vanished in a recess by the window.

Concerned for the safety of his other children, Swifte raced upstairs to their room and told the nurse who was with them what had just taken place in the sitting room. The other servants had by this time hurried into the parlour, where Mrs. Swifte gave them a full account of the experience. What Edmund found strangest of all was that although he and his wife clearly saw and, in her case, *felt* the weird object, neither his son nor his sister-in-law could see it.

Swifte's account of this strange misty object bears a strong similarity to whatever it was that the three friends encountered on their lonely Maltese road. Swifte recounted one more sinister story, another event that took place during his time at the tower. In connection with this account, it should be borne in mind that the tower was a menagerie for many years before the animals it once housed were transferred to Regent's Park to become the nucleus of the London Zoo.

A sentry was keeping guard in front of the Jewel House door, a door that stood in the shadows under a stone archway. Swifte described it "as ghostly a door as ever was opened or closed on a doomed man." The figure of an enormous bear poured out from under the door — much as Aladdin's genie had done when he had emerged from the magic lamp. Desperate but determined, the sentry struck at it with his bayonet. He struck so hard that the bayonet stuck in the oaken door behind the apparition. Just like the man who had been overwhelmed by the strange spectre of the woman in white, this Jewel House door guard also collapsed unconscious. The sound of his cries and the impact of the bayonet on the door had alerted his companions, who ran swiftly to his aid. There was no question of the unconscious man being either asleep or drunk. Only a few minutes before the supernatural bear had emerged the sentry had spoken perfectly normally and in a brisk, alert fashion to a fellow soldier passing the door. The Jewel House door guard himself had a deservedly high character for courage and good conduct. When Swifte interviewed him the following morning the man was shaking uncontrollably and bore a look of mortal terror on his face. *Three days later he was dead.* He was buried with full military honours in the Flemish Cemetery attached to St. Katherine's-by-the-Tower.

Animal ghosts are by no means uncommon. There are many tales of the "Black Shuck" from Norfolk and Suffolk — although this should never be confused with "Old Shuck" (which appears to be an innocuous domestic canine ghost, said to run loyally between the graves of his two drowned masters).

A mysterious hound is also said to haunt Oak Island in Nova Scotia.

The old west-country ballad tells of Tom Pierce's (or Pearce's) grey mare at Widdecombe, which appeared in ghostly form, and Dartmoor has a strange tale of a ghostly sow accompanied by its equally insubstantial litter of hungry piglets. Borley Rectory, in Suffolk, has its tales of headless horses controlled by a headless horseman who drives a phantom coach.

If there is any mileage in the theory that extreme emotions at or near the point of death can result in impressions being recorded in the surrounding fabric, is it possible that when bear-baiting, a cruel sport for both bear and dogs, took place as part of the "entertainment" in the tower menagerie, the desperate and agonized bear would leave psychic impressions of itself in those ancient stones? Or could it even be that the ghost of the tormented animal had returned? In the days when the Lion Tower housed the menagerie, James I is said to have provided a display of bear-baiting for his guests.

One of the famous ghosts of those executed in the tower was that of sad little Lady Jane Grey, granddaughter of Mary Rose, who was the youngest sister of Henry VIII. When Edward VI died in 1553 Lady Jane Grey was legitimately one of those who could have been considered as being in line for the throne, although Henry's daughter Mary, by Catherine of Aragon, had a closer claim. Plotters proclaimed Jane as Queen, but the poor girl was arrested and Mary took the crown. On the February 12, 1554, Guilford Dudley, Jane's husband, was executed and his ghost has reportedly been seen on numerous occasions in the Beauchamp Tower — part of the Tower of London complex. Dudley's ghost sobs quietly to itself as though expecting to be executed. Lady Jane died the same day and her ghost has been reported on many occasions.

It was on February 12, 1957, four hundred and three years after Lady Jane's execution, that Guardsman Johns on duty in the tower was convinced that he saw her on the battlements just above him. He immediately alerted a fellow guardsman who also saw what he reported to be Lady Jane's ghost. The restless, unhappy spirit of Anne Boleyn, Henry VIII's second wife and mother of Queen Elizabeth I, has frequently been reported by observers from the family home, Blickling Hall in Norfolk, and from Hampton Court, where several of Henry VIII's unfortunate wives seem to return after death. Anne has also been reported from the Tower of London itself, where she has allegedly been seen by numerous witnesses as a headless female figure who usually appears near the Queen's House where she was confined before her execution.

The great old building conceals numerous mysteries of different kinds. Do the mysterious "lower levels" of which Sid, Lionel's Fleet Street photographer friend, spoke really exist? And, if so, what's concealed down there? Who was responsible for the deaths of the two tragic young princes? And what of all the other strange psychic events that have been so frequently reported by reliable witnesses for so many centuries? The Tower of London is an old and extremely mysterious site.

Chapter 20
The Mystery of Slane in Ireland

The picturesque village of Slane, one of the most beautiful in the whole of Ireland, stands at the crossroad that links Dublin with Derry and Drogheda with Navan. Four fine old Georgian houses stand across the corners of the intersection.

The village has many historical associations with Saint Patrick, who was said to have lit his great fire on the Hill of Slane in the year AD 433. King Laeghaire had lit an equally impressive fire at Tara as an integral part of a major pagan festival he was celebrating. The royal command was that as long as the Tara fire was burning at the king's pleasure, no other should be lit within sight of it on pain of death. According to tradition, seeing Saint Patrick's fire burning fearlessly on the Hill at Slane, King Laeghaire rushed over in his chariot to discover who it was who had dared to defy him. Patrick was duly summoned to appear before the king and explain his fire of Slane.

The local Druids had ordered that no one was to show any respect or honour to Patrick, but one bold Irishman, Erc, stood proudly and resolutely to defy them and to give Patrick the respect he deserved. Erc was totally contemptuous of the Druids' orders. Following this courageous declaration for Patrick, Erc was converted to Christianity and became one of the saint's most loyal servants. Not long afterwards Patrick appointed him as a *Breitheamh* — or judge — and Erc remained one of Saint Patrick's staunchest and most trustworthy friends throughout the whole of his strong, purposeful life. Patrick appointed Erc as the first bishop of Slane, where he died in the year 514. Muirchu records that Erc was always closely associated with the history of the church at Slane and other, more recent, evidence shows that Erc, the first great bishop in the entire area, is still honoured there today.

A curious tomb dating from very early times stands in the graveyard on top of the Hill of Slane. Its design is remarkable for its gable-shaped ends. Until a few years ago, at funerals in Slane it was the practice to carry the coffin three times round the Bishop's Tomb, as it was known, and to set it down there for a brief interval before its interment. The tomb on the Hill of Slane is sometimes referred to as Erc's Tomb and sometimes as the Bishop's Tomb.

Other old religious sites in Ireland have similar "saint's tombs" shaped almost like miniature houses. Some historians believe that they may originally have served as shrines and were used as sacred reliquaries of notable saints and holy men from the earliest days of the Irish Church. It is particularly interesting to discover that boys are still christened "Erc" in Slane — but the name is almost unknown in other parts of Ireland.

Close to the Slane Hill graveyard are the remains of a Franciscan friary. It stands on the site of a *much earlier* religious building that Erc himself founded. It was this *first* monastery that housed the great central mystery of Slane and its connection with the ongoing mystery of Rennes-le-Château in southwestern France.

The early French historian Mézeray wrote his *Histoire de France* in 1685. He was particularly critical of the confusion and uncertainty he felt the early chroniclers seemed to have had about important events which took place in and around the year AD 650. Mézeray believed that King Sigebert of Austrasie (sometimes rendered Austrasia) died in 650 when he was only 21 years old. His kingdom was then located in eastern Gaul, and Metz was its capital city. Despite dying so young, Sigebert had a son named Dagobert who was barely 2 or 3 years old when his royal father died.

Mézeray's account maintained that Grimoald, who held the vitally important position of mayor of the palace, had carefully spread the word that before his own son had been born, young King Sigebert had legally adopted Grimoald's son, Childebert, to follow him as king. As soon as Sigebert died, Grimoald sent the rightful heir — young Prince Dagobert — to Slane in Ireland, where he was carefully hidden until such time as Grimoald could get his own son Childebert safely established on the Austrasian throne.

The Austrasian lords, however, were furious with the mayor of the palace — whose forces, unfortunately for him, were not adequate to meet theirs. Grimoald was sent as a prisoner to Paris to be judged by King Clovis II, who promptly executed him.

Mézeray puts some significant historical analysis into his account at this point. He examines the motives of the Austrasian seigneurs who made it their business to have Grimoald's unfair treatment of Dagobert II dealt with by Clovis II. In Mézeray's view their action was not based on any love or loyalty which they felt for young Dagobert II. It was merely the local lords' reaction to one whom they considered only their equal who had outraged them by endeavouring to seize the kingship over their heads. None of them, as Mézeray points out, went to any lengths at all to persuade Grimoald prior to his execution to say *where* the young King Dagobert had been sent or even whether he was still alive. Nor did any of the Austrasian seigneurs go looking for Dagobert in order to give him the throne which they had snatched back so self-righteously from Grimoald and Childebert.

Again according to Mézeray's account, there were years of misrule and disorder until, having finally discovered where Dagobert was, the Austrasian nobility brought him back from Ireland and acknowledged him as king. It was a time and place for short turbulent reigns: in Mézeray's account Dagobert was on the throne for less than four years.

Mézeray was undoubtedly justified in his complaints about the fluidity and unreliability of the Austrasian historians as far as the middle years of the seventh century were concerned. Somewhere legend and history came apart as frustratingly as a fisherman's line when he is attempting to land the catch of the decade. Dagobert II and his hypothetical Merovingian descendants drifted mysteriously out of history and into legend. If the mystery of Rennes-le-Château and its legendary treasure is to be placed in perspective and linked effectively with the mystery of Slane Monastery and Dagobert II's time there, it is necessary to digress briefly into the character of the enigmatic nineteenth-century priest of Rennes-le-Château, Bérenger Saunière. Was there a treasure or great secret he found at Rennes? Another equally puzzling mystery is how he — ostensibly just a simple village priest — was able to stand up so effectively against the weight of an intolerably pompous Church hierarchy and his many other critics and opponents.

It seems that as a child young Bérenger had his imagination fired by stories of the ancient treasure of Rennes-le-Château and the heroic deeds of Frankish, Merovingian, and Carolingian kings who had once ruled in southwestern France. The wreckage of the Western Roman Empire left in its wake one of the most confused and least-known epochs of European history. The United Roman Empire was terminated formally in AD 395 when Arcadius and Honorius, the sons of Theodosius I, took the Eastern and Western halves of the old empire respectively. The Western Empire sputtered into extinction ignominiously when Odoacer disposed of Romulus Augustulus, its last emperor, in the year 476. The Byzantine half of the empire, over in the East, managed to survive until AD 1453 when its last emperor, Constantine XI, succumbed to the Turkish conquest of Constantinople. The events that occupied the last years of the decaying Western Empire left their legacy of mystery in the region of Carcassonne and Rennes-le-Château.

From 462 to 486 the great kingdom of Gaul was nominally under the control of Syagrius, a more or less independent Roman governor. The first Frankish dynasty, the Merovingian, was already well rooted. Clovis I, grandson of Merovech — also known as Mérovée — married a Christian princess, was converted by her, and went on to dispose of Syagrius, the last Roman governor, in AD 486. He then established his court at Paris and did his best to unite the entire Frankish race into one large powerful kingdom; he almost succeeded.

To the east and to the north of Paris was the great Frankish kingdom of Austrasia, to the south and west of Paris lay the Frankish kingdom of Neustria, south of Neustria — all the way from Spain to southern Burgundy — lay the Visigothic realm containing the citadel of Rhedae, which was destined eventually to become the mysterious little hilltop village of Rennes-le-Château.

Some researchers into the Rennes mystery have maintained that ancient manuscripts were discovered in Saunière's church, which proclaimed that the treasure of Rennes belonged to King Dagobert II, that he had died in the year 681, and that the treasure was concealed somewhere near the king's body. Find the mysterious tomb of Dagobert II, and the wealth of Rennes would be yours. Bewilderingly, however, these supposedly ancient coded parchments were ambiguous over the question of the French phrase "*il est la mort.*" This could mean "he is there dead," implying that the body of

Dagobert II is concealed somewhere beside the treasure of Rennes, or "it is death," suggesting a curse similar to the one alleged to accompany Tutankhamun in his Egyptian tomb would descend upon any who interfered with the mysterious treasure of Rennes-le-Château. It is the date 681 on the coded manuscript — supposed to have been found in a Visigothic pillar in Saunière's church at Rennes — that causes the problem.

Traditional historians place Dagobert II's short reign a few years *earlier* than the 681 on the controversial Rennes parchments, but in a period when accurate records were rarer than snowflakes in a blast furnace, a gap of only three years is not an insuperable problem.

Romantic and chivalrous traditions worthy of anything in the Arthurian court tell how Dagobert II, a noble and altruistic young warrior-king, faced death after being trapped in an ambush set by treacherous enemies. These same traditions tell how Dagobert, recognizing that the situation was hopeless, chose to hold off the enemy in a narrow canyon while his most trusted companion in arms escaped taking with him Dagobert's five-year-old son. One tradition maintained that this boy grew up to become King Sigebert IV and was finally buried in the wall of the ancient church of St. Mary Magdalene at Rennes-le-Château alongside his murdered father's vast royal treasure.

It must be assumed that the secret of that same royal treasure was imparted to the faithful but nameless companion-in-arms who had saved young Sigebert's life while his father gallantly held the pass. Such a man must have been a friend in a million if the desperate, doomed Dagobert II dared to trust him with his son *and* the royal treasure.

These ancient Merovingian kings were Christians of a kind but their faith was not necessarily an orthodox one. Many of the more interesting early versions of Christianity — damned as heresies by self-appointed truth-keepers and timidly orthodox theologians — laid particular stress on the importance of ethical behaviour in general and loyalty and fidelity in particular. The later Albigensianism (or Catharism) in particular regarded the earth as a battleground between God and the Devil, a battleground in which ethical conduct, loyalty, and honesty struck powerful blows against a tangible personalized force of evil. Empty creeds, liturgies, and religious ceremonies and rituals did not satisfy these early heretics. Their powerfully practical version of the Christian faith affected the way a person lived. This could go some way towards explaining Dagobert's total trust of his loyal lieutenant and its subsequent justification.

There is a considerable body of evidence suggesting that Dagobert II was not popular with the local bishops and other church leaders of his day. Their complaint was that far from being the puppet-king or figurehead they had rather hoped for — a monarch who believe in laissez faire — he was a real king who did not hesitate to demand his royal taxes, rights, and fiscal dues. His problem seems to have been that he did not have the necessary military strength to reinforce his legitimate royal claims. This was a situation that a strong, ambitious, young king would find frustrating in the extreme. It could well be that Dagobert turned to powerful heretics for financial and military support against his troublesome orthodox clergy.

If legend and tradition are to be believed, Dagobert II in an impatient moment of military madness (reminiscent of Custer's tactics at the Battle of the Little Bighorn) led a strategically inadequate group of his knights and royal guards on what was intended to be a punitive raid into hostile territory. He detected the fatal ambush when it was too late to escape it, sent his staunchest companion-in-arms galloping to safety with the infant Sigebert, while he himself — warrior-king to the last — turned to face the ambushers, slew as many as he could, and effectively blocked their pursuit of his son and the secret of the royal treasure. Exciting and romantic as it is, the legend does not clarify *why* the infant Sigebert had been taken along on such an inherently dangerous mission.

One of the most helpful and informative books on the subject is J.M. Wallace-Hadrill's work *The Long-Haired Kings*. He refers to Dagobert II's twenty-year exile at Slane in Ireland, his restoration by Saint Wilfrid to the throne of Austrasia in 676, his subsequent death and Saint Wilfrid's hearing the news in 680 from an irate bishop who compared Dagobert to Rehoboham, the son of King Solomon.

There is other evidence connecting Rennes with Dagobert II and his violent death. Among the many curious items in the museum is the *Dalle de Chevalier* — the knight's tombstone. This very ancient stone carved in bas relief *seems* to depict a crowned head on horseback on its left side and a mounted knight carrying a child on its right. The carving is ancient and primitive and it is far from easy to decide what these figures really represent. Some researchers who have studied the Dalle de Chevalier suggest that it is a religious carving showing the flight of the Holy Family into Egypt as they escaped from King Herod's massacre of the Innocents in Bethlehem. The carving *might* possible represent the infant Jesus, Mary, and Joseph — but given the location in which it was found and the history of the Rennes area, it seems more probable that the Dalle de Chevalier tells the story of Dagobert II and the escape of young Prince Sigebert. Rennes villagers certainly prefer the idea that the stone was once mounted horizontally along the side of Sigebert's tomb and does depict Dagobert II and his infant son. The sixth-, seventh-, and eighth-century records of the Merovingian Dagoberts and Sigeberts do not accord with the Rennes-le-Château legend. There are historical records that suggest that the third and final Dagobert survived until AD 715 and does not seem to have been connected in any way with ambushes, hidden treasures, or the coded date of 681 on the ancient manuscripts. Were Sigebert, or Dagobert, or *both* of them buried in some secret crypt below the ancient church at Rennes, and was their treasure buried with them?

The mystery of Slane focuses on the ancient tomb of Bishop Erc and the role the quiet and beautiful Irish monastery may well have played in the unsolved mystery of Rennes-le-Château and the unknown source of Bérenger Saunière's incredible wealth. The researcher is left to wonder what strange secrets Dagobert II learnt in the ancient monastery of Slane. This beautiful, historic village is well worth a visit.

Chapter 21
The Mystery of Saint Nectan's Glen

It is almost as difficult to date the legendary Saint Brychan as it is to date Saint George with his dragon or King Arthur and his Knights. There is less doubt of his existence than of his precise era. He was, according to tradition, a pious Welsh king who was also connected with the early Church in Ireland. He is remembered for the size of his enormous family almost as much as for his piety. The lowest estimate puts his children into double figures and the highest reaches a tentative three score! In the hard and difficult Celtic days through which Brychan reigned, death, and not divorce, was the great breaker of marriages.

This powerful, wise, but saintly old king was a veritable Irish Solomon and had no time for the pious nonsense of celibacy. Brychan had at least three wives — each of whom produced a large brood. Their descendants included four saints: Clether, Morwenna, Endellion, and Nectan, who gave his name to the mysterious glen in Cornwall with its unique waterfall. As with all early saints, traditions differ about Nectan. He is described as a Welsh hermit saint who settled in his hermitage near Hartland in north Devon, England, and was ironically murdered by robbers whom he was trying to help after they had stolen his cattle.

The famous twelfth-century Gotha Manuscript describes Nectan as the oldest and most famous of Brychan's twenty-four children. At some time during the sixth century — for Nectan is a *little* easier to date that his prolific paternal parent — accompanied by several members of his family, Nectan left his beloved Wales for his new home in north Devon. He found himself a suitably lonely spot in the middle of what was then dense and dangerous forest and arranged with his family that he would see them at his hermitage on December thirty-first each year.

After several years of isolation and lonely prayer Nectan answered a call for help from a swineherd who was looking for his pigs. This man had a grateful employer who sent a present of two cows to Saint Nectan as a token of his gratitude for the help the saint had rendered to his swineherd. The cows did not last long. According to this version of Nectan's life the cows were stolen by cattle thieves whom Nectan promptly pursued. As well as being a saint, a hermit, and a contemplative holy man, the blood of a Celtic king still ran in Nectan's veins. He was not the kind of man whose cattle you could steal with impunity. Far from dealing with the cattle thieves as a Welsh warrior-chieftain would have done, however, Nectan confronted them with the moral issue — as the fearless prophet Nathan had once confronted King David, or as Elijah had confronted Ahab. (Nectan would have done far better to have used the tried and tested Welsh warrior approach!) The cattle rustlers were not impressed by an unarmed holy man who had no fighting men to back him. Nectan's relentless sermon and earnest attempts to convert the thieves to Christianity surprised and irritated them to such a degree that they beheaded him. According to the Dark Age legend, Nectan promptly picked up his severed head — just as the famous Green Knight did after his encounter with Sir Gawain in the Arthurian romances — and carried it back with him to the river beside his hermitage. What effect this posthumous demonstration had on the cattle thieves is not recorded.

Saint Denys, patron of France and bishop of Paris in the third century, was also beheaded alongside his loyal companions: the deacon Eleutherius and the priest Rusticus. Their bodies were found in the River Seine and the great Abbey of St. Denys — the traditional burial place of French royalty — was built over their tomb.

A similar story of beheading became attached to Saint Decuman, who was the patron of Watchet and Saint Decuman's in Somerset. He too was a Welsh monk who allegedly came from what was then known as Rhoscrowther, better known as Llandegyman, in Dyfed and made his way to a hermitage near Dunster in Somerset. Like Nectan he lived a blameless life as a pious hermit and met his death at the hands of an unprovoked assassin while he was praying. Following his decapitation he picked up his head, as Nectan was credited with doing, and carried it to the nearest well.

Saint Nectan had a large medieval following in the West Country. Lyfing, who was bishop of Crediton in the early part of the eleventh century, supported Nectan's cult and provided generous financial support for Hartland Church. A beautiful reliquary, some valuable lead to keep rain from the roof, and a splendid peal of bells were all included in Lyfing's generous patronage. Nectan's simple wooden staff was overlaid with gold and silver and set with jewels. The church was also reinforced against attacks from the Irish pirates who came from the Viking settlements there. Celebrated patrons of Hartland included King Harthacanute and Earl Godwin.

The other version of Nectan's life and death tells how the saint arrived sometime towards the end of the fifth century and

Mysterious waterfall in Saint Nectan's Glen. He lies buried in the river bed just below it.

built his hermitage alongside the River Trevillitt. He placed it just above the spectacular waterfall and kieve, or basin, in the glen which is now named after him. Nectan constructed a chapel there with a tall tower in which he placed a great silver bell with a penetrating tone that carried a great distance. It was said that he rang the bell to warn sailors of the treacherous coast they were approaching. It was also used to fetch help from what was thought by some historians to have been an ancient Celtic monastery at Tintagel. Great controversy rages — and looks like continuing to do so — over the real origins of these stark coastal ruins. A representative of the robust old Celtic Christianity, Nectan found himself caught up in the angry altercations which arose between the recently arrived Roman Catholic missionaries and the far older Celtic-British religious traditions. His death in this version was a very different affair from the story of his having been beheaded by cattle rustlers.

As he lay dying, Nectan prophesied that the older Celtic Christian faith would one day come back into the ascendant, and he vowed that his great silver bell should only be rung by true believers. His disciples carried him to the river bank above the deep kieve, and from there he dropped the great bell into the depths of the basin. As with every other legend of submerged towns, villages, chapels, and castles, the bell still rings from below the water, and, as in Nectan's day, its tones are a grim warning.

There are also reports of Nectan's monks being seen still chanting their sacred songs as they walk the beautifully wooded valley paths.

The mystery surrounding Nectan's death deepens when the legend tells of two mysterious women — presumably his sisters — who arrived and took possession of the saint's chapel. Nectan had left special instructions about the disposal of his body, and, acting on these, his sisters placed him in a sturdy oak chest along with the sacred vessels he had used during his long, lonely life as a religious hermit. The sturdy and industrious women then diverted the river after the old Visigothic style of burial, dug a grave in its bed somewhere below the kieve, and placed their brother reverently in it. The dam was then broken and the river returned to its original route flowing over Nectan's last resting place. The two sisters then took up a hermit's life for themselves in the shelter Nectan had built.

They did not make any regular contact with their neighbours, who became suspicious and hostile. The two hermit nuns were regarded as demons, witches, or worse, and were blamed for every local epidemic, or accident, that befell the villagers or their animals. One finally died and the villagers saw the other — terminally ill herself — weeping over her dead sister.

Overcoming their fear and suspicion at last, the kindly villagers gave the two poor women Christian burial, and tradition has it that their bodies lie in Nectan's valley under a great flat marker stone within the sound of the fall. There are reports of two grey ladies who haunt Genver Lane close to Nectan's Glen. Is it possible that these are the shades of the saint's devoted sisters? After their deaths what had once been Nectan's chapel and hermitage gradually became a ruin, but in the mid-nineteenth century a cottage was built exactly on its site.

The sturdy old walls, which the saint had constructed so well almost fifteen hundred years previously, were a metre thick and still strong. They were incorporated into the Victorian cottage. The building was enlarged in 1900 but it is still possible to trace the outline of Nectan's original chapel and hermitage — and it seems likely that the massive rock on which the kitchen stands today may once have been the foundation for the great tower from which Nectan's warning bell rang to help sailors to avoid the dangerous coast.

As with any building of such great age, the hermitage site underwent a number of different uses. At one time it turns up in the record books as an outpost for the pre-Norman castle *believed* to have occupied the site of the Tintagel castle currently associated with the legends of King Arthur. Many of the old Arthurian traditions associate Nectan's Glen and the remote hermitage, the strange waterfall, and the mysterious kieve with King Arthur, the Grail legends, and the romantic adventures of the Knights of the Round Table.

Is it *really* Nectan, the holy hermit, who sleeps in his oaken coffin below the clear waters of the Trevillitt River? Who *were* the mysterious grey ladies? The river burial tradition they employed is Visigothic. Alaric, the Visigothic conqueror of Rome at the beginning of the fifth century, was buried in just such a way. It is suspected by numerous Rennes-le-Château researchers that a similar Visigothic burial chamber exists somewhere in the bed of the river near the tomb of Arques. Does the strange tale of Nectan the saint camouflage the last resting place of one who was far more famous?

Chapter 22
The Vampire of Highgate Cemetery

To find Highgate Cemetery, take the Northern Line on the London Underground, alight at Archway Station, and walk up Highgate Hill — which is quite a climb. Where Highgate Hill joins High Street, turn left into Waterlow Park, and continue through the park itself until you emerge on to Swains Lane — where the main entrance to Highgate Cemetery is situated.

Highgate is by no means an ancient or even a medieval cemetery.

By the 1750s there was considerable public concern because burial places in city centres were reaching crisis point. From the beginning of the nineteenth century the press was taking an active interest in the unhygienic state of many London churchyards and parliamentary committees were also investigating them. Under the pavements of many churches and their limited surrounding areas, the vaults were literally crammed with coffins. The air in many of the buildings was so badly polluted that it was a major source of death and disease. In the churchyards themselves coffins had to be piled one above the other until they were within a few inches of the surface; ground level frequently had to be raised to correspond with the sills of the churches' lower windows in order to cram in even more coffins. Crafty sextons surreptitiously removed bones and decaying remains to make room for fresh interments, and in all too many such instances bodies were simply tipped out into pits nearby. The gravediggers' perks on these sordid occasions were the coffin plates, nails, and handles that they salvaged and sold for their scrap metal value. Consequently, churchyards and their immediate environs became dangerously unhealthy and hideous eyesores.

This was the situation in many major cities in the first few decades of the nineteenth century. Because of its vast population and high mortality rate London suffered worst of all. The old churchyards were finally closed by Act of Parliament and the cemeteries on the city periphery took over from them. Kensal Green cemetery, for example, is roughly the same age as Highgate and dates from 1832.

Highgate itself goes back only as far as 1836 when Steve Geary of the London Cemetery Company bought just under twenty acres of land on a hillside there. For almost a century things went very well indeed with the new burial site. Expert landscape gardeners worked hard to create a peaceful and beautiful setting to ease the grief of families, loved ones and friends who came there to mourn and to remember. Well-placed and well-tended trees and shrubs added to the quiet, dignified ethos that then prevailed.

Many of the good, the great, and the famous were buried in Highgate, including: Sir Alfred Barratt, chairman of the international sweet manufacturing company, Catherine Booth-Clibborn, a Salvation Army pioneer, Sir George Barclay Bruce, the railway designer, Cherkassky, a concert pianist, William Clifford, the mathematician and philosopher, Leslie Hutchinson (always known as Hutch), a cabaret singer and pianist, Elizabeth Lilley, midwife to Queen Victoria, Karl Marx, philosopher, economist and politician, Sir Ralph Richardson, the actor, Christina Rossetti, the poet, Thalden-Ball, a renowned organist, Topolski, the painter, Max Wall, the comedian, and fearless Ed Woodham, who rode in the Charge of the Light Brigade at Balaclava and lived to tell the tale.

It was not until World War One that things began to go badly wrong at Highgate Cemetery. It was no longer possible to obtain enough staff; very few plots were left for sale; and cremation was proving a popular alternative. Neglect and vandalism inevitably followed — reaching a level that forced the cemetery to close to the public in 1975.

In response to these problems, a group of public-spirited volunteers known as The Friends of Highgate Cemetery was created in an attempt to do something about the problems of neglect, overgrown graves, and chronic vandalism. They coped exceptionally well with a long list of daunting tasks, and when we made a research visit to the cemetery in 1998, we found their representatives very helpful, informative, and co-operative.

It was in the bleak and desperate period before the Friends began their immense work of restoration that stories of the Highgate Vampire began to circulate.

But a general look at vampire myths and legends is an essential introduction to the specific Highgate Cemetery episodes, if the Highgate reports are to be understood and placed in their proper perspective.

In popular mythology and legend, a vampire is described as an evil entity that sucks the blood from its victims, and infects them with its own vampirism in the process. During early periods of dangerous religious obsession and fanaticism, vampires were alleged to be the returned, satanically animated corpses of heretics, criminals, or suicides.

Like werewolves, leopard-people, and other shape-shifters, the vampire is credited with the ability to change its bodily form: a bat being a favourite alternative. According to the "rules" of this traditional vampire folklore, the vampire must be safely back within its grave, or tomb, before dawn breaks. Sunlight is fatal to it. When travelling, it needs to be accompanied by its coffin containing soil from its original burial place to provide it with this essential diurnal refuge.

Although widely known throughout Asia and Europe, the vampire legends were particularly prolific in Slavic and Hungarian mythology, and a great many cases were reported.

In May of 1730, the Austrian Count de Cadreras turned up at the University of Fribourg in Switzerland, where he allegedly dictated notes to the university's librarian, notes which became the notorious Cadreras manuscript, and told an amazing story of apparent wholesale vampirism.

Some ten years earlier, the Habsburg Empire of Austria — having fought long battles against the Turks and the French for several years — was enjoying a period of relative peace and tranquillity. The army was quietly being brought up to strength and retrained. It was during this period of calm that a young Austrian soldier from Vienna was stationed at the village of Haidam near the Hungarian frontier. The soldier's name was Joachin Hubner, and he was billeted with a friendly, local farming family. Joachin was drinking wine with the farmer and his teenaged son, while the ladies of the house were clearing away the evening meal in the adjacent kitchen. The farmer was facing the open doorway. His son and the young soldier had their backs to it. The farmer broke off what he was saying in mid-sentence and froze with a look of horror on his face. The boy turned to follow his father's gaze and did the same. Joachin then craned round and saw only a harmless-looking old man moving slowly into the room. He touched the farmer's shoulder and then walked silently away. Joachin saw him vanishing among the gathering shadows outside.

The farmer, normally robust and vigorous, staggered upstairs as though he had aged forty years in as many seconds. His teenaged son and the women ran up after him. The farmer died during the night. Horrified, Joachin asked who the old visitor had been, and whether he had had anything to do with his host's death.

"He was my grandfather," replied the teenaged lad, *"and he has been in his grave for ten years."*

When Joachin Hubner's story went the rounds, the Count de Cadreras — a capable, sensible, and experienced commander of an Alandetti infantry corps — was sent to investigate. He took several other officers with him, plus a military doctor and a lawyer. Hubner and the farmer's family were closely interrogated. A solemn party gathered at the cemetery and the grandfather's corpse was exhumed. Despite being buried ten years previously it looked as though it had been dead only a few hours. The amazed military doctor made a small incision in one arm. According to the Cadreras manuscript, fresh red blood trickled from the cut. The body was duly staked through the heart, decapitated, and reinterred.

When Cadreras made his official report, its impact was so sensational that it reached the emperor, Charles VI, who reigned from 1711 to 1740. Charles was a particularly pragmatic, shrewd and able statesman who developed a much improved banking system and recognized the importance of Austrian sea trade — developing Trieste as the Empire's major port. He also reorganized and consolidated the territories recently recaptured from the Turks. Not surprisingly, this practical and prosaic ruler was disinclined to believe the bizarre evidence which Cadreras had laid before him. A Royal Commission was established and charged with the task of reinvestigating the Haidam phenomenon — the implication being that should this commission fail to confirm

Cadreras' findings, the Count would be looking for another job. The commissioners were highly sceptical during the long journey to Haidam, but when they arrived they were confronted by a greater and more sinister mystery than that which young Hubner claimed to have witnessed in the farmhouse.

Many cottages had been abandoned; others had their doors barred and their windows shuttered. There was scarcely a soul to be seen and only a handful of men had remained loyal to their officers in the small garrison. Despite the severe penalties for desertion, many of the troops had simply run away from the village. The commissioners were amazed. Scepticism turned to fear and credulity. The few villages whom they could find along with the remaining members of the garrison told incredible tales of long-dead relatives from the cemetery visiting family members who died shortly afterwards. It appeared that the village, according to the witnesses, was being attacked by a battalion of reanimated corpses.

The commissioners made a careful list of the alleged "undead," opened their graves, and staked and decapitated each occupant in the prescribed manner. On every occasion it was reported that the bodies so dealt with had been found in an unusually good state of preservation. There were no further reports of vampire problems from Haidam after the grisly work in the cemetery had been done.

Understandably the story grew in the telling and became distorted and wildly exaggerated. Cadreras, in an effort to clear his name, asked Charles VI to publish the Royal Commission's findings, but the politically astute old Habsburg remained obdurately silent. It was that stubborn silence that sent the Count to the University of Fribourg to record the facts as he understood them and to preserve the report for academic posterity.

No survey of vampirism would be complete without reference to its psychotic "founding father," Vlad the Impaler. Born in 1430 in the old Transylvanian town of Sighisoara, he was the second son of Vlad II, the Prince of Walachia, and came to the throne himself as Vlad III. His father had been known as Dracul, meaning "the devil," and he himself was known as Dracula, "son of the devil," or as Tepes, "the impaler." During his stormy and belligerent reign, Dracula was a political weathercock who changed his allegiances more frequently than his underwear. When it suited him, he supported Turks, Hungarians, the Roman Catholics, the Orthodox Church, and the Islamic Ottomans. He reached the throne of

Walachia in 1448 with Turkish support after his father and brother had been assassinated by the Hungarians. Not trusting the Turks either, Vlad abandoned the throne but reclaimed it in 1456 with the support of the Hungarians. His cruelties and atrocities, his executions and assassinations, would easily fill a lengthy volume by themselves — and it is thought by some historians that Tsar Ivan the Terrible of Russia took Vlad as a role model.

A curious irony connecting the historical Vlad with Bram Stoker's fictional Dracula is that the real Vlad was best remembered for staking other people — whereas Stoker's imaginary monster was vulnerable to being staked. A further interesting point, which may go some way towards explaining Vlad's immense international notoriety, is that his reliance on mayhem, murder, and terror coincided historically with the relatively recent invention of the printing press. A contemporary German pamphlet concerning his many depravities contained the words: "... the shocking story of a monster and berserker called Dracula ..." Understandably, that sensational little publication was widely distributed.

In 1746 Dom Calmet, a French monk, studied vampirism and became something of an authority on it. According to Calmet there was adequate evidence that what he called the walking dead were able to return and drain the blood of both men and beasts. He also subscribed to the popular theories of vampire disposal involving staking, decapitating, and burning.

Much more remarkable is the evidence for vampires presented by Jean-Jacques Rousseau, who wrote, "if ever there was in the world a warranted and proven history, it is the history of vampires ... the judicial evidence is all-embracing ..."

Montague Summers, a clergyman, and the Reverend Neil Smith of Hampstead both studied vampirism in some depth — broadly concluding that in all probability the creatures really had existed in the past, and might still be around today.

Returning to the modern vampire of popular legend, much is owed to the depiction of Dracula in Bram Stoker's novel of that name published in 1897. The theatrical version of the story reached the stage in 1927 and was followed by Tod Browning's film, which starred Bela Lugosi in 1931. It was characteristic of this stereotyped stage and screen vampire to have a pale face, protruding fangs, and glaring eyes.

Such stereotypical vampires cast no shadow and have no reflection. Like the werewolf they can be killed by silver and warded off by a cross, a crucifix, or plenty of strong garlic. They are unable to cross running water, have an allergy to light, and invariably die if exposed to sunlight.

Another famous and well-documented vampire report in Britain concerns the mysterious attack on Amelia Cranswell of Croglin Grange, near Penrith, which is dealt with in full in one of our earlier Hounslow Press volumes, *The World's Greatest Unsolved Mysteries*.

In a number of pieces of relatively recent fiction, reference has been made to a creature known as a *drud* — a vampire's vampire — which is said to live on the refined blood of the vampire itself. It is possible that the drud, the vampires' predator, has some tenuous basis in myth and legend rather than being only a creation of fantasy fiction. As far as is known, the drud resembles a normal human being in most respects and is entirely benign to Homo sapiens, whom it protects. Its only distinguishing feature is a total absence of eyebrows. According to this tradition, vampires are terrified of the drud.

Sinister Highgate Cemetery in London, where a vampire is alleged to prowl.

241

Researcher David Farrant reports that he was called in to help a number of residents in the Highgate Cemetery area in 1969. These witnesses told Farrant that they had seen a tall, dark, cloaked, human shape — almost seven feet high — in the vicinity of the cemetery. Their reports included details of its ferocious, glaring red eyes — a feature that Amelia Cranswell also reported in connection with the Croglin Grange vampire attack many years before. The reports that reached David Farrant also said that the strange, cloaked figure had faded mysteriously into the darkness after being observed.

On a bitterly cold December night in 1969, Farrant went to the Highgate Cemetery entrance, where several witnesses had reported seeing the bizarre figure. David's main motive at the time was to see whether there was some rational, physical, or logical explanation for the strange reports that had reached him. As he passed the cemetery's top gate on his way down Swains Lane, he reports that he saw a tall shape in the darkness. It seemed so real at the time that he was convinced it was someone dressed up to play an unwelcome practical joke to frighten passers-by.

David reported seeing two red eyes set in a dark object looking only vaguely like a head. This globular, dark object was not easy for him to describe. He felt that it was strangely *vague*, neither opaque nor translucent, but quite definitely *alive*, sinister, and very hostile. It seemed to him to be hovering above the ground and to be shaking or vibrating in a very menacing manner. He also reported a sharp drop in temperature — noticeable on even such a cold night. To him the glaring red eyes seemed wolf-like, baleful, and malign. David was convinced that he was in the presence of some very real and particularly foul, evil entity. He reports feeling that he was very definitely exposed to some sort of dangerous psychic attack, and instinctively exerted his will-power against his supernatural antagonist — exactly as Lionel recalls doing against the powerful, evil opponent with dangling seaweed "hands" in the nightmare he had after visiting Bowden House. David reported that as he focused his own spiritual and mental powers against the sinister Highgate entity, it slowly faded and vanished into the darkness.

In 1970 the *London Evening News* published a front page account of a hundred-strong vampire hunt in Highgate Cemetery — which must have looked very similar to the finale of a classical

Hammer horror film. Despite their enthusiasm — and a formidable array of sharpened stakes and heavy mallets — the Highgate vampire hunters did not meet with any notable success. The *Evening News* report made reference to the possibility that the supposed vampire sightings had been the result of a cine club using the cemetery to make a film called *Vampires at Night*.

No cine club was involved in another very strange episode connected with Highgate Cemetery that preceded the 1970 "vampire hunt" by about a century.

The artist and poet Dante Gabriel Rossetti had buried his beloved Lizzie Siddal there and had placed a manuscript of his poems in the coffin with her. Unfortunately, these were the only copies in existence and as his literary career took off he needed them. With the help of a young friend called Howell, who obtained permission from the home secretary for the exhumation to take place, the vital Rossetti manuscripts were duly recovered. Rossetti himself had remained at Howell's house while the work took place. Howell assured him that Lizzie's hair still retained its original beautiful colour and that her body was not corrupted.

There have been other cases of inexplicably uncorrupted bodies over the centuries. The Princess Withburgha of East Dereham in Norfolk was one, and Saint Edmund was another. Where artificial means such as embalming fluids have been ruled out by scientific tests, researchers are left to contemplate the possibilities of abnormal conditions in the tomb such as natural currents of warm dry air or even abnormally high levels of background radiation. Where all other explanations fail, paranormal possibilities may be considered.

There are other rumours and legends of Highgate that also predate the great 1970 vampire hunt. Some refer to a spectre with a top hat and cloak reported from two local pubs: "The Flask" and "Ye Olde Gatehouse." This latter hostelry is also alleged to be haunted by the ghost of Mother Marnes, who always appears dressed in black gliding along a gallery. According to the legend, the old lady was murdered there along with her pet cat by a callous thief who killed her for her savings. Perhaps because of the old lady's love of animals, it is generally maintained that her wraith will not appear if children or animals are in the inn. Ye Olde Wrestlers pub, which dates from the seventeenth century, is a reminder that Highgate was once an important point on the drovers' road There was a rather curious initiation ceremony conducted there at one time known as "Swearing on the Horns." Although this is generally thought of as a drovers' custom, it is possible that it is the vestigial trace of something far older and more sinister. Might the horns in question have been those of Hern the Hunter? Or of the terrifying horned god of the witches, Cernunnos of the Celts? Yet another possibility is that swearing on the horns is connected with Mithras, a god of light, in whose honour a bull was slain. A cattle cult such as Mithraism might have remained underground for centuries with the droving fraternity, and thus have survived the inroads made by the early Christian Church.

Some researchers have suggested that Highgate Cemetery was once the site of an ancient manor house rather than empty hillside land. It was also suggested that this ancient manor, like Medmenham Abbey (the haunt of Sir Francis Dashwood and his cronies), was a focal point for many hidden evil deeds. Suppose that like Hagley Hall near Rugeley in Staffordshire, there was a weird subterranean temple or shrine in its grounds. There are rumours of a mysterious coffin having been transported from the East and buried somewhere in or near this sinister old manor house. According to other legends, when the real, historical Vlad Dracula died during the fifteenth century, he was buried on the island of Snagov. But there were sensational reports from the island in 1931: *when his tomb was opened it was found to contain the remains of a bull.* So where was Dracula? Was it the mysterious "father of all the vampires" who had been transported to the weird old Highgate manor in that legendary coffin? And what became of him when that eldritch manor became part of Highgate Cemetery?

Bram Stoker, who wrote his bestseller *Dracula* in 1897, is said to have written it while living in Highgate. Other strange rumours and legends link the Highgate vampire with Jack the Ripper, the notorious Victorian serial killer.

Queen Victoria employed Robert James Lees as a medium, and according to the records left in his diary, Lees had visions of the Ripper. It was said that he eventually led the police to Dr. Gull's house at 74 Brook Street. It was subsequently suggested that a false funeral took place and it was further hypothesized that the real Dr. Gull was buried under the name of Mason some years later — in Highgate Cemetery. On the basis of this version it has been suggested that the Highgate vampire-spectre is none other than the ghost of Jack the Ripper.

So what conclusions can be drawn concerning all the varied vampire stories circulating around Highgate Cemetery? The location is undoubtedly very atmospheric and mysterious. The human mind seeks to create explanations for stimuli that can, in fact, have sources that are perfectly normal and innocent. It is possible to sit in a train and to interpret the rhythmic rattling of the wheels over the tracks as speech patterns. It is equally possible to see everything from enchanted castles to flying monsters in cloud formations and glowing coals in an old-fashioned grate. The branches of trees combined with glowing cigarette ends in the distance could possibly be interpreted as a strange creature with malevolent red eyes. *But is there more to it than that?* An experienced investigator like David Farrant reports that he felt an evil presence and a dramatic drop in temperature. Many other sane and sensible witnesses have described inexplicable sightings in the vicinity of Highgate Cemetery. If there really *was* an ancient manor on the site centuries ago, does something weird and dangerous still linger in the area? The Highgate Cemetery vampire has not yet been laid to rest. The data is well worth further investigation.

Chapter 23
The Easter Island Mystery

The mystery of Easter Island is inextricably intertwined with the mystery of Fernandez the navigator who was sailing between Callao and Valparaiso in 1576. Juan reported that he had found a large island inhabited by a people of pale complexion who seemed to have a culture at least the equal of the civilizations of the Peruvians and Chileans. Fascinated by what he had found, Fernandez reluctantly continued his trip to Valparaiso determined to return as soon as he could and examine the island in detail. Death beat him to it.

A century later Captain John Davis was looking for anything of interest in the area when, according to his log, he reached latitude twenty-seven degrees twenty minutes south and saw great flocks of birds apparently coming from a mountainous land to the west of his position. Davis made a note of it in his log accordingly, named his discovery Davis Land, and sailed on. Almost half a century passed before a Dutch admiral named Ruggewein went looking for Davis Land. He failed to find it, but on Easter Day he found the island Fernandez had seen two hundred years before.

It is geologically possible — though difficult to explain satisfactorily —that if Davis Land had existed where Davis thought it was, it might have vanished under the water before Ruggewein went looking for it. Macmillan Brown records the case of the disappearing island of Tuanaki, not far from the Cook Islands. Two Mangaians reported to some local missionaries that they had found an island they called Tuanaki where no missionary had previously been. Excited by what the Mangaians told them, the missionaries duly headed their schooner towards Tuanaki. They searched for it for weeks — *but there was no trace of it*. Had it not been for an account given by two citizens of Rarotonga that one of them had actually *lived* on Tuanaki and the other distinctly remembered *visiting* it, there might be cause for doubting that the Mangaians had ever seen the place. Is it possible that the island Captain John Davis saw and named had disappeared like Tuanaki before Ruggewein went looking for it?

When the bold and competent Dutch admiral reached Easter Island in 1722, he reported that the island had a population of six or seven thousand and that they seemed to be of different ethnic types and colours. What impressed Ruggewein even more than the people, however, were the great stone idols. As he described them, they were of "the figure of a man with very long ears, his head covered with a red crown." Before the end of the century Captain Cook, Lapérouse, and Gonzales had all landed on Easter Island and explored it.

The visitors were similarly amazed by the great stone idols that confronted them and did not seem to be known anywhere else at all. Almost two hundred and fifty of these strange stone carvings are to be found on the slopes of Rano Raraku, the extinct volcano, and they stand like guards of honour along the ten kilometres of ceremonial riad making its melancholy way to the tribal cemetery.

For some reason known to the original sculptors and their contemporaries, but now lost in the mists of time, those who cut these great statues hacked them out of the solid rock of the dead volcano and separated them from the rock as each was completed. It was as though their makers intended to give the impression that these were gods of stone being born from the rock rather than mere statues made from it.

The great Easter Island statues vary in size and weight from a little under twenty tonnes to as much as sixty or seventy tonnes. Just as the great trilithons of Stonehenge give modern civil engineers food for thought, so anyone who is called upon professionally to cut stone from a quarry and then transport very heavy blocks of it would be interested in learning how the ancient Easter Islanders not only did it — but did so *repeatedly*.

The great statues have no legs. They begin from below the waist and this gives them the uncanny look of weird gods of the earth rising out of their native element to rule over and terrify humanity. Each has the same strange-looking face: the forehead slopes backwards, the chin juts forward, and the mouth has a look of cruel command, almost of disdain, and of hyper-confident, social superiority. There is an odd feature to the tip of the nose — but the most noticeable characteristic is the length of the ears, which reach down almost to the jaw. Many researchers who have studied the stone faces of Easter Island believe that they are looking not so much at a *likeness*, but at a recognizable *caricature*, exaggerating the prominent features of the individual, or race, it is meant to represent. British cartoonists during the Second World War tended to show Winston Churchill as a very muscular bulldog, and Hitler as a rat or a snake. A cartoon can be complimentary as well as offensive.

The most frustrating part of the Easter Island mystery is that the answers probably still lie there hidden below the soil of the island. The Easter Islanders have their own unique script. Some scholars have recorded a remarkable similarity between it and ancient texts from the Indus Valley. This is a fascinating nexus, but it poses more questions than it answers. The present inhabitants of Easter Island are unable to read or understand their island's own written language, and when asked about the original text they answer by saying: "It is here but not here." This seems to suggest that it is hidden on the island *somewhere*. (It is possible that only the Long-ears only could read the script, and that they had travelled the great distance from the Indus Valley. It is worthwhile comparing the ear lengths depicted on some of the Indian statues with those on Easter Island.) Various copies of the original stone *Rongo-rongo* tablets have been made on bark and wooden disc, but these copies — however faithful and accurate — have not as yet been deciphered.

It has been suggested by linguistic scholars that the Oak Island Tablets were mnemonic in form and that when the "reader" looked at one of the symbols, he would tell the story, or give the information, which went with that symbol. Only those who had been taught the oral tradition which went with the mnemonic script could ever hope to make sense of the Rongo-rongo tablets.

Although they are unable to read the records of their history (if it is, in fact, theirs), the Easter Islanders have an enormous wealth of oral traditions, stories, myths, and legends from which a shadowy central narrative can be distilled. The heart of this narrative is that far to the west of Easter Island was a great kingdom called Maraerenga. When its ruler died his sons fought over the inheritance. Hotu Matua, who was one of those competing sons, took his family, his guards, and his personal followers and sailed away eastwards in the hope of finding somewhere to live. They came at last to their new home — Easter Island — which they called Rapa Nui. Here they planted the seeds they had brought with them and prospered because the land had fertile valleys. Hotu Matua was venerated as a great national hero-ruler and when he felt that his life was drawing to an end, he abdicated and became a holy hermit. The legends describe him as a tall, imposing figure with the characteristically long ears that, according to the legend, belong to kings, princes, and chiefs. He wore a cloak and a hat of crimson feathers as his regalia of leadership. The Easter Island legends make it clear that in addition to these long-eared aristocrats who resembled Hotu Matua there were a great many short-eared people who seemed to do most of the work. The legends go on to tell that rather like the events in Israel and Judah after the death of the wise King Solomon, his son Rehoboam became something of a tyrant and antagonized his people. The result of the Jewish rebellion was that the ten northern tribes declared their independence from Rehoboam — who was left only with the two small southern tribes and the city of Jerusalem. After the death of Hotu Matua on Rapa Nui the aristocratic long-eared class became greedy tyrants to a degree that led to a revolution by their short-eared servant race. The revolution, according to some of the legends, was a total success and the Long-ears were wiped out.

These legends and the tales of the original settling of Easter Island explain the great statues as the work of an inspired sculptor named Rapu, who felt that it was his sacred duty to glorify Hotu Matua. Thus inspired he ascended Rano Raraku, the extinct volcano, and carved Hotu Matua's likeness from the rock of the mountainside. The legends go on to tell how the people came to marvel at Rapu's work and to admire it. In accordance with their wishes he cut the statue's base free of the mountain while the jubilant citizens prepared a thick mud slide so that it could be taken safely down.

According to these old Easter Island folklore tales and traditions, the statue Rapu had created was believed to have some important defensive purpose and he was commissioned to make more. When everybody was satisfied that enough guardian statues now protected the coast of the island, more had to be made to honour and protect the dead. More statues were duly carved and hauled up to Tongariki and the sacred burial ground. (Some researchers think that this phase of statue carving and moving may have resulted in the removal of many, if not all, of the trees on Easter Island.)

A major tragedy hit the island in the second half of the nineteenth century. Slavers came to abduct labourers to work at the guano deposits in Peru. They took about a thousand Easter Islanders including, it was suspected, *the very last of those who knew how to read the Rongo-rongo script*. When the Peruvians sent the surviving Easter Islanders back again, nine hundred of the original thousand were already dead. Small pox killed 85 percent of those on the ship and the pathetic handful who landed again so feebly on the shores of Easter Island brought the disease with them. It spread like wildfire and thousands died.

Another of the unsolved mysteries of Easter Island — apart from the purpose of the statues and the meaning of the weird Rongo-rongo script — is the riddle of the burial ground. The vaults contain vast quantities of bones — the remains of *many thousands* of people. The graveyard is many times bigger than it would need to be if the story of Hotu Matua and his seaborne followers is a truly accurate and historical account. How could Easter Island have supported such a huge population from its own natural resources? Was it once, along with vanished Davis Land, the vestigial remains of an enormous Polynesian empire that was submerged by a disaster of Atlantean proportions?

There are other strange signs on the island — almost as there were on the *Mary Celeste*, and in the deserted Inuit village on the shores of Lake Angikuni in Canada. It was here that Joe La Bell found no sign of his friends in the village at all — but every indication that they had left in a very great hurry. Unbelievably, the hunters had left their rifles behind; the dogs lay silent and dead where they had been left tethered, and the vital canoes, kayaks, and umiaks lay derelict and deserted by the shore of the lake. The abandoned Easter Island statues in the quarry gave much the same impression as the suddenly abandoned *Mary Celeste* and the suddenly deserted Inuit village. The great Easter Island statues — over a hundred and fifty of them — lay all over the quarries in varying states of completion. Some had just been begun, others were practically finished but had not yet been separated from the rock. The quarrymen's tools had been dropped around their work as though they had left it in a desperate hurry.

One theory is that it was the Long-ears who were making the statues, or having them made to their direction, and the Short-ears who rebelled and wiped out the master sculptors and their work.

The adventurous pioneer, Thor Heyerdahl, took on the immense task of demonstrating that even with primitive stone tools and the level of technology that would have been available to the early Polynesians on Easter Island, it was perfectly possible for enough determined men to carve and transport the statues. Heyerdahl's investigations also proved (as conclusively as such things can be proven centuries after the event) that there was a very strong possibility that the Easter Islanders had in fact come *westwards* from Peru at some remote period in the past.

And so the mysterious statues still stand challengingly around their island and line the road to the ancient cemetery. As computer technology advances by leaps and bounds — both with the power of its processors and its scanner inputs — perhaps, in the not too distant future, the Rongo-rongo tablets may yet yield their secrets to the Pentium chip.

Chapter 24
The Bermuda Triangle

There is a challenging and mysterious section of the western Atlantic. It lies off the southeast coast of the United States and extends from Bermuda to southern Florida and then through the Bahamas and out past Puerto Rico to somewhere around longitude forty degrees west. Several other areas have a grim reputation for lost ships, planes, and people — but the Bermuda Triangle is the best known of them all.

One of the most disturbing accounts is the first-hand, eyewitness testimony given by Martin Caidin. He wrote up his experience for *Fate* magazine. Caidin reported that it had taken place on June 11, 1986. The weather was warm and clear. It was a perfect day for flying. Caidin and his companions were going from Bermuda in the direction of the naval air station at Jacksonville in Florida. They had sophisticated modern electronic navigational equipment on board, and they were receiving satellite photographs of the area through which they were flying.

For some totally inexplicable reason Caidin found that he was no longer able to observe part of his plane's left wing. A moment or two later part of the right wing also became invisible. All his electronic data from the satellite told him that there was no mist, nothing to hide, or obscure, any part of the plane. He saw next that the clear blue sky seemed to have turned to an almost custard yellow. Caidin reported it as something like a "white out" except that it was this creamy custard yellow instead of white and the instruments were all behaving erratically and abnormally.

As Martin looked up he saw what he described as a tunnel, a hole, or a vortex, immediately above the plane. Through that aperture the normal blue sky remained visible in spite of the creamy yellow opacity everywhere else. He then looked down and found that through a similar aperture the sea was visible. These gaps in the creamy yellow opacity surrounding their aircraft were somehow keeping up with the it — as if the plane was *somehow dragging them with it.*

Caidin's wife was with him, as well as the whole aircrew. All personnel on board remained steady and cool-headed and continued their flight doggedly — as though everything was normal. There can be little doubt that this calm professionalism played a major part in saving them all from becoming additional victims of the weird Bermuda Triangle phenomena. The extraordinary creamy yellow disturbance and the apparent "tunnels" through it cleared as suddenly as they had begun — and Caidin and his companions found themselves flying through what he described in his subsequent report as perfectly normal, clear air.

They turned the plane swiftly to try and see what it was that they had come through, but everything now looked clear and normal behind them. It was as if the creamy yellow blankness had never existed. All the electronic equipment began behaving normally again and they landed safely at their destination.

There have been literally hundreds of strange reports and tragic losses of ships and planes in the Bermuda Triangle for years. As far back as 1928 on a flight from Havana to Florida, the great pioneer aviator Charles Lindbergh experienced double compass failure and reported something which he described at the time as heavy haze or mist *completely blocking out all vision.*

In 1968, flying from Nassau to Palm Beach, Jim Blocker's radio and navigational system failed while he was in a cloud bank. Early in the 1970s the USS *Richard E. Byrd* experienced a total failure of its communications systems and navigational aids while en route to Bermuda. The problem lasted for over a week before the *Richard E. Byrd* was able to re-establish communications.

During the closing months of World War II, Captain Joe Talley was on board the *Wild Goose*, which had experienced problems and was being towed by another ship, the *Caicos Trader*. Talley found the *Wild Goose* suddenly going down and he, himself, was deep under water before he fully realized what was happening. A strong and resourceful sailor, Talley grabbed a lifejacket and kicked his way desperately up to the surface fifty feet and more above his head. The *Caicos Trader* was herself in danger of being pulled down by the *Wild Goose* and had to sever the tow line as an emergency measure while they picked Talley out of the Atlantic. The *Wild Goose* went down like a lead weight, sinking at far higher speed than could be reasonably explained. (There is a folk tale in this region that speaks of *"Him-of-the-hairy-hands"*— an undersea monster that is supposed to drag boats down into the depths of the sea.)

In balancing the picture it needs to be remembered that the Bermuda Triangle mystery statistics are slanted to some extent by the very large number of aircraft and vessels that are to be found crossing that area. A number of recreational sailors lack experience, and it must also be noted that there is allegedly a considerable amount of drug traffic making its dangerous and illegal way across those waters — in addition to significant numbers of potential illegal immigrants.

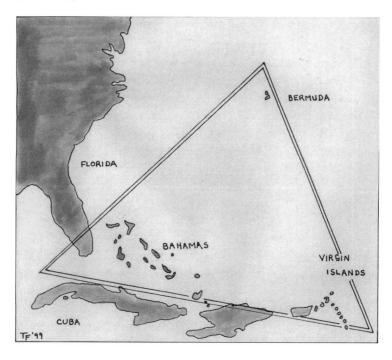

The Bermuda Triangle. Drawing by Theo Fanthorpe.

One of the most remarkable of all the Bermuda Triangle tragedies was the loss of Flight 19. In May 1991 five TBM Avenger aircraft were discovered in nearly three hundred metres of water only ten miles from the Florida coast. Was the mystery of the missing Flight 19 finally solved? The ill-fated Flight 19 was made up of five Grumman TBM-3 Avenger torpedo bomber planes belonging to the navy. They were on a routine training flight that left Fort Lauderdale's naval air station in Florida at two o'clock in the afternoon Eastern Standard Time. The date was December 5, 1945. Lt. Charles Taylor was their flight instructor and leader. Two hundred and fifty hours of flying experience would have made the average pilot more than competent to tackle such a mission. None of the trainees had less than three hundred, and flight leader Taylor had two and a half thousand — ten times the minimum competency level. The basic idea was to fly a triangular route heading out towards the Bahamas from Fort Lauderdale, to turn, and then to come back to the same naval air station.

A TBM-3 Avenger could carry more than enough fuel for two thousand kilometres. Flight 19 was scheduled to do barely five hundred. Worked out on the basis of timing rather than air miles, the whole exercise should have taken only an hour and a half: two hours at an absolute maximum. Each of the TBM-3's had enough fuel aboard for six or seven hours. When Flight 19 took off at approximately two p.m. weather conditions were fine and clear. Meteorologically, it was a good, safe flying day.

Shortly before four o'clock, however, a senior flight instructor at Fort Lauderdale, Lt. Robert F. Cox, overheard a call on the radio training flight frequency that sounded to him like Lt. Taylor and one of the other pilots on Flight 19, Captain Powers. Cox was on a training flight with some of his own trainees at the time that he overheard the broadcast, which he felt certain was coming from Flight 19. Cox reported that he had heard something, the gist of which was: "We must have got lost after the turn. I'm not sure where we are." Flight leader-instructor Charles Taylor was then heard to say that both his compasses were malfunctioning. The implication had to be that Powers' compass was malfunctioning as well. If that actually was the case, there is some reason to suggest that an external force working in the sinister Bermuda Triangle had possibly neutralized the compasses on *both* TBMs.

The logical thing for an experienced aviator like Taylor to have done would have been to ask one of his trainees to take over navigation and lead the flight back home. The fact that he did not seem to do so would suggest that *all* compasses on Flight 19 were by then malfunctioning. Wouldn't such accidental multi-malfunctioning be asking a great deal of the long arm of coincidence? *It is infinitely more probable that some external force was the stimulus for such general malfunctioning.*

Realizing that his comrades on Flight 19 were in some sort of serious trouble, senior flight instructor Cox announced that he would go south to meet them and then lead them in. Had Flight 19 been anywhere near the location they thought they were in and where, from what he had overheard on the radio Cox thought they were in, as he flew south he expected that their radio links would have improved. They didn't. They faded.

One pivotal point of the mystery of the lost Flight 19 is whether or not Taylor had become so disorientated that he simply panicked. There is evidence that Taylor instructed his students to fly *east*. He had at this point, it seems, believed himself to be somewhere in the Gulf of Mexico and flying north with the Florida peninsula on his right. If he was *already* to the east of the Florida peninsula, turning east at that point would take him and his students out over wide, empty stretches of the Atlantic. What did that snatch of Taylor's conversation mean, when he commented that the ocean didn't look *right*? How much stress was Taylor under? And, if there was some malign and dangerous external influence, had it affected his mind as well as his compass? Despite his two and a half thousand flying hours, he was evidently under some kind of stress.

The logical conclusion was that when that ill-fated Flight 19 eventually ran out of fuel it was somewhere north of the Bahamas over deep water and a long, *long* way from where it should have been. By the time their fuel did run out the sea was rough, the weather was foul, and the TBM-3's would not have lasted long on the surface.

There is always a doubly tragic corollary to a disappearance mystery when those who have gone to seek for that which was lost are themselves doomed. Part of the search and rescue activities connected with the loss of Flight 19 was a huge Martin Mariner sea plane. It was piloted by Lt. Walter Jeffrey who took off at approximately seven-thirty in the evening eastern standard time.

He should have reported in at eight-thirty p.m. — *he didn't*. The crew of the *Gaines Mills* reported seeing a huge explosion in the air shortly before eight p.m. and also thought they had see a plane crashing into the sea. Their sighting links reasonably well with the location the Martin Mariner *ought* to have reached by that time. If it *was* the Martin Mariner rescue plane exploding and going down that the crew of the *Gaines Mills* actually saw, what caused it? Martin Mariners had a reputation as flying "gas tanks" and were very vulnerable to anything that would set off their cargo of highly inflammable fuel.

Doctor Richard McIver proposed a logical theory to the effect that there could well be dangerous deposits of toxic gases under the seabed in the area of the Bermuda Triangle. If, theorized McIver, frozen methane was down there, it could be released quite naturally in sufficiently large quantities to disturb the water. The methane might even rise high enough to interfere with aircraft. In support of his theory, McIver notes cases of drilling rigs and oil exploration ships being damaged in this way. The release of the methane seems to affect the density of the water causing both swimmers and their ships to sink far more speedily than would be the case if they were cruising in water of normal specific gravity.

Captain Shattenkirk was on a flight between Puerto Rico and New York when he observed vast white bubbles surging up to the sea's surface. Suppose that these dangerous gases were able to rise to the height of an aircraft and starve its engine of oxygen?

The equally mysterious Welsh Triangle was the scene of a great many UFO sightings during the late 1970s. Restaurateur Louise Bassett, a sensible and reliable witness from Carmarthen, was driving home from her restaurant in the early hours of the morning when she saw what she described as a brownish mass whose flat blue lights were flashing intermittently. She said that it seemed to be hovering rather than resting on the ground, and as she approached it the car radio stopped working. Louise drove on towards Towy Castle and observed that the lights she had seen earlier seemed to be gliding in the direction of Trimsaran. Many other witnesses had experienced severe radio interference in that area at that time.

In June of 1976 Brian Guiver, from Surrey, was on holiday in Wales and driving down the A4086 from Cym-Y-Glow to Llanrug. He could clearly see Mount Snowdon from where he was on the road, and while observing Snowdon, he saw a strange object in the sky moving towards the peak of the mountain. A while later when he was actually climbing Snowdon and admiring the birds in flight above him, three strange aerial objects appeared at a height he estimated to be in the region of seven hundred metres. He described these objects as typically saucer-shaped.

Phil Vaughan and Llew Davies, both from Bridgend in Wales, saw a strange, flying, cigar-shaped object low on the horizon and travelling towards the southeast.

These are only a few examples of the hundreds of sightings made over this particularly strange area known as the Welsh Triangle.

One of the weirdest mysteries of the Bermuda Triangle was the experience reported by pilot Bruce Gurnan who was only 29 at the time when it happened. He was flying his Beechcraft Bonanza from Andros Island in the direction of Florida. Everything was normal; the weather was good; the plane was behaving perfectly: then Bruce saw a weird, oval-shaped cloud ahead of him that seemed to be matching his speed as he climbed.

The thing was of vast size and looked as if it went all the way down to the surface of the sea. Gurnan did his best to fly clear of it but found himself in what he described as a rotating tunnel completely enveloped in cloud. As with Flight 19, his instruments ceased to function and radio contact was lost. Bruce also had a strange feeling of weightlessness. He noticed a small island below him, its outline vague through the clouds, and he guessed — according to what he estimated as his flight time — that it *should* have been Bimini. Less than five minutes after this sighting he re-established radio contact and was told he was now over Miami. *He knew this to be utterly impossible.* The top speed of his little Beechcraft Bonanza was less than two hundred miles an hour. Somewhere thirty minutes had vanished. His tank gauge told him that the Bonanza had used only twenty-eight gallons of fuel when it normally took forty.

He was not alone in this weird time-gain experience in the Bermuda Triangle. One of a group of four U.S. Air Force planes engaged on a NATO mission gained almost four hours over the rest of its group after flying into a strange area of cloud in which it was impossible to distinguish sky and sea. John Sanders, a steward aboard the *QE II* at the time was heading for New York from Nassau when he and other members of the crew saw a small light aircraft appear and fly directly towards them at lower than a thousand feet. As Sanders and his companions watched, it dived straight into the sea. They heard no splash, no explosion, no sound at all. In John Sanders words, "the sea simply opened and swallowed the plane." They brought the huge liner around and the rescue boat went out. It found nothing: there was no wreckage, no debris, no oil slick. The plane had simply vanished into the water as though it had never existed.

An interesting scientific theory put forward by Richard Sylvester from the University of Western Australia centred on the idea that the mysterious sinkings and swallowings of ships and aircraft in the Bermuda Triangle can best be understood in terms of whirlpools. Sylvester's research focuses on the Sargasso Sea, which is well to the east of the Bermuda Triangle. Vast amounts of seaweed accumulate in the centre of the Sargasso where powerful currents slowly circulate. The weed behaves in a manner similar to froth draining away down a plughole in a sink.

According to Sylvester's theory the huge whirlpool centred on the Sargasso is capable of creating smaller ones that travel out from it and arrive eventually in the Bermuda Triangle. In Sylvester's hypothesis these whirlpools are powerful enough to make a ship rotate, and then to drag it down.

In the same way, he speculates on the existence of miniature cyclones in the air above the Triangle that are just as capable of pulling a plane from the sky as the miniature whirlpools are of pulling a ship from the surface of the sea down to the ocean bed. When the unfortunate ship or plane has been dragged all the way to the ocean floor it continues to be pulled along by the swirling water and either buried beneath the sand of the ocean bed or spun out of the vortex again a great distance away.

In Sylvester's view this explains the mysterious absence of wreckage or debris of any kind from the vanished ships and planes.

The journal of Christopher Columbus provides an interesting entry for the year 1494 when he wrote of an unusual "whirlwind" that he said had sunk three ships by spinning them several times. Experienced sailor that he was, Columbus also noted that the sea was calm at the time.

These are a few facts and pointers, theories, and hypotheses relating to the mystery of the Bermuda Triangle. Some actuaries and statisticians would argue that it is neither more nor less dangerous than any other area of the oceans, and has simply acquired its sinister reputation because of the natural love people have for unsolved mysterious and the paranormal. Is there something under the Bermuda Triangle *that was left there by the ancient Atlantean civilization?* Is there some strange mystery below those waters that is of extraterrestrial origin? Are there huge bubbles of methane rising from the ocean bed? Are there vast but perfectly natural magnetic forces that are as yet only partially understood? The Triangle exists. Tragedies affecting ships and aircraft exist within it. The mystery is far from solved. Much more up-to-the-minute data and detailed on-site research is needed before a definitive answer can be put forward. Even with the limited information available at present, the authors would not be surprised if it eventually turns out that the Bermuda Triangle harbours a mystery of great age and immense power.

Chapter 25
Tintagel

The ruins of great ancient cities can be buried below mounds of earth or hidden by the rain forests of the Amazon. Teeming civilizations that reached unsuspected levels of technology and culture can be overwhelmed by encroaching desert sand. For millennia, the nomads who pass that way are naturally preoccupied with the desperate business of survival in a harsh environment, and have no suspicion, save perhaps in their most ancient myth and folklore, that a civilization of astounding complexity lies unseen beneath their feet. Evidence of other great civilizations lies below oceans and lakes.

What may well prove to be one of the most historically important sites in the world — Tintagel in Cornwall — could well be hidden under a twelfth-century Norman castle and have been totally misunderstood even by the most academic and able archaeologists. It is often regarded simply as a Celtic monastery.

There can be little doubt that King Arthur, a great figure of *more* than myth and legend, was closely associated not only with numerous sites in Wales and with Glastonbury, but perhaps most closely of all with these mysterious ruins of Tintagel. As far as orthodox history and archaeology are concerned, Tintagel Castle was built in the middle of the twelfth century by the Earl of Cornwall, Reginald, who was the illegitimate son of King Henry I. Richard, a later Earl of Cornwall, was the brother of Henry III and he added to Tintagel Castle a century after Reginald had built it. Another century passed and Tintagel became the property of the Black Prince.

By the 1500s the gap between the island where the castle stands and the rugged Cornish mainland had been widened by wind and sea. The site was gaunt, bleak, and derelict. Of far greater interest than the ruin of the Norman castle are the *older* ruins, which suggest that the site was occupied before the Romans left and certainly during the period most closely connected with King Arthur. The link between Arthur in Wales and Arthur in Tintagel is supported by the existence in the vicinity of the "ruined monastery" of structures of the type found on the hills of Glamorgan in South Wales.

This monastery theory of Tintagel's ruins is linked to the work of Saint Juliot who was said to have been connected with Nectan of Nectan's Glen fame. Nectan's hermitage was practically in sight of Tintagel, and Juliot was yet another descendant of Nectan's royal father: the wonderfully prolific Brychan. If there *was* a religious community at Tintagel in those early days, then its members were likely to have been of a wilder and stronger type than the later monastic orders — most of whose members' lives were circumscribed by the triple follies of poverty, chastity, obedience — and by chronic misery. If there *was* a religious community in those early days at Tintagel, it would probably have been based on the spiritually adventurous pattern led by Saint Patrick and Saint Columba rather than that of the later Benedict.

But suppose for a moment that both the Norman castle and the pious tales of an ancient Celtic monastery at Tintagel were little more than veils of stone obscuring the adventurous, romantic, dynamic existence of a real historical Arthur: a great war leader whose court and headquarters moved as circumstances necessitated from Tintagel to South Wales and then across to Glastonbury.

In August of 1998 one of the most significant archaeological finds of the decade was unearthed at Tintagel. It was a piece of slate some fifteen hundred years old bearing the name Artognov. Scarcely eight inches by fourteen, the stone was brought to light by archaeologist Kevin Brady from the University of Glasgow. The rest of the inscription referring to Arthur reads "Pater Coliavificit Artognov." One possible translation is: "Artognov, father and/or descendant of Coll has constructed this building." Is it then some sort of *foundation stone* that Brady and his colleagues turned up at Tintagel? Artognov refers to the Bear Tribe, or Bear Clan — and they go back into the mists of time. Whatever it was that Artognov constructed at Tintagel was destroyed in battle, damaged by wind and storm — or was simply neglected after his death and allowed to fall into disrepair. For whatever reason, Artognov's building had gone by the seventh century, so when something new was then constructed on the site it looks as though the old foundation-slate bearing the vital inscription was demoted to the role of drain cover. But it is not only the Arthurian inscription on that stone that makes it so fascinating: *there are older letters and symbols cut into that historic piece of slate.*

What are believed to be the ruins of Arthur's Castle at Tintagel.

Our great friend and valued research colleague, George Young, of Queensland, Halifax County, Nova Scotia, is among the most distinguished Ogham experts available. Following careful study of the inscription on the Arthur stone from Tintagel, George detected the Ogham symbols for the god Bel and the name Hew. In his opinion, and it is one we strongly endorse, the stone was intended as a memorial to Hew and invoked the name of his Middle Eastern god, Bel. Some long time after this old Ogham memorial inscription had been made for Hew, the later Artognov message in Latin was inscribed over on the same stone.

George's intriguing translation of the ancient Ogham symbols makes the Arthur stone of even greater importance than it already

Co-author Lionel Fanthorpe at what are believed to be the ruins of Arthur's Castle at Tintagel.

merits through its association with Arthur of the Britons and Tintagel. But the Ogham mystery at Tintagel does not end there. It has a fascinating trans-Atlantic connection as well. In the beautiful Colorado countryside on a shelf below the tableland of Mesa Verde are the mysterious ruins of a cliff dwelling — very similar to the ancient, houselike tombs cut into the cliffs at Myra in Turkey.

One of the most interesting things about working on the unexplained and the paranormal is that you so frequently encounter other researchers — as though by something *more* than coincidence — who have recently discovered just that one vital piece of information that helps you to further your own current investigation. Time and time again we have come across friends who have either written to us as a result of our radio and television programs, who have attended our lectures, or read our books — and have pointed us in the direction of some new mystery they have researched. In other instances they have helpfully provided us with further data connected with the case we were then studying. Whatever coincidence or synchronicity *really* is, it has been our experience over several decades that it works out too well and too often to be simply random chance. Such was the case with the information that came to us from John and Jean

The rugged coast of Tintagel: did Arthur's Knights once ride here?

Copland, who have the same high regard and admiration for George Young that we have.

In October of 1995, John and Jean were on holiday at Tucson, Arizona, from where they toured Texas, New Mexico, Utah, Nevada, and Colorado. When they were at Spruce Tree House, Mesa Verde, in the Colorado National Park, they noticed a piece of stone that was in use as an unsecured step over some foundations of the ancient Spruce Tree House. The stone was rectangular and honey-coloured and as John looked down to examine it he saw an inscription on the surface. He felt instinctively that what he was looking at was something far more significant than random damage. It was then that he remembered what George Young had told him about the ancient Ogham script.

The park ranger in charge of the area gave John permission to copy the marks on the stone. The copy was duly made and John added a note about the shape and size of the Mesa Verde stone. It was two feet long by a foot wide and between four and five inches thick. It seemed to him to have been reasonably well dressed for its probable date. He spotted several other similar stones around the canyon and got the impression that they had been used as covers for storage rooms in which grain, hay, fruit, and vegetables could be kept.

On reading John and Jean's comments about the Mesa Verde stone, we were particularly interested to note that its shape and size made it very similar indeed to the stone that had been discovered in the early nineteenth century at the hundred-foot level of the Oak Island Money Pit — another unsolved mystery on which George Young is also a leading authority.

After studying the copy of the Mesa Verde stone, which John had made for him, George wrote back advising John that the message was indeed in Ogham and outlining his findings. With the kind permission and enthusiastic support of both John and George, we are able to include their comments in this volume. John's discovery of the Ogham stone and George's analysis of it give the Mesa Verde ruin a secure place among the world's most mysterious sites.

George told us that on receiving John Copland's letter and sketch of the Mesa Verde stone with its deeply incised markings, he compared them with the Ogham writings and translations found in the ancient *Book of Ballymote* in the library of the Irish Academy in Dublin. The *Book of Ballymote* was put together in the fourteenth century by combining a large collection of much earlier documents comprising some 502 folio vellum pages. The vital page containing the translations of earlier Ogham writings by Celtic monks carries the heading "Languages that we know of but are no longer used." Each of the marks inscribed on the Mesa Verde stone from Colorado matched a letter in the Ogham tract known as Ogham consigne. Like many early writings, the vowels had to be inferred. Also like many of the ancient writings, this one needed to be read first by reading the lower line from left to right and the one above it from right to left.

As on the Arthurian stone discovered at Tintagel, one very important word at the upper right quarter of the Mesa Verde stone is *Bel*. The name — among several other similar deities — of the Celtic sun god. (In Latin, Bel is one of the gods of war, and Arthur may well have been a *dux bellorum* or warlord rather than a king.)

The message on the Mesa Verde stone says simply, "... a prayer for Gil son of Lew from ..." and then there's a gap. The language spoken by the ancient people who inscribed the Mesa Verde stone appears to have been a form of ancient Gaelic, a language developed by the early Celts and brought with them in their migrations across Europe to the eastern shores of the Atlantic Ocean, long before the advent of Christianity.

Another fascinating link with George Young's expert analysis of the Mesa Verde stone is that scholarly Abbé Boudet from Rennes-les-Bains near Rennes-le-Château spent much of his life working on a remarkable book called *Le Vraie Langue Celtique et le Cromleck de Rennes-les-Bains*. Boudet believed that the ancient Celtic language had much in common with other languages that had spread from the East to the West. It should also be noted that the Rennes area south of Carcassonne was at one period in its early history inhabited by a Celtic group known as the Tectosages, literally, the "wise or clever builders." The ancient Gaelic that George had deciphered on the Mesa Verde stone was a language developed by early Celts of this same type and, in his view, there is plenty of evidence to support the theory, that this mysterious language had been brought with them in their migrations across Europe to the shores of the Atlantic Ocean long before the Christian era.

Their cherished god Bel was probably synonymous with the god Baal, frequently referred to in Old Testament times. It was this same Canaanite fertility god Baal whose priests were the opponents of the prophet Elijah during the great contest on Mount Carmel.

George's researches have convinced him that a large Celtic colony existed in ancient times in the area now occupied by Vermont and New Hampshire in the United States. His first reaction on studying the inscription on the Mesa Verde stone was that the message it contained must have been written by explorers from that very early Vermont Celtic colony.

George's work reinforces that of Professor Barry Fell who, with several academic colleagues and co-investigators, had

The Artognov Stone from Tintagel. Drawing by Theo Fanthorpe.

discovered and examined many similar stones in the United States inscribed in this same early Celtic language. In George's view it is perfectly possible that the sites Barry Fell investigated were identical with the "Greater Ireland" described and referred to on numerous occasions by early European writers. (Brittany, in France, for example, used to be known as Lesser Britain to distinguish it from the British mainland.)

Further investigation, however, led George to the conclusion that the area where the stone was found in Colorado had probably been visited and occupied by a band of Gaelic-speaking Celts at some period between 300 BC and AD 100. His theory was that their journey had started from what is now the Iberian Peninsular and that they had been attempting a voyage to Greater Ireland either in the hope of settling there, or to trade with the existing settlers. George also conjectures that they were possibly fleeing from political or religious problems that had already driven many of their people over to Ireland itself.

When evaluating George Young's exceptionally interesting views on the routes these early travellers might have taken across the ocean, it must be borne in mind that he writes of these voyages not only as a scholar who is versed in ancient history, but as a retired officer of the Royal Canadian Navy with an intimate practical knowledge of the sea and its currents. George believes that these ancient Celtic peoples sailed a westward route similar to that taken by Columbus centuries later in 1492. Instead of staying in the islands, however, they visited or passed by them, and continued in a westerly direction across the Gulf of Mexico. Arriving at the mouth of the Rio Grande, they navigated this great waterway for over a thousand miles. This brought them to what is now New Mexico in the U.S.A. There they could have met up with the indigenous peoples already occupying that area. George's theories at this point tie in very closely with the discoveries that the authors made during their research visits to White's City in New Mexico, where the museum contains the bodies of indigenous Americans who lived around the Carlsbad Cavern area seven thousand years ago.

George believes that these early Celtic travellers would have settled peacefully among the indigenous Americans in the New Mexico area, marrying into their tribes and eventually being absorbed by them — as has happened many times throughout history.

The Celtic Tectosages from the Rennes-le-Château area had an extensive knowledge of building and construction practices as they were carried on in southern Europe and on the African shores of the Mediterranean. Did they bring with them the knowledge of the use of mud bricks? It is worth noting that the Hebrew slaves during their period of captivity in Egypt had to make mud bricks for the great Egyptian structures that they were required to build. It is, therefore, not only feasible but probable that the Celtic travellers (possibly the Tectosages from the Rennes area) were the ones who introduced brick-making involving mixtures of mud and straw to the indigenous Americans in the Colorado area, and farther afield. If the Celts had in fact brought this new building technology to the Colorado area, it would have enabled large villages to be constructed under overhanging cliff faces in these regions.

Although the peoples who occupied these areas had numerous individual names for their tribes, they are generally referred to as Pueblo. This word refers to the type of construction they used for their villages. Is it possible that they learnt it from the Celtic immigrants who settled among them? The strong likelihood that there is a connection between the inscribed stone at Square Tower (Spruce Tree) House in Mesa Verde, Colorado, and the Arthurian stone in Tintagel is an intriguing one, and George Young's unique exploration of these ancient and widely scattered Ogham inscriptions merits close attention and further investigation. We are deeply indebted both to him and John Copland for placing this information with us and generously allowing us to include it in the present volume.

No survey of the Arthurian legends and their link with the enigmatic Tintagel ruins could be complete without some passing reference to the possibilities of reincarnation and its ancillary mysteries. In the course of half a century of investigating and researching paranormal phenomena and unsolved mysteries, the authors have met many strange and fascinating characters — none more so than a man who believes himself to be the reincarnation of King Arthur himself. He is certainly an attractive and charismatic personality. It was co-author Lionel's privilege in December of 1998 not only to meet him but to be knighted by him as a Quest Knight of his Loyal Arthurian War Band. During the interview "King Arthur" said: "I have been Arthur and led the

Co-author Lionel Fanthorpe with the amazing man who believes himself to be the reincarnation of Arthur, the once and future King.

life of Arthur since 1986. During that time I have lived the life of an impecunious mendicant. I have never taken any state benefits whatsoever and once having taken that leap of faith that I truly *was* the reincarnation of King Arthur, I have never looked back. On my epitaph I wish it to be carved that I have no regrets. I was faced with a choice in 1986 and I knew that there would be no turning back. In the twelve years that have passed since then, I hold title and office and am recognized by ten Druid orders and three covens of magicians. I am generally accepted as the Pendragon, the Battle Chief, the once and future king. In me the cauldron and cross unite. Christian and pagan can fight together side by side for the great cause: the land, nature, and the future of our earth. During these years the magic has sustained me. I believe in *three* Arthurs, the pre-Roman life, the post-Roman, and my current life. I remember Camelot as a nomadic court. It was situated in many hill forts. The Arthur of that day commanded a light cavalry unit and told his local chieftains to build fortresses. He and I stand for the principals of truth, of honour and of justice and I believe that all three are worth fighting for. I am asked sometimes if King Arthur ever existed historically and I answer this: 'If he didn't — he does now.' In so doing I echo Winston Churchill's words: 'If King Arthur never existed he should have.'"

There is something undeniably impressive about this wild, free, honourable, and unorthodox man.

We wish him well in his quest.

272

Chapter 26
The Tomb of Saint Nicholas

When Dickens wrote his *A Christmas Carol,* one immortal truth emerged very clearly from his inspired fiction. Whoever and whatever the original Saint Nicholas, or Father Christmas, might have been — and this was the subject of our recent *Fortean TV* Christmas Special investigation on Channel 4 — the *spirit* of Christmas, the *ethos* of Christmas, the *character* and *atmosphere* of Christmas, are undeniably *real* and a massive force for good in a dark world.

While we were filming this particular show we flew out to Turkey to examine the tomb of the historical Saint Nicholas, who became Santa Claus. The ancient church bearing his name is rich in atmosphere and some of the timeless magic of Christmas seems to linger on in its ancient stones. Saint Nicholas died in the fourth century. Yet standing beside his tomb gave the very clear impression that this tomb was empty — the spirit of the man lived on. It is something of a surprise to learn, as we did in the course of our research beside Saint Nicholas's tomb, that this great-hearted and generous saint — who is eternally associated with celebration and festivity and the giving of gifts in happy family situations — was among other things the patron saint of harlots.

According to the ancient tradition attached to Saint Nicholas, it came about like this. He was a wealthy man who rode a magnificent white horse, and it was very much part of his nature to give generously and spontaneously whenever and wherever he felt there was special need. It came to Nicholas's attention that there was a local merchant whose trading ventures had failed disastrously. He had fallen hopelessly into debt and in accordance with the legal practices of the day he and all that he had — including his three attractive teenaged daughters — were to be sold into slavery to pay what he owed. The old merchant accepted his personal fate with resignation, but it was a great cause of grief and anxiety to him to think that his three girls would almost certainly be purchased by the local brothel keeper.

The night before his creditors enforced the sale, however, Nicholas, who followed Christ's teaching about doing his charitable works in total secrecy, rode quietly past the window of the merchant's house from which the girls had hung the clothes they had just washed — including their stockings. Saint Nicholas placed a bag of gold in each. The money was sufficient not only to clear their father's debts, but to provide each of them with the dowry they needed in those days to secure a good husband and a happy marriage. It is still part of the Christmas tradition that stockings are hung in order that gifts can be placed in them — as happened in the merchant's house in the fourth century.

But as well as containing the tomb of Saint Nicholas, the ancient Turkish town of Myra is also famous for its astonishing rock house-tombs built into the hillside, — and bearing a strong resemblance to both Petra and the Mesa Verde ruin in Colorado.

Mysterious ancient house-tombs at Myra in Turkey.

Co-author Lionel Fanthorpe researching the ancient Roman amphitheatre at Myra in Turkey.

Mural of Saint Nicholas painted in his church in Myra in Turkey.

The religious tradition among these very early Turkish tomb builders and the loved ones whom they buried there in these strange little houses of the dead was that the higher up the mountain they were, the more easily their spirits would ascend to the heavens.

It was one of the earliest Lycian cities and during the days of the Lycian federation, Myra was regarded as one of their most significant cities and it was accorded three votes in the federation's council. The city is so old that the precise date of its foundation is not known. But its ruins, its rock tombs, and many of the ancient inscriptions found in the area would place it well before the birth of Christ — perhaps five or six centuries earlier, or even longer. In the year 18, the famous Roman Germanicus, and his wife, Agrippina, paid a visit to Myra and in the year 60, Saint Paul called at the city on his way to Rome. During the fourth and fifth centuries when the Byzantine Empire was flourishing mightily, Myra became the focus of religious and administrative affairs in this part of Turkey. It was then that Saint Nicholas became its greatly revered and admired bishop.

No saint before or since has been credited with greater mystical powers than his. His Diocese in southwestern Turkey was known as Mugla. Many church historians are of the opinion that he was one of the early Christian fathers present at the Council of Nicea in the year AD 325 and he was also alleged to have been imprisoned at one time during the Diocletian persecution of the Christians.

The Church of Saint Nicholas in Myra in Turkey.

The Tomb of Saint Nicholas in the Church of Saint Nicholas in Myra in Turkey.

There is ample evidence of his cult being established throughout the East by the middle of the sixth century. Methodius, who wrote in the early ninth century, was responsible for a biography of Nicholas that may not have been entirely accurate in all points. As a result, however, the Nicholas tradition had become well known in Western Christendom by the tenth century.

Myra was captured by the Moslems during their expansionary period and the holy relics of Saint Nicholas were transferred to Bari in 1087. There was already a large Greek community there. A beautiful new church was built to accommodate Saint Nicholas's relics and Pope Urban II came himself to the opening of the church. Once this new centre at Bari had been established Saint Nicholas's devotees became ubiquitous throughout Western Christendom. His reputation as a worker of miracles was second to none, and working on the principle that where there is a mass of smoke there may well be at least a tiny fire, it is interesting to speculate about how many of them were genuine and how many were the product of the imagination of writers like Methodius. Many different groups adopted Saint Nicholas as their patron: perfumiers, apothecaries, pawnbrokers, unmarried girls, sailors,

277

merchants and children, as well as harlots, all eagerly adopted him as their patron.

The "magical" number three crops up again and again in the Saint Nicholas stories of magic and miracle. He is said to have restored life to three boys whom an evil butcher had murdered in a brine tub. His intervention saved three condemned men who had been wrongly accused and unjustly sentenced to death. He saved three sailors from drowning off the rocky Turkish coast.

After his bones had been transferred to Bari, a mysterious substance — like a fragrant myrrh sometimes referred to as "manna" by his devotees — was said to have emanated from the saint's tomb. It was this beautiful fragrant essence in his shrine that made him the patron saint of perfumiers. Whatever the real source of the mysterious substance with its attractive odour, it brought a great many pilgrims to Bari.

It is interesting to note that the old church at East Dereham in Norfolk is dedicated to him and it was in the churchyard there that the spring of healing water arose after the body of Princess Withburgha was stolen by the monks of Ely and taken to their sanctuary in the heart of the East Anglian Fens to lie with the remains of her two royal sisters.

The life of Nicholas is carved on the front of Winchester Cathedral and on an ivory crosier from the twelfth century, which is currently preserved in the Victoria and Albert Museum in London. Saint Nicholas was especially popular in Holland, Belgium, and Luxembourg — where he was known as Santa Clause. When Dutch Protestants arrived in New York — then known as New Amsterdam — they brought with them some fascinating Nordic folk tales of a midwinter magician who rewarded good children with presents, but was stern with those who had misbehaved.

Saint Nicholas's patronage of children and his generous gift-giving formed one part of this tradition. But the arcane Nordic folk tale of the midwinter magician was far, far older.

Although the saint's mortal remains are no longer in it, his ancient tomb in Myra also remains one of the world's strangest and most mysterious sites.

Chapter 27

The Colossus of Rhodes

In the fifth century BC, Pindar, the poet, wrote:

Out of the ocean depths came forth the island Rhodes
Born of Aphrodite goddess of love and bride of the sun.

According to tradition and legend, the Colossus of Rhodes was a vast statue of the sun god Helios — some forty metres high and standing on a great white marble plinth another ten metres high. The stormy history of the Island of Rhodes and its many wars needs to be understood if the mystery of the colossus is to be seen in context.

Roundabout 1200 BC Rhodes appears to have been part of the Dorian Empire. By 400 BC approximately they had left the Athenian League and life on the island was very largely a struggle for independence. Mausolus, ruler of the Kingdom of Lydia, took Rhodes, as did Alexander the Great midway through the fourth century BC. When the great Macedonian died, however, Rhodes reasserted its independence and seems to have been able to undertake advantageous trade with the Egyptian Ptolemies. Ptolemy I of Alexandria was engaged in a long and bitter struggle against Antigonus who had assumed the Macedonian throne. Rhodes — probably because of its trading links with Egypt — threw in its lot with Ptolemy and defeated Antigonus, at sea. Antigonus decided that diplomacy might serve him better than a naval battle and sent his son Demetrius to try to persuade Rhodes to change sides and join Macedon against the Egyptians.

Rhodes, however, preferred to stay with Ptolemy and when Demetrius' diplomacy failed, the Macedonian army — nearly fifty thousand strong — launched an attack on Rhodes. Never an easy people to conquer, the Rhodians were again victorious and the island stayed independent for the time being.

Following their defeat of his army, the Rhodians concluded a treaty with Antigonus while maintaining their important trade with Alexandria and Ptolemy. According to the legend it was to celebrate their great victory and their hard-won independence that the Rhodians created the colossus. The gigantic statue was said to represent Helios their sun god who was venerated in all three districts of Rhodes: Kemeiros, Ialysos, and Lyndos. According to tradition their huge bronze statue of Helios took over ten years to build and was said to have been made from gigantic pieces of bronze bolted together.

A sculptor from Lyndos, one Chares by name, was said to have made each section by casting it individually before bolting them all together to form the vast image of Helios.

The sealed door to the weird subterranean temple under the site of Hagley Hall, Rugeley, England.

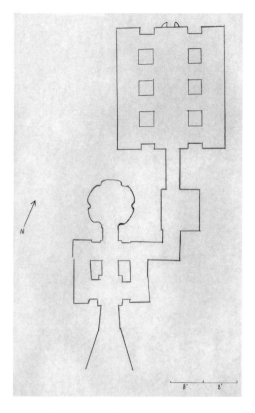

Artist's impression: stylised plan of the mysterious underground temple at Hagley. Drawing by Jane Fanthorpe.

Chares' design was said to have included diagonal iron struts reinforcing the interior of the statue. But according to at least one version of the legend of the colossus it was far *more* than a mere statue.

Rhodes had been the cockpit of the struggle between Macedon and Alexandria for a long time. Weapons and technology were much in the islanders' minds. War is the great breeding ground of invention: it is the blood-stained catapult from which new technology is launched. Some traditions assert that the interior of the colossus was no mere reinforcing work of iron diagonals to hold the great bronze shell, but was rather an ingenious system of pulleys and gears *that enabled the arm of the colossus to be raised and then dropped by gravity to deal a ponderous blow at any invading ship in the Rhodian harbour.*

281

Effective as the early Greek engineers were, and advanced as their mathematics was, their civil engineering was not, at that time, up to the standard of their imaginative ingenuity. According to one version of the legend, the mechanism for raising the great weapon-arm worked perfectly: it was the momentum the down-swing would generate that was not taken fully into account in the Rhodian mathematicians' calculations.

Strabo recorded that the colossus fell in a great earthquake in 226 BC less than a century after it was constructed. But *was* it an earthquake or was it the vast weight of the down-swinging weapon arm that brought the statue toppling forward to its doom? Strabo goes on to record that an oracle had warned the Rhodians that it would bring evil fortune to their city if the statue was ever raised again.

If, indeed, it had been a weapon whose engineering and balance was faulty, then raising it and attempting to swing the arm down again would have seemed very likely to cause further disaster. According to Strabo, the Rhodians decided to let the colossus lie where it had fallen .

Nothing more happened until the middle of the seventh century AD.

It was generally believed that the Saracens had salvaged the valuable bronze and sent it to a wealthy merchant in Edessa. It was also believed that hundreds of camels conveyed the broken pieces of the once so glorious colossus to ignominious resmelting sites in Syria.

Reinforcement for the idea that the Colossus may actually have been a weapon comes from an examination of the Pharos lighthouse that stood on an island close to the harbour at Alexandria. The original structure apparently had four storeys. The great rectangular base contained the accommodation for the engineers and their assistants.

There are suggestions that the thoughtful Pharos designer, Sostratus, had installed some kind of hydraulic apparatus by which fuel could be lifted to the top of the lighthouse. According to the legends surrounding the Pharos and its contents, the lens at the top could be used to observe ships while they were still a long way away, but — far more importantly — it could also focus the rays of the sun on them and cause fire to break out on board.

The Byzantine court was noted for its guile and subtlety and one ancient tradition suggests that a particularly devious Byzantine emperor was hoping to attack Alexandria, but had heard of the secret weapon that could set fire to ships from the top of the lighthouse while an invading fleet was still a long way from attacking Alexandria itself. It the story is true, this cunning Byzantine infiltrated the caliph's court with one of his own very persuasive secret agents who managed to convince the caliph that a vast treasure, once the property of Alexander the Great himself, had been concealed *deep below the Pharos lighthouse*.

The caliph was apparently taken in, and the excavation he ordered to retrieve Alexander of Macedon's hypothetical treasure was well under way before the vulnerable upper sections of the lighthouse — including the deadly lenses that could detect and ignite enemy shipping at a distance — had collapsed and been destroyed. If the Pharos lighthouse was as technologically advanced as the legends suggest, then the necessary skills to have constructed the Colossus of Rhodes as a gigantic and devastating weapon would most probably have been available to the Rhodians.

At this distance in time and in the absence of firm archaeological evidence nothing can be proved about the colossus. Yet it is not beyond the bounds of possibility that it was built as a highly imaginative weapon that was destroyed, not in an earthquake, but by the faulty mathematics and physics that underestimated the effect of the momentum of the down-swinging arm.

BIBLIOGRAPHY

Andere, Mary. *Arthurian Links with Herefordshire*. Great Britain: Logaston Press, 1995.

Ashe, Geoffrey (Ed.). *The Quest for Arthur's Britain*. London: Granada Publishing, 1972.

Attard, Joseph. *The Ghosts of Malta*. Malta. Publishers Enterprises Group Ltd., 1990.

Bacon, Francis. *Essays, The Wisdom of the Ancients and the New Atlantis*. London: Odhams Press Ltd., 1950.

Bergamar, Kate. *Discovering Hill Figures*. Great Britain: Shire Publications, 1997.

Berlitz, Charles. *The Bermuda Triangle*. London: Granada, 1979.

Betjeman, John. *Collected Poems*. London: John Murray, 1988,

Bezzina, J. *The Ggantija Temples*. Malta, 1995.

Blashford-Snell, John. *Mysteries: Encounters with the Unexplained*. London: Bodley Head, 1983.

Bonanno, Anthony. *Malta: An Archaeological Paradise*. Malta: M.J. Publications Ltd., 1993.

Blouet, Brian. *The Story of Malta*. Malta: Progress Press Co. Ltd., 1993.

Bord, Janet and Colin. *Mysterious Britain*. Great Britain: Paladin, 1974.

Boudet, Henri. *La Vraie Langue Celtique et le Cromleck de Rennes-les-Bains*. Nice, France: Belisane, 1984 reprint.

Bradbury, Will (Ed.). *Into the Unknown*. New York: Readers Digest, 1988.

Bradley, M. *Holy Grail Across the Atlantic*. Toronto: Hounslow Press, 1988.

Briggs, Katharine M. *British Folk Tales and Legends: A Sampler*. London. Granada Publishing in Paladin, 1977.

Brookesmith, Peter (Ed.) *Open Files*. London: Orbis Publishing, 1984.

Buren, Elizabeth Van. *The Dragon of Rennes-le-Château*. Vogels, France: 1998.

Camilleri, George. *Realms of Fantasy: Folk Tales from Gozo*. Camilleri Victoria Gozo, 1992.

Cavendish, Richard (Ed.). *Encyclopaedia of The Unexplained*. London: Routledge & Kegan Paul, 1974.

Childress, David Hatcher. *Lost Cities of Atlantis, Ancient Europe, and the Mediterranean*. USA: Adventure Unlimited Press, 1996.

Clark, Jerome, *Unexplained*. USA: Gale Research Inc., 1993.

Cohen, Daniel. *Encyclopaedia of Ghosts*. London: Guild Publishing, 1989.

Dixon, G. M. *Folktales and Legends of Norfolk*. Minimax: 1983.

Dunford, Barry. *The Holy Land of Scotland*. Scotland: Brigadoon Books, 1996.

Dyall, Valentine. *Unsolved Mysteries*. London: Hutchinson & Co. Ltd., 1954.

Encyclopaedia Britannica: Britannica Online: http://www.eb.com

Eysenck, H.J and Sargent, Carl. *Explaining the Unexplained*. London: BCA, 1993.

Fanthorpe, Lionel and Patricia. *The Holy Grail Revealed*. California: Newcastle Publishing Co. Inc., 1982.

Fanthorpe, Lionel and Patricia. *The Oak Island Mystery*. Toronto: Hounslow Press, 1995.

Fanthorpe, Lionel and Patricia. *Secrets of Rennes le Château*. USA: Samuel Weiser Inc., 1992.

Fanthorpe, Lionel and Patricia. *The World's Greatest Unsolved Mysteries.* Toronto: Hounslow Press, 1997.

Fanthorpe, Lionel and Patricia. *The World's Most Mysterious People.* Toronto: Hounslow Press, 1998.

Flem-Ath, Rand and Rose. *When the Sky Fell: In Search of Atlantis.* Toronto: Stoddart, 1995.

Forman, Joan. *Haunted East Anglia.* Great Britain. Fontana, 1976.

Fortean Times. London: John Brown Publishing Ltd.

Fowke, Edith. *Canadian Folklore.* Toronto: Oxford University Press, 1988.

Godwin, John. *This Baffling World.* New York: Hart Publishing Company, 1968.

Graves, Robert (Introduction by). *Larousse Encyclopaedia of Mythology.* London: Paul Hamlyn, 1959.

Gribble, Leonard. *Famous Historical Mysteries.* London: Target Books, 1974.

Guerber, H.A. *Myths and Legends of the Middle Ages.* London: Studio editions Ltd., 1994.

Haining, Peter. *The Restless Bones and Other True Mysteries.* London: Armada books, 1970.

Hancock, Graham. *Fingerprints of the Gods.* New York: Crown Publishers, 1995.

Hapgood, Charles. *Maps of the Ancient Sea Kings.* USA: Adventure Unlimited Press, 1996.

Hitching, Francis. *The World Atlas of Mysteries.* London: Pan Books, 1979.

Jeffrey, Adi-Kent T. *The Bermuda Triangle.* London: A Star Book, 1975.

Knight, Gareth. *The Secret Tradition in Arthurian Legend.* Great Britain: The Aquarian Press, 1983.

Lacy, N. J. *The Arthurian Encyclopaedia.* Woodbridge, Suffolk, UK: Boydell Press, 1986.

Lampitt, L.F. (Ed.). *The World's Strangest Stories.* London: Associated Newspapers Group Ltd., 1955.

Mack, Lorrie et al (Ed.) *The Unexplained.* London: Orbis, 1984.

Maziére, Francis. *Mysteries of Easter Island.* England: Wm. Collins Sons & Co. Ltd., 1968.

Metcalfe, Leon. *Discovering Ghosts.* UK: Shire Publications Ltd., 1974.

Michell, John and Rickard, Robert J.M. *Phenomena: A Book of Wonders.* London: Thames & Hudson, 1977.

Moss, Peter. *Ghosts Over Britain.* Great Britain: Sphere Books Ltd., 1979.

Muck, Otto. *The Secret of Atlantis.* London: Collins, 1978.

Paget, Peter. *The Welsh Triangle.* London: Granada, 1979.

Pohl, Frederick J. *Prince Henry Sinclair.* Canada: Nimbus Publishing Ltd., 1967.

Poole, Keith B. *Ghosts of Wessex.* Canada. Douglas David & Charles Ltd., 1976.

Porter, Enid. *The Folklore of East Anglia.* London: B.T.Batsford Ltd., 1974.

Rawcliffe, D.H. *Illusions and Delusions of the Supernatural and the Occult.* New York: 1959.

Reader's Digest Book. *Folklore, Myths and Legends of Britain.* London: The Reader's Digest Ass. Ltd., 1973.

Reader's Digest Book. *Strange Stories, Amazing Facts.* London: The Reader's Digest Ass. Ltd., 1975.

Ritchie, Anna. *Picts.* Scotland: HMSO, 1993.

Rolleston, T.W. *Celtic Myths and Legends.* London: Studio Editions Ltd., 1994.

Russell, Eric Frank. *Great World Mysteries.* London: Mayflower, 1967.

Bibliography

Saltzman, Pauline. *The Strange and the Supernormal*. New York: Paperback Library, Inc., 1968.

Sampson, Chas. *Ghosts of the Broads*. Norwich: Jarrold & Sons Ltd., 1973.

Sharper Knowlson, T. *The Origins of Popular Superstitions and Customs*. London: Studio Editions Ltd., 1995.

Sinclair, Andrew. *The Sword and the Grail*. New York: Crown Publishers, Inc., 1992.

Snow, Edward Rowe. *Strange Tales from Nova Scotia to Cape Hatteras*. USA: Dodd, Mead & Company, 1946.

Spencer, John and Anne. *The Encyclopaedia of the World's Greatest Unsolved Mysteries*. London: Headline Book Publishing, 1995.

Strong, Roy. *Lost Treasures of Britain*. USA: Viking Penguin, 1990.

Tesla, Nikola and Childress, David. *The Fantastic Inventions of Nikola Tesla*. USA: Adventures Unlimited Press, 1993.

Tomas, Andrew. *Atlantis: from Legend to Discovery*. London: Sphere Books, 1974.

Trench, C.E.F. *Slane An Taisce Meath Association*. Slane Co. Meath. 1987

Wallis Budge, E. A. *The Book of the Dead*. Secaucus, New Jersey: The Citadel Press, 1984 reprint.

Welfare, Simon and Fairley, John. *Arthur C. Clarke's Mysterious World*. England: William Collins Sons & Company Ltd., 1980.

Whitehead, John. *Guardian of the Grail*. London: Jarrolds, 1959.

Whitehead, Ruth Holmes. *Stories From The Six Worlds*. Nova Scotia: Nimbus Publishing Ltd., 1988.

Wilson, Colin, and Damon. *Unsolved Mysteries Past and Present*. London: Headline Book Publishing, 1993.

Wilson, Colin, Damon, and Rowan. *World Famous True Ghost Stories*. London: Robinson Publishing, 1996.

Wilson, Colin, and Dr. Evans, Christopher, (Editors). *The Book of Great Mysteries*. London: Robinson Publishing, 1986.

Young, George. *Ghosts in Nova Scctia*. Halifax: George Young, 1991.

Young, George. *Ancient Peoples and Modern Ghosts*. Halifax: George Young, 1991.

Zammit, Prof. Sir Themistocles. *Prehistoric Malta*. Malta: Valletta, 1994.

Zammit, Prof. Sir Themistocles. *The St. Paul's Catacombs*. Malta: Valetta, 1980.